TRAVELLERS ON A TRADE WIND

Marcia Pirie

Seafarer Books

Sheridan House

First published 1992
Frontier Publishing

This edition published in 1998
in the UK by Seafarer Books
2 Rendlesham Mews
Rendlesham Woodbridge
Suffolk IP12 2SZ

in the USA by Sheridan House
145 Palisade Street, Dobbs Ferry,
N.Y. 10522

UK ISBN 085036 471 X
USA ISBN 1 57409 065 8

British Library Cataloguing in Publication Data
Pirie, Marcia, 1942-
Travellers on a trade wind.
I. Title
910.09164

Printed in Finland by WSOY

CONTENTS

1. Half a World Away 1
2. Illegal Entry 11
3. Isle of Ill-repute 21
4. Trade Wind Passage 32
5. Gauguin's 'Savage Paradise' 39
6. Polynesian Make Believe 55
7. To Ua Pu for a Ukelele 59
8. Imperfect Paradise 60
9. Playmates 69
10. Into the Trade Winds - And through the Doldrums 79
11. Re-entry Rituals 90
12. Hurricane in the Wind 99
13. Goodbye to the Trade Winds 110
14. Winter Arrangements 115
15. Heroes in the Flesh 121
16. Beyond Desolation Sound 131
17. Islands of the Haida 147
18. Ice in the Drinks at Last 159
19. South to Sitka 180
20. Running (and Beating) Down to 'Frisco 189
21. Urban Adaptation 192
22. Tupperware Tinseltown 207
23. The Fleet Prepares 220
24. Back before the Trade Winds 230
25. Changes 233
26. Memorable Yachts 245
27. To the Tikis 254
28. Heyerdahl's Virgin Island 256
29. Village on a Coral Strand 263
30. Raw Edges of Paradise 279
31. One Atoll, One Family 292
32. Paradise - Lost or Found? 305
33. Half a World Nearer 319
Appendix 330

1

Half A World Away

It was almost a year to the day since I'd hung up my business suit for the last time; eight months since I'd held a telephone, sat in a car, read a newspaper, had a hot bath. The only one I missed was the hot bath.

These thoughts belonged to the dark hours of a moonless Equatorial night. The three hours of my watch seemed interminable. I wriggled restlessly on the wooden seats of the cockpit. Beads of moisture glazed the varnished coamings and the air felt oddly chilly. It was a sure sign that we had the Antarctic-born waters of the Humboldt Current under us. At least it meant we were moving, even if it didn't look like it. *Moongazer*, her sails furled, bobbed gently on a satin sea. The sounds of the night were light and sporadic: the splash of something leaping for its life; the snoring of David, lying on the saloon bunk, hands folded on his chest like a tombstone effigy of a Norman knight.

We were on the threshold of an ocean and a hemisphere that were new to us. Twelve days before, we had sailed from Balboa into the Gulf of Panama, bound for the Galapagos Islands. The thousand miles should take us about ten days, according to our usual average. We started promisingly, with a light following wind and fairweather skies. The Gulf teemed with birds and fish. For two days we were entertained by diving cormorants and plummeting pelicans. Then suddenly the wind disappeared, as did the birds and the leaping fish, and we were left to wallow, apparently the only souls on the planet.

The log notes read:

TUE: Breeze died at dawn. Sails flopping around so took them down. Sea very calm, no swell so life could be worse. Good day for chores. Baked bread. Washed hair and selves, signal for sun to disappear.

WED: Grey drizzly dawn with breeze from the S.W. Sails up, can't make the course, but at least we're moving. Noon: breeze dies, sun comes out. David gets a reasonable sight. Hot. Have a tepid can of beer with lunch (bread and pate and half of our last tomato).

3 p.m: Drifted through a school of sperm whales basking and blowing and totally ignoring us. David is excited. I would like to be but am nagged by reminder that around here several yachts have been attacked and sunk.

4 p.m: Sun shows itself again, just in time to provide a sight. David plots it with our noon position and marks a cross on the chart. Disappointing progress.

THUR: Squalls last night. Damp and chilly, but sails up again and moving, 3-4 knots! Sea getting rougher. 5 p.m: wind increasing, darkness soon, so we put a reef in the main. Just after supper the wind dies. Sails down again. I start a dialogue with the heavens and then think the better of it.

1 a.m: On watch, I put on headphones and listen to BBC World Service. Am astonished to hear the familiar voice of a friend giving a by-election victory speech. Suddenly I feel very far away.

FRI: Another gloomy dawn. Breeze from N.W. this time, but swell is from the S.E. and increasing, more like the ocean now.

11 a.m: A freighter heading east passes close-to, flying the Red Ensign. The Halifax Castle, *David calls it up on the VHF and the first mate is very chatty. Wants to know all about our trip, and about our boat. We talk for twenty minutes until the signal fades as the ship disappears over the horizon.*

The Mate on the *Halifax Castle* seemed as excited as we were to talk to another human being. He was also a yachtsman, planning a long trip one day. We could tell that from the barrage of questions. David shot back the answers, packing in what he could while the radio signal lasted.

'It's an Endurance 35, ferrocement. We bought the hull and built the rest from the deck up. Eighteen months spare time project. No, we've had no real problems; left Plymouth eight months ago; Spain, Madeira, Canaries, Barbados and up the Antilles Chain. Now we're on our way to Vancouver, via Marquesas and Hawaii. After that? No idea. Rough weather? Not much so far. A bit brisk in Biscay. The worst was from the Virgins to Panama, four days of running before a gale with big seas. Nothing we couldn't handle. The Atlantic passage was slow, 27 days. Flukey winds for the first ten days, but the rest was a milk run.

'Yes, We'd given up our jobs and sold our house. We bought another one, renovated it and rented it out to give us some income. It's surprising how little we can manage on. Altogether, a great way of life. Beats going to the office, hands down.'

As the white superstructure of the freighter to disappeared over the horizon, the VHF signal faded and the conversation ended in an unintelligible crackle. David called once more, unsuccessfully, and hung up the mouthpiece. I had shown uncharacteristic restraint during the conversation, but I was ready to make up for it.

'You made it sound like we'd just sold up and sailed away,' I said.

'Well didn't we?' The answer to that, I thought, depends on whether you are able to direct your focus only on life's simplicities, or whether, like me, you let yourself get distracted by its complexities.

'Anyway,' David added, 'no-one wants to hear the dreary bits.'

Even we had preferred to let time obscure the dreary bits. It was six years since the embryonic *Moongazer,* in the form of a ferrocement shell, was lowered into our garden and I had already forgotten how powerfully it dominated our lives. The hull was right outside our bedroom window and for the next eighteen months it all but stepped in and shared our bed. I'm not quite sure why David embarked on the project, as we already had an adequate, though smaller, boat at the time. My experiences in the Irish Sea had not fostered any great enthusiasm for extended blue water sailing and that aspect had never been discussed when we designed the construction of *Moongazer*. Had we done so, I reflected now, we would have a less suffocating cockpit, with seats long enough to lie full length. *Moongazer's* cockpit was designed to keep the cold sea spray at bay and we had never for a moment imagined wanting to sleep in it.

It was through the notion of greater comfort that David sold me the idea of building a boat. Anything that could make a nasty night on the Irish sea more bearable was worth eighteen months hard labour.

Even after she was completed and launched, *Moongazer* continued to govern our lives. We found ourselves locked into an annual ritual of laying her up in the Autumn, repairing and maintaining during the winter, painting and anti-fouling in the rain during Easter and launching again on Spring Bank Holiday. Then began a summer of weekends where every Friday night we struggled through the traffic for three hours to Anglesey, snatched a Saturday sail if the weather permitted, and struggled back again on Sunday night. For our first summer cruise on *Moongazer* we spent most of the two weeks against a harbour wall in the Isle of Man, drying with the tide, while David rebuilt the engine. The second summer we spent mostly at anchor in Tobermory Bay listening to the endless rain drumming on the coachroof and the equally endless gale forecasts on the radio. We put up with it all because, strange as it seems now, we didn't think there was any alternative.

As the next few years went by, we gained in experience and the Irish sea became friendlier. In the comfort of a larger boat we ventured further, to the west coast of Ireland and there developed a taste for Guinness and wild spots. We met our first long-distance cruisers, a Canadian couple in an old wooden boat. They showed how an enviable quality of life could be supported by the slenderest of means. We began to read books about cruising in warm, gale-free waters. Friends began to send us letters from the Caribbean. Another friend had his retirement dream shattered by sudden and serious illness. We felt ourselves to be victims of a conspiracy of events which was gathering pace. I'm not sure when we made the decision, because like most of the turning points in our lives it emerged by some tacit understanding, intuitively and without much discussion, surprising for two people who, in the course of their work, often had to alert the less enlightened to the merits of systematic and consultative decision-making.

And so without much discussion of the 'if', we found ourselves one winter, straight into the nitty gritty of the 'how'. It's at this point of implementation that our approaches tend to diverge. David likes to 'get on with the job'. I prefer to ease myself in, though that's not how he describes it.

Herb Payson wrote in *Blown Away* that he was impressed by the aptness of a motto carved in a friend's deck beam: *Between The Dream And The Deed Lie The Doldrums*. For us it was more like being engulfed by a typhoon. The words had rolled off David's tongue when he told the mate we'd given up our jobs, sold the house, bought another, done it up and rented it out. He didn't add that it had been the most exhausting three months of our lives. Not because we had been preparing *Moongazer*. She was ready and tugging at her mooring. Her owners, in their search for a simple, low-maintenance dwelling suitable for letting, had been ensnared by the crumbling charms of a most unsuitable Cornish cottage. Part of the attraction was that the cottage was only a dinghy-ride away from river moorings and we could live on the boat while we did the necessary renovations. The other part of the attraction eludes me but it could only have appealed to that masochism which I now know for sure lurks near the surface of our souls.

Few details of that summer clamour for recognition, except for that hard-won day of departure when we wearily released *Moongazer* from her mooring and ourselves from our frenetic labours and endless lists. (But only for the time being: frenetic labours and endless lists were to be our customary companions for all subsequent departure preparations.) With a sharp eye on the weather we lumbered out of Plymouth Sound in early September in a grossly overladen boat. We felt not at all liberated but merely that we had exchanged one tyranny for another. From that moment on, we were the submissive slaves of the weather gods who dictate where and when small yachts might go.

We fell in with the fleet, cruising just ahead of the Autumn gales, from Spain to Madeira and on to the Canaries. There we waited until the danger of Caribbean hurricanes was over in November, preening and preparing *Moongazer* for her first ocean crossing. It was from the luxury of hindsight that David was now telling folk, 'It was a milk run. No problems at all.' I knew the 3,500 miles of trade wind crossing was known as the M1 to the Caribbean, and that we wouldn't fall off the edge at the other end, but like the sailors on the *Santa Maria* I continually prepared myself for possible catastrophe. It was a wearying effort, and quite unnecessary (as David frequently reminded me). The main problem was that I had not yet learned to ignore the often apocalyptical look of tropical skies. It was surely for my benefit that Joshua Slocum wrote: 'To know the laws that govern the winds, and to know that you know them, will give you an easy mind on your voyage round the world; otherwise you may tremble at the appearance of every cloud.'

There were irritating moments for David when things stuck, or broke or wouldn't work, but he pounced on them with the enthusiasm of the born engineer and as quickly as they were fixed they ceased to be problems. Discomfort and tedium varied from day to day until the day of landfall when everything seemed wonderful.

For a few weeks after arrival in Barbados I floated on air. There were no oceans I could not conquer, and in this vulnerable state I discovered that we had made another of those unspoken conjugal decisions. We seemed to be talking about 'when we get to Vancouver.' Along the way we had met several couples from Western Canada who were sailing their European-bought boats back home. All of them left us in no doubt as to the splendours of cruising in British Columbia, but just to make sure, some slipped us the most gloriously seductive books and brochures. An added enticement was the opportunity to get some skiing in (another of our enthusiasms). The opportunity most needed, that of earning money, came way down our list.

In this post-arrival mood of exuberant confidence we

consulted our copy of *Ocean Passages Of The World.* Published by the Hydrographic Department, this dour-looking volume has been the inspiration of countless heroic voyages of the mind. You can plan, from your sitting room in Swindon, your sailing route from Valparaiso to the Sunda Strait; or perhaps from the Beagle Channel to the South China Sea. Our 'route for sailing ships' from Panama to Vancouver tracked west into the Pacific and north via Hawaii. It covered over 7,000 miles, a mere sweep of the hand across the chart. 'See,' said David, his other hand occupied with a rum punch, 'We can be there by this September.'

And so we slid round the corner of another critical turning point in our lives. It had always been an option that we might spend the season in the Caribbean, then move up to the U.S.A. and sail home the next summer. It was a popular circuit and two years was not too long an absence to pick up on things back home. It was only when they heard that we were going on to Western Canada that it dawned on our parents and friends that we had really sailed away. Just what a commitment we had made by sailing into the Pacific began to be apparent to us: the further we ran before a trade wind sea the more difficult it was to turn back. Our first reminder came just after we had surged past the breakwaters, storm sail still set, into the huge harbour of Colon, at the eastern end of the Panama Canal. In a corner of the bleak, open anchorage known as The Flats was a forlorn huddle of yachts that we learned later had been waiting for two months for the wind to ease to allow them to get out into the Caribbean.

In Panama we stayed a few days at the Colon end, transited the canal and spent a week at Balboa. The dreary bits I've almost forgotten because it was an exciting time, full of promise, the start of real adventure. When the swirling waters of the great sea-lock decanted us out into the Pacific and we motored under the Bridge of the Americas down to Balboa, I felt for the first time that this was what *Moongazer* was built for. Those are the moments of flash-back when folk like the mate on the *Halifax Castle* ask, 'what's it like, this cruising life?', and I reply, 'wonderful!' Either I answer in one word or in thousands – which is how I come to find myself writing all this, a personal account of how it was for us, so that those who want to know can find their own own answers.

However far off our ultimate destination, I always only ever looked forward to the next landfall. The Galapagos were only 1,000 miles away, but we expected the winds to be inconsistent. (That had turned out to be an optimistic view.) The old Conquistadors had every reason to be terrified of these waters. In the sixteenth century the bullion galleons lumbering up from Peru to Panama hugged the mainland coast, a difficult and laborious route which made them easy prey for privateers. But to be caught in an offshore current in windless waters was to be swept off to oblivion. There lay in wait monstrous whirlpools, unchained leviathans, and certainly eternal perdition.

Occasionally a ship lumbered back to Panama from oblivion and reports began to filter through about strange islands to the west. They had peculiar birds and reptiles and giant tortoises, *los Galapagos*. But there was no gold, little water and no souls to save. So while the Manila Galleons opened up the trans-Pacific route to the Orient, the tortoises continued to munch cacti undisturbed. The Galapagos were only of interest to people with something to hide, like the buccaneers. Navigation was so imprecise and the currents were so wayward that even they had difficulty finding the islands. Some swore that they moved position and they became known as the Encantadas, the 'Bewitched Islands'.

Now, only 400 miles away, I was becoming increasingly impatient to get there. I implored the grey expanse above me: 'Please! Just a nice little wind, we only need it for a couple of days.' I looked in vain for even the tiniest crack in the clouds or ruffle on the water. I wasn't expecting the heavens to part to angel choirs but I was dispirited by the total lack of response. I was still an initiate in the hard school of living close to nature. I would learn that whatever I wanted was totally irrelevant. It didn't come easily to a pampered product of the twentieth century who liked to have more control over events.

David was more able to transfer his frustrations. He was taking the autopilot to bits. We only used it when under engine and it had packed up while motoring through the Gatun Lake. I took the hint and dug out my most formidable tome on Contemporary Art. By the end of the daylight I had worked my way through three pages of mind-numbing text. David had fared little better with his fault tracing. And then we heard the faintest murmur, a rustle of water on the hull. Wind! We rushed to put some sail up. It came from our bow quarter but we could hold the course. A golden glow came from the sun on the west horizon. It looked promising but we knew that trick.

The breeze persisted. For two days we carried on with our tasks, ignoring it as we expected it to die at any minute. It carried us on across the Equator and into the Southern Hemisphere. Even the sun became obliging and allowed David to put a confident cross on the chart.

'Tomorrow,' he said, 'we should see land.' Such optimism made me nervous.

'If all goes well,' I cautioned. 'And the islands haven't moved.'

2
Illegal Entry

What we eventually saw, on the fifteenth day out from Panama, looked very firmly fixed in position, some forty sea miles south of the Equator. It was San Cristobal, the most easterly island of the Archipelago de Colon (the official name bestowed by Ecuador in 1892) and it looked desolate and unwelcoming. We gazed at a long-dead eruption of cones and craters. It was a landscape that, in 1835, reminded the young Darwin of '...those parts of Staffordshire where the great iron foundries are most numerous.' We could only imagine the comparison and agree with him, that '...nothing could be less inviting than the first appearance.'

The desolate scene suited us. We were in no hurry to encounter human activity, since we had come illegally, without a permit. The islands, which belong to Ecuador, are almost wholly a National Park with restrictions on the movement of tourists and yachts. Permits for cruising had to be applied for, months in advance, accompanied by a good reason for the visit. Only the very energetic bothered to apply and most of their applications were swallowed without trace. Our experience with bureaucracy had taught us that the situation in practice was likely to vary from season to season.

That year the consensus in the yacht club bar at Panama was that we should just arrive and plead the need for engine repairs or water or whatever. 'After all what can they do to you but send you on your way?'

Now, after fifteen days to reflect, we could think of quite a number of things a South American military government could do: especially if one had a nice yacht to confiscate.

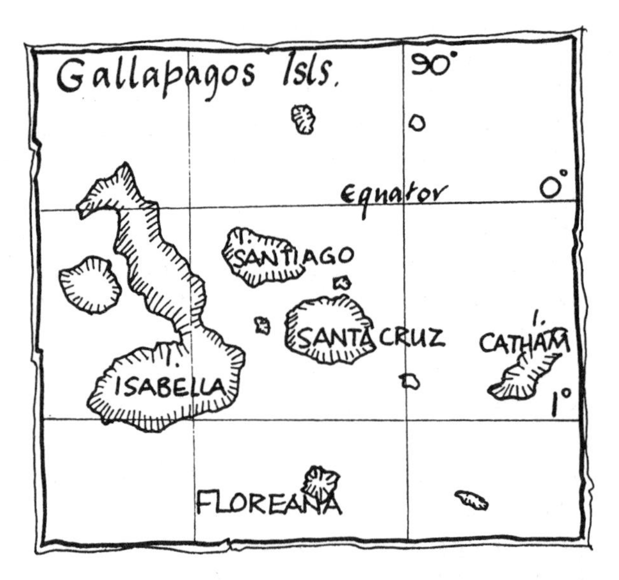

We decided to make our arrival, not at the administrative centre on San Cristobal Island, but at the smaller settlement on the Island of Santa Cruz, a day's sail further to the east. Possibly the authorities might be less bureaucratic there. Neither of us had ever visited a country which was governed by the military. Our impressions of juntas were formed mostly from pictures of bemedalled generals in *Time Magazine*, so we were definitely nervous.

We drifted in the night between the two islands and at first light made toward Santa Cruz. It seemed another heap of spent volcanoes. The bleakness of the scene made me edgy. I jumped when David broke the silence.

'We've got company.'

My disbelieving eyes focused on a boat about half a mile behind us. Through the binoculars I could see that its hull was dark, and that its bow was high and flared, and emblazoned with an eagle-like insignia.

'Lord, a patrol boat, ...altering course ...straight for us.' Instantly a vision of our fate flashed before me. Would we languish in gaol here or on the mainland? David, ever the pragmatist, was more concerned with our immediate position.

'We'd better get some clothes on,' he said, disappearing into the forepeak.

Clothes? Ah, yes. I was topless, possibly a worse crime than being permitless.

David emerged, clad in shirt and shorts (amazingly, without the usual preamble on 'have-you-seen-my-etc.'...).

'I've got the ship's papers and passports ready. Sit in the cockpit and don't look behind. Pretend you haven't noticed anything.'

I draped myself beside the tiller with the contrived nonchalance of a model in a yachting advert, but I felt more like a nervous horse with its ears pinned back. The roar of engines was uncomfortably close – and still at full throttle. Surely they wouldn't ram us?

Also racing at full throttle was my heart, and my attempts at a relaxed pose were weakening. Our pursuer was coming up parallel with us, only a few metres off, but still at speed. We could no longer pretend we hadn't noticed, and I threw a sideways glance, as if to remark, 'Goodness me, the Ecuadorian Navy!'

But the figures I saw clustered on the deck were not clad in navy grey. They were clad in very little and what there was, was crisp and colourful. About thirty camera lenses zoomed in on us, followed by cheery waves and they were gone, leaving a wake of white water.

'Tourists, bloody tourists,' we exploded, with relief.

We followed behind, and arrived in the anchorage at Academy Bay several hours later. It was an exposed and lonely place with only a couple of unattended boats on moorings. We felt conspicuous. There was still no sign of a Naval Presence but with every minute we expected to see it come steaming round the headland.

I had just put on the kettle for our ritual afternoon tea when I heard David on the foredeck, mutter, 'Visitors.'

'Uh-hu,' I thought. 'Here we go.' I looked out of the window and saw only a man and a boy in a rowing boat.

'*Buenos Dias*.'

'*Buenos Dias*.'

Just a split second before we issued an invitation they started to climb on board. Our man was small and worried-looking and wore a check shirt and baggy trousers. '*Buenos Dias*' had used up half our Spanish vocabulary, which was at least 50 per cent up on our visitors' English, so it was with gesture and mime that we continued our exchange. It seemed he was some sort of official.

'*Passeportes*?' O.K. no problem. '*Permiso*?'

'*Permiso*?' We echoed, in what I hoped sounded like surprise. '*No Permiso*.'

He shook his head and tutted and the frown on his forehead deepened. He indicated, a shade timidly, that he would like to inspect the interior of the boat and after some cursory poking around asked if we had any beer. To avert any misunderstanding as to whether he meant now or later, he produced a bag. But '*Si, gracias,*' he'd have one now as well. We also managed to find a can of fizzy soda for the boy who sat silent throughout the proceedings. We had no clear idea whose emissary he was, but he was one with a spare Sunday afternoon to fill. It was dusk when he finally left, impressing upon us that we had to come tomorrow at *ochos horas* to *el Capitano del Puerto.*

I slept lightly, dreaming of gun-boats and grizzlefaced *capitanos.*

A few minutes before eight o'clock, we presented ourselves, neatly attired, in the yard of the naval barracks. A bunch of shaven-headed cadets was drilling in front of a small figure, resplendent in white uniform. He turned to greet us. It was our worried-faced visitor of the previous evening, transformed by the mantle of authority! It seemed he was the assistant Port Captain, but the port Captain himself? ...well, he wasn't here yet, but perhaps if we came back in *una hora*?

For the next *una, dos* and *tres horas* we trudged up and down the dusty dirt road that serves as Puerto Ayora's main street, wondering if the Port Captain's non-appearance was the start of a make 'em sweat routine. We finally found him, having coffee in one of the little bars, laughing and chatting with a group of friends. Amid much smiling and buenos dias-ing he invited us, and them, to accompany him up the road to the barracks. This naval commandant bore little resemblance to the swarthy bull-headed figures of our imaginings. He was young and slender and with his white uniform jacket draped elegantly over his shoulders, looked more like an up-market fashion model.

Doing our theatrical best to reflect his easy, relaxed manner, we settled ourselves down in his office and finally got around to the purpose of our visit. In mime and pidgin Spanish we explained about our engine. 'About two days to repair.' He listened as if he'd never heard this story before, his big brown eyes clouding with concern. Our tale over, he smiled reassuringly. '*No problema.*' There would be charges to pay of course. He pointed to a document on the wall as if to indicate they were official. And as we had arrived on a Sunday there would be overtime. But there was no hurry. All we needed to do for the present was to get our passports stamped at the police station next door.

The police station was a primitive affair but the yard in front of it had been converted to a volleyball court, presumably to relieve boredom. There was no-one at home and it took a day and a half before we found a policeman. Then he couldn't find the key of the drawer where he kept the rubber stamp, so could we come back the next day? This we did, interrupting a poker game, and when he saw us he immediately remembered that he had forgotten all about the key... 'Manana por favor...'

We didn't mind, the more excuses to extend our stay the better. But just in case the Port Captain was getting restless we took him a bottle of our duty-free whisky. He seemed genuinely pleased and delighted. We told him our engine repairs were progressing and he said, '*No Problema.*' We were learning the rules of the game. Step by step; day by day. Don't rush it; don't force a commitment. Keep it open; no-one has to say yes or no. Don't worry about the objective; concentrate on the process.

Puerto Ayora, in spite of its frontier-town flavour, is the economic centre with a population of 4,000. Here, the Charles Darwin Foundation built a research station in the early sixties, with the assistance of UNESCO and others. Its small staff carry out numerous conservation programmes and research studies in conjunction with the National Parks Dept. In 1959 the Ecuadorian Government declared most of the Archipelago a National Park, and a staff of Park Wardens now looks after the conservation management. This includes the control of tourists and only Warden-led parties are allowed to tour the islands.

One morning we were wakened by the arrival of one of these parties in a battered-looking passenger ship from Guayaquill. This turned out to be the New York Natural

History Society, slumming it in the search for knowledge. The sight of the ship disturbed me with strange stirrings of nostalgia. Its homely lines were somehow familiar and certainly at odds with the name *Buccanero* emblazoned on its stern. I found out later that it was formerly the old well-loved *St Ninian*, a mail steamer in the Western Isles of Scotland, on which I'd travelled as a child.

The members of the New York Natural History Society attacked their task of learning about the Galapagos with formidable zeal. Clad in various designs of crisp safari outfits and festooned with binoculars and cameras they stepped out briskly for the Research Station the instant they were put ashore. I was doing the washing at the time, in the public washing place. I had climbed up into the washing trough and was trampling the sheets when I saw a group returning from their visit to the tortoise corral. The party leader was steering them around the spiny undergrowth, pointing out the passing fauna.

'Look, one of Darwin's famous finches – *Geospiza magnirostris*.'

The Natural Historians scribbled on their clipboards.

'And see there, a lava lizard – *Tropidurus*.'

More fervent scribbling on the clipboards. Then two less attentive ladies caught sight of me and drifted over.

'Excuse me, but we're curious to know what you're doing.'

'I'm washing my sheets.'

'Well well, I never!' Wrinkled faces gazed up at me in wonder. They even looked as if they might write my answer in their clipboards.

Some more of the group spotted us and came over followed by others anxious not to miss out on anything. The questioning became rigorous. These folk were relentless in their pursuit of knowledge. 'How did we allocate our water supply and in what proportions? What specific type of bean did we sprout?' Standing three feet above everybody with my feet in the water trough, I was captive material. I felt I was facing the Board of Examiners. They were clearly enjoying themselves. Some of them even took photographs. Mercifully, no-one peered at me through binoculars.

Release came when they were recalled to the cactus thicket and they trickled away, almost reluctantly. Even for naturalists, human interest beats animals. We too were discovering that. We had come to the islands to see the wildlife. The guidebook spoke of the '...unusual physical circumstances and peculiar inhabitants...' This reference, we assumed, was not intended to include the human inhabitants but we found the life history of the Giant Tortoise dull stuff compared to the gossip on some of the resident *Homo sapiens*.

A collection of Europeans existed in the 'suburbs' of Puerto Ayora, on a rocky peninsula amid a tangled forest of cacti and thorn bushes. Some had been in residence since the 1920s and '30s and some were more recent pioneers. They lived in a varied assortment of structures, from dug-out caves to high-tech greenhouses. Most of the dwellings were modest affairs assembled from lava blocks which gave them the appearance of growing out of the bedrock. At one with this lunar landscape were an Englishman and his German wife, who had lived there with their family for fourteen years. Within their calcined walls they had created a little culture warp. The rooms would have been quite at home in an attic flat in Fulham. Only the sun-scorched view from the windows spoiled the illusion.

They were planning to move soon from the islands. He had just completed a survey for the British Government on the possibilities for tourism in an even more remote corner of the world.

'Where is there left?' we asked.

'The Falkland Islands. I can see a lot of possibilities there.'

Further afield, in the hills among the cloud and drizzle, a colony of Norwegians has farmed and raised cattle for several generations. Scattered among the other islands are a few small clusters of descendants of other seafaring Europeans.

The history of colonization has been fraught and turbulent, almost as if the islands actively resisted human intrusion. One defeated settler wrote, '...(the Galapagos) were one of those parts of the earth where humans were not tolerated.'

The first visitors were buccaneers, whalers, and sealers, not interested in settling, but in the early nineteenth century the governments of first Peru, and then Ecuador, made several ill-fated attempts to colonize the islands with convicts. Equally shrouded in tales of dark deeds were the efforts of a motley succession of shipwrecked sailors, desperadoes, hermits, and would-be emperors, all attempting to wrest a living or act out a fantasy amid the thorn and clinker. A sprinkling of tenacious settlements persisted and by the 1930s the stable population exceeded 800. World War II brought the temporary presence of the American Forces to Santa Cruz and left it with improved communications, an airport and an increased awareness of its scientific importance. It was only a matter of time before the outside world would beat a track to its shores.

The first cruise ship arrived in 1970 with sixty passengers. Since then, both the tourist influx and the Ecuadorian population (swelled by immigrants fleeing the poverty of the mainland) have soared. The delicate balance between man and environment is endangered. Only four of the nineteen islands are permanently inhabited, but these support eight 'towns' with a total population of 10,000. The authorities are struggling, despite political and commercial pressures, to regulate the number of visitors and establish a just-manageable annual quota of 25,000.

We lingered on at Academy Bay for over a week, and when our policeman finally found the key to his stamp drawer it was time, by our own schedule, to move on. We presented our freshly embellished passports to the Port Captain, paid our dues and, amid much smiling and bowing, exchanged *Adios*'s.

But this was not yet goodbye to the Galapagos. Our clearance papers allowed us to stop at the island of Floreanna and we planned to spend a week or so there. We knew that it had a dark, unsavoury past and that local fishermen avoided it. But it was on our way and we were curious.

3

Isle Of Ill-repute

'Ra-ta-ta-ta' rattled back at us from the empty hills. Another few fathoms of chain clattered over the bow roller. The echo's reply was swallowed by a burst of reverse engine. The anchor dug and held and the silence returned to Post Office Bay.

It was too late to go ashore. The sun was definitely over the yard-arm (or would have been if we'd had one). We settled in the cockpit to survey the darkening bay. David stirred his iceless gin and tonic and said, 'Up early tomorrow to see the sights.'

'The sights?' I looked at the barren landscape.

'Haven't you read the guide book?'

Glossy guide books, I was disappointed to discover, were on sale at Puerto Ayora. It was a reminder that the islands were a marketable commodity, which for me, robbed them a little of their mystery. However I had bowed to progress and enlightenment and bought one.

'You must mean the Post Office barrel, seeing as we are in Post Office Bay?' I'd read many accounts by yachtsmen about the famous barrel. Whaling ships had long ceased to anchor in the bay and use the barrel as a mail drop, but yachtfolk still made a pilgrimage to it.

David nodded. 'And... somewhere near the beach are the ruins of a fish factory.' He made it sound as if another

Delphi was awaiting discovery.

I was in a mood for absorbing local colour. From our overstuffed bookshelves I prised out *The Shorter Novels of Herman Melville* and burnt the midnight paraffin. Herman Melville came to the Galapagos in 1841, but his ship avoided Floreanna (or Charles Island, as it was then called). He tells, in his sketches entitled *The Encantadas*, of drifting near the island one night and seeing a lighted beacon on the shore. The mate asked the skipper if he should put out a boat to investigate, but the old captain '...laughed rather grimly, as, shaking his fist towards the beacon, he rapped out an oath. '"No! That is Charles Island; brace up Mr. Mate and keep the light astern."'

It seemed that the island was one that decent men avoided, or as Melville more colourfully put it: '...it had become...Anathema – a sea Alsatia – the unassailed lurking place of all sorts of desparadoes.'

A few years before, it had been the 'kingdom' of a character from Peru who arrived with eighty would-be settlers and a bodyguard of ferocious dogs. The unfortunate subjects were directed to build a city from the clinker and any dissenters were hunted down by the canine cavalry. When the supply of human quarries ran low he replenished it with young sailors lured from visiting whaling ships. Each new arrival was at first pampered and petted, but eventually the Pretorian Guard turned on their Emperor and instigated the much over-due rebellion. After a bloody battle on the beach the few surviving dogs and their master were pursued into the bleak interior to meet with a grisly end.

Melville had more tales to tell of enslavement and malevolence, but already I fancied I could hear the cackle of mad laughter from the darkened shore. I blew out the light and snuggled down beside my snoring husband.

A bright and sunny morning greeted us with comforting

signs of exuberant life. Birds were everwhere on the look-out for breakfast. Frigate birds, identified easily by their angular silhouette, soared high above. A trio of brown pelicans glided across the shallows in single file formation. Around us, boobies and tropic birds squabbled over the spoils of their dive-bombing. A pack of sea lion cubs frolicked beside us as we rowed to the shore. We beached the dinghy and put on our shoes under the stern, unblinking gaze of booby birds with bright blue feet.

Almost immediately we found a well-trodden path leading into the scrub bushes. After about a hundred metres it ended, in a clearing. There, in the centre, was an assemblage which would have been the pride of a modern sculpture gallery. At its core sat the object of our quest, the barrel, festooned with layers of bric-a-brac bearing the names of the yachts that had come that way. It was a version of Kilroy-was-here in 3D graffiti. Two of the names were very recent. They had left Panama only a week before us so we had just missed them.

We had brought our own little contribution to the vandalising and David tacked it in place. 'Right,' he said, looking around. 'Done the barrel, now for the ruins.'

But the Tourist Trail went no further, for reasons which began to be painfully apparent. Ahead stretched a giant jumble of angular lava blocks, bristling with thorn bushes. We prised and crawled our way uphill, making slow progress under a blistering sun. After a couple of hours I ground to a halt. David was ahead by a couple of blocks and a deep fissure.

'How're you doing?' he called.

'As happy as a parched pincushion,' I replied. 'I don't care if the tombs of the Pharaohs are up ahead. I quit.' He looked relieved.

We had found not one trace of the past – of the penal colonies, the dog-king's lava palace, the hermit's cave or even the fish factory. Some would be much further up the hillside, others swallowed forever by the thorn bush.

Back in the cosy sanity of our floating home, I reflected, without answer, why anyone would actually want to settle in such a hostile place. It didn't strike me just then that some people ask a similar question about those who cross oceans in small boats.

We spent the next few days enjoying the living present. We wandered among the sea-lion colonies. The cubs milled around us, showing off shamelessly while the adults dozed, unconcerned. We took close-up photos of fearless birds, who almost posed for us. We tramped for miles along a sandy beach furrowed with the trails of sea turtles. They'd dragged themselves above the high water mark to lay and then bury their eggs. Of those that hatched only a few would make it to the sea as baby turtles. We crept to the edge of a salt lagoon to watch shy flamingoes roost at sunset, a riot of gilded crimson.

It was all magical but curiously unnerving. We felt we were intruding, so after a few days we tiptoed away and left Post Office Bay to its sea-lions and the silence.

Morbid curiosity was not the only reason that brought us to Floreanna. There was also the rare and surprising opportunity to treat ourselves to dinner in a restaurant. On the west side of the island, by the shores of a rocky inlet, lived Frau Wittmer. Although in her seventies, we were told she was still indefatigably producing delicious meals at her Pension Wittmer and was always pleased to have customers. This now-legendary lady was the sole survivor of another of Floreanna's dark episodes, so we went, almost as pilgrims, to pay our respects as well as to sample her cooking.

When Margaret Wittmer landed on these bleak shores in 1932 with her husband and stepson, she was young, unworldly and five months pregnant. But with Teutonic fortitude she flourished where most had despaired or even perished. I had read an account by Miles Smeeton who sailed that way in 1952. He described Frau Wittmer then, as a '...middle-aged German *Hausfrau*, plucked from her natural environment and transported to the wild.'

At that time Herr Wittmer was alive and he looked after the 'farm' about 300 metres up on the hillside. Here the cloud-drizzle, deposits of rich soil, and fresh water springs allow the cultivation of a wide variety of fruits and vegetables. Smeeton was amazed when he saw it:

> I had expected to see a vegetable garden, but here were acres of cultivation, as if Mr Wittmer expected an American fleet to anchor in Black Beach Bay... this was a market garden – without a market. It takes men of vision to colonise a country and we felt Mr Wittmer's vision was ahead of its time.

We pulled our dinghy up on the beach of black basalt pebbles and were directed by one of a handful of Ecuadorian neighbours to the Pension Wittmer. It was, like the other houses, assembled from packing cases, driftwood and corrugated iron but rambled on across a courtyard into numerous outbuildings. As we entered the yard two huge Alsatians sprang to life, barking and baring most unfriendly fangs. They stopped immediately on command when Frau Wittmer bustled out to greet us. Miles Smeeton's middle-aged *hausfrau* was now an elderly *hausfrau*, but standing there in her carpet slippers, white hair rolled in a bun and wiping her floury hands on a large apron, she could easily have just popped out from her Bavarian bakery.

'Oh, I am so pleased to meet you, have you just arrived?' she asked as if we were guests just off the train.

'You will have some tea with us ? Please sit down.'

She plied us with delicious home baking and insisted we try her recently made wine.

'We came to ask if we could have dinner here tonight,' we said.

She raised her hands to her head. 'This morning I had thirty-five people to breakfast, and last night to dinner there were over forty.'

She was talking about the passengers on the *Buccanero* and on its sister ship the *Iguano*, which was busy with the Audubon Society. Evidently a highlight of the cruise was a stop-off for home cooking at the Pension Wittmer. The market garden had found a market. Time had finally caught up with the vision.

'You come tomorrow evening and I will cook a nice dinner. My daughter-in-law and grandchildren are here just now so I have help. No, no, for the tea this afternoon there is nothing to pay, that is my pleasure.'

Dinner the next evening was a memorable occasion. By a happy coincidence we dined in company. A French couple sailed in that afternoon, hungry, like us, for good food and conversation.

We sat in a room straight out of a Bavarian guesthouse. We ate pork, sauerkraut and kuchen and I was sure if I looked out of the window I'd see snow-covered mountains. We washed it down with *kirsch* and *kafe* and reflected that every single drop and morsel of that meal was home produced. Not just the major ingredients, but the salt, the pepper, the sugar, the coffee, and the flour. 'But I like to work,' the indefatigable Frau told us. Just as well. The trip up to the farm in itself was an arduous couple of hours by a winding rocky track. And the only help was from mules and donkeys.

There was something bizarre about the everyday banality of the scene. Somehow it made the sinister history of the settlement quite credible.

The Wittmers were not the first Germans to arrive as would-be settlers in Floreanna. Hacking out an existence on the upper slopes was a Dr Ritter of fanatical inclinations and his helpmate, the hapless Dora. They had come to the Galapagos to lead a life of contemplation. So far, it had been one of ceaseless toil, just to survive. Nonetheless they did not welcome the Wittmer intrusion and had little to do with them.

Shortly after the Wittmers settled into their hillside cave and prepared for the arrival of their baby, there was another, ruder intrusion on the scene. This was the self-styled Baroness Eloisa Bosquet Von Wagner and her retinue of three submissive admirers. Described in one account as a '...spoilt, demanding lady of fortyish with prominent teeth,' the Baroness established her *Hacienda Paradise* and proceeded to shock and enrage the neighbours with her scandalous behaviour. In November 1934 she suddenly and mysteriously disappeared, along with her favourite of that time, a young Englishman. The remaining inmate of her household, a meek and tubercular Austrian, left a week later in an open boat with a Norwegian fisherman. They, too, disappeared and months later their bodies were found on another island.

Within four days of this discovery Dr Ritter died suddenly, his life's work still left undone. The distracted Dora was given shelter by the Wittmers until a ship came and took her off.

To this day no trace of the Baroness and her lover has ever been found. There have been several investigations into the events surrounding the disappearance but the truth has eluded them all.

Whatever the dark secret, it did not evidently haunt the homely little grandmother who bustled and fussed around us that evening. But as we made to leave, her Alsatians rose up and escorted her across the courtyard and as we said our last *Auf Wiedersehen* and turned to the darkness, we heard the noise of bolts being slid home and the snapping shut of well-oiled locks.

The rest of that night remains etched in my memory as miserably sleepless. The anchor chain ground up and down on the rocky bottom and with each lift of the gentle swell, wrapped itself around the lava blocks. Every few minutes, to a nerve-jarring clank, there was a sharp tug downwards on the bow, as if we were in the grip of some spirit of the deep.

When daylight finally came, it took David, with the help of scuba tanks, over half an hour of groping in the murky water before he could unravel the chain and release us from Floreanna. We escaped to the open ocean with unusual feelings of relief. Often, during our visit I had been disturbed by a sense of foreboding. Maybe it was the effect of the desolate landscape, the black rocks, the gloomy skies, or maybe Herman Melville had fed my imagination with such lines as: 'And all about it wandring ghosts did wayle and howl.'

Either way, I felt malevolence in the island's sullen brooding, of a kind I had never experienced in the ocean, even in its ugliest of moods.

As we left the grey outline of Floreanna astern I could just make out a red and white speck disappearing into Black Beach Bay. It was the tourist boat again. Frau Wittmer would be busy in her kitchen, preparing lunch for fifty.

BROWN PELICAN

Since that visit I have come across a number of written versions of the happenings at Floreanna, including Margaret Wittmer's own story *Floreanna*, which has recently been reprinted. The most evocative for me was a book by Dr Ritter's disciple Dora, published in 1935, poignantly entitled *And Satan Came To Eden*. It is written earnestly, as if to set the record straight.

Her account of the first few years sounded like penal servitude, but although she had her moments of doubt, Friedrich did not waver in his purpose. Which is only to be expected of someone who, before leaving Germany, Dora tells us: 'had employed a system of eating which required extensive mastication of each mouthful and had worn his teeth to stubs. He had the stubs removed to see if gums, once toughened could be a substitute for chewing.'

They had eloped to the islands, after providing their respective spouses with an arrangement to look after one another. When the scandal was discovered the resulting publicity produced a rash of Germans seeking a similar salvation in Paradise. On arrival, most of them needed only one glance to realise that Floreanna was not the sort of salvation they had in mind, so when the Wittmers arrived Dora did not expect to have to share their Eden for long. Dora, from her lofty spiritual position found Frau Wittmer, 'a rather ordinary sort of woman. We felt that life in the wilderness would soon lose its charm for her.'

Dora rarely condescended to visit the Wittmers' dwelling but when she did she noted that: '...the interior was immaculate! Frau Wittmer was undoubtedly a gifted housewife.'

Then the Baroness and her retinue arrived and during the next two years a sequence of events unfolded that would have done credit to Iris Murdoch – but without the sex. On that subject Dora could only bring herself to make veiled disapproving references: 'Cruelty and evil passions ran wild, with no Police or Public Opinion to check their wild excesses.'

Other characters flitted in and out of the drama and we get an interesting glimpse of the travellers who frequented those parts in the inter-war years. A number were that vanished breed of sea captain entrepreneurs who plied their old rusty tramp steamers ever searching for The Venture that would make their fortune. The others were the yacht parties, in the days when the word Yacht meant at least 60 feet with paid crew. Vincent Astor called several times in *Nourmahal.* There were the *Mary Pinchot* and the *Mizpah* and the ubiquitous schooner, *Yankee.* The Baroness liked to entertain these visitors and go aboard their yachts. In Electra Johnson's book, *Westward bound in the Schooner Yankee* there is a rare photo of the Baroness and her retinue on the deck of *Yankee*.

Inexorably, the drama wound towards a climax and Dora pinpoints the day of most significance, 19th March 1934. It was an intensely hot day in a period of drought and scorching winds. The noon-day silence is shattered by a long, drawn-out shriek. A few days later Dora is told that the Baroness and the Englishman have left in an American yacht, but she is surprised to find that the Baroness has left all her personal belongings behind.

Dora, faithful to her master's training, records only her observations and leaves us to draw our own conclusions. Ritter himself seemed unconcerned by the affair and threw himself into a fury of writing, as if in a race against time. He was, Dora tells us: 'Striving to overcome the world of appearances and illusion to merge intellect and spirit in the rhythmical movement of the Impersonal All'.

The effort was evidently too much and two months later he suffered a stroke and died, 'twitching'. It came almost as an anti-climax and although the description of his end bears a remarkable similarity to the effects of food poisoning Dora gave no suggestion of foul play. She was concerned more about her fitness to inherit The Great Task. Her tale ends on a brave note of self-encouragement (or possibly self-flagellation, as it's a common sub-theme in this story) '...Friedrich Lives through Dora!'

Certainly he has won a measure of immortality as each new generation stumbles across the story and writes it up. Not that it has brought us any nearer to knowing what really happened. That is something I expect the little old *hausfrau* will take with her when she goes to the Great Guesthouse In The Sky.

4

Trade Wind Passage: Galapagos to Marquesas

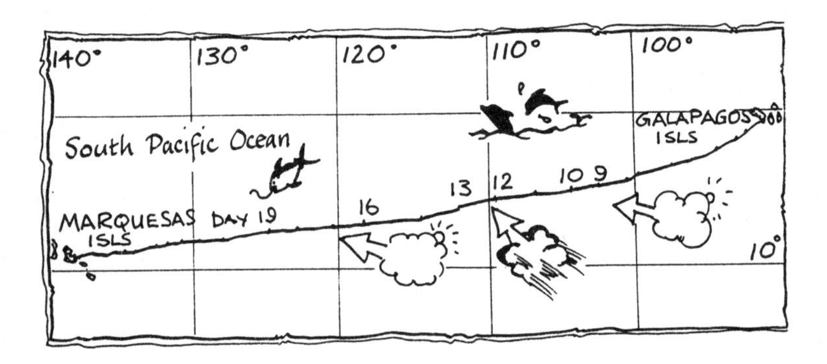

There are 3,000 miles of empty ocean ahead and thousands more to the north and south. We are a little dot between Antartica and Alaska. No shipping lanes come this way; we are probably as far from our fellow humans as we shall ever be. I have anxious thoughts about drifting in the liferaft. David points out that even a dustbin would drift westwards on the wind and current – like the *Kon Tiki* raft, until (like the *Kon Tiki*) it piled up on an island in its path. We are moving along one of the earth's most consistent weather belts. There should be no doldrums, no gales, and the current is with us.

The Pacific is getting into its stride slowly. We are one day out now and the famous swell is beginning to make itself felt. The wind is still light, coming over the stern. We are slipping gently into ocean-going mode. Through the night we keep a cursory watch, changing every three hours. Squalls, wind shifts and unusual boat noises are, for half the night at least, not my worry (unless wakened to help deal with it). On the Atlantic passage we tried doing without night watch-keeping. We would both lie awake listening to noises which clamoured for attention, each sure it was the other's turn to see to it.

I take the watch which sees the daybreak in. Just before six, the sky suddenly lightens from the east and a cold yellow light flushes out the indigo of night. If I'm lucky I'll see a molten sun burst above the horizon. More often the horizon will be decorated with a dark frieze of billowing cumulus and I have to make do with watching peach-gold streaks fan out and spread across the sky.

Six o'clock and David is waking up for the day. We exchange brief greetings and I slide back into my bunk for a last luxurious snooze. Soon the sun's heat will make sleep impossible. David puts on the headphones and fiddles with the radio, searching for the 'ham' bands. I slip into dreamland.

Dreamland starts to disconnect as the sun's rays climb and I remember where I am. My space is narrow, airless and it slowly heaves from side to side, every few seconds without respite. My crumpled sheet is sticky with sweat and so am I. Lethargy clamps me to my bunk and I try not to think of the daily sameness of weeks ahead. Instead, I think of all the books I'm going to read; of the projects I've set myself. Four uninterrupted weeks? I should see it as a luxury of opportunity.

Breakfast is tea, orange, boiled eggs, homemade bread and canned butter. The eggs (if they are fresh when bought) should keep for over a month. We coated each one in a thin film of Vaseline which seems to keep mould and staleness at bay. Citrus fruit and tomatoes we wrapped individually in plastic-wrap.

We tidy up and David takes the morning sunsight. He's

reduced all the mumbo jumbo of celestial navigation to a painlessly low-tech simplicity. At the same time as he measures the sun's altitude with the sextant, he logs the exact time (his watch is checked regularly against the radio time signals) on a little car mileometer gismo which he's glued to the side of the sextant. No notebook, no pen, but don't bump the sextant on the way into the cabin or the reading could shift. He sits at one end of the saloon table, which at sea is divided into sections with movable battens. One half serves as the navigation area with sections for the almanac, sight tables, pencils and rulers and the chart itself, protected by a sheet of transparent plastic.

For a few minutes David's head is bowed over the sight reduction tables. His foot is braced against my bunk to steady himself. On a tiny notebook he works out three simple sums, draws a line on the chart, notes it in the log and replaces the books and chart cover. Five minutes work at the most. The noonsight, which takes even less time to work out, will give our latitude. The morning position line is projected forward. A small X marks where it crosses the noon sight line, about ninety miles westwards from the previous X. It's slowish progress. The trailing log spinning out behind us is registering about seventy miles. The rest of the lift is from the current, about a knot. A twenty-four hour average of 100 miles suits us. Not too fast or too slow – both are uncomfortable. Discomfort takes on a whole new meaning out here. There's no going off home at the end of the day.

Mealtimes are a big event. One o'clock: time for a lunch of bread, oily cheese, marmite, half a tomato and two slices of cucumber. Water, enlivened with a squeeze of fresh lime, helps it slip down, especially when the vegetables run out. We're low on bread already. Must bake some tomorrow. My loaves are much lighter now than the cement blocks I first produced. The breakthrough was reading that Susan Hiscock had the same problem until she found that in the tropics, a wet sticky dough gave better results. The cake tin is full of sweet-tooth treats, but we keep these for the ritual of tea-time, with refreshing green tea and the ubiquitous slice of lime.

David will have woken from his snooze and taken the afternoon sight before tea. From then on the sun, too low for an accurate sight, drops into the clouds on the western horizon. By six o'clock a deep gold stain is spreading through the clouds. The stain reddens and the sky is showered with little streamers of pink and orange. The colours cool off, running into the pale green-blues of oncoming night. The planets and the early stars are twinkling, like pinpricks in a curtain.

We see the day out, wedged against the cockpit coamings, enjoying our sundowner, a gin and tonic for David, a whisky and lime juice for me. (The tonic is made from concentrate and water, carbonated by an old fire extinguisher which David has adapted to squirt into a glass.)

I go below to finish cooking the evening meal. It's my turn tonight; we've been taking it in turns for years. The one who doesn't cook makes the coffee and washes up. There is a good smell coming from a spiced stew of potatoes, onions, canned tomatoes and sweetcorn. David takes a walk around the deck checking things. The twin jibs are poled out, pulling us steadily along. We're undercanvassed in this wind of about twelve knots, but speed is not our goal. To arrive safely with everything in one piece will be all that we ask of the month ahead.

The night sky envelops us. The moon rises late tonight. David washes up, using salt water that is almost warm. The kettle is on for coffee. I take a last look outside; no sign of squalls. I brush my teeth, using just a squirt of fresh water. With another squirt I wipe my face. In a few days time I'll treat myself to a shower on deck. I sip my coffee in the dark cabin while we listen to the BBC World Service. We are avid

fans. No other broadcasting service comes near to it. There is an hour or so before my watch. I drift into a doze. David, stretched out on the day bunk puts on the headphones. *Moongazer* rolls on. The second day has passed... and the third... and the fourth... Each different in detail, in essence the same.
The log notes read:

MAY 4th: DAY 4: Wind light, swell gentle – means a busy day. Oiled rigging, baked bread, washed hair & selves.

D. fixed sewing machine, patched No.1 jib, repaired flag & made 2 sundresses (for me!)

Also made lure for fish hook using spinnaker cloth. Chose orange for this month's colour.

DAY 9: Sail astern! huge spinnaker. Spoke on VHF radio – 35 metre ketch, Lord Jim. French owner Brit. crew. Left Galapagos only 5 days ago!

6 p.m. Disappeared over horizon – lost radio contact.

DAY 10: Trade wind well set in now. 15-20 knots E.S.E. steady progress. Current helps, 20-35 n. mls. per day. But yesterday we had a counter-current!

DAY 12: Rolling along from side to side. Hot and uncomfortable – no signs of life – no birds, fish, rubbish. Perhaps we are sole survivors of the planet?

DAY 13: Wind shift to S.E., strong gusts, sea lumpy. Main up – 2 reefs. Lots of little petrels. (Storm petrels?)

DAY 16: Sea eased – wind to E.S.E. Twins up again. Ship passed in night. (must stop snoozing on watch).

Much reading and mind improving. Quality deteriorates with weather. On fair days – Literature & Learning. On foul days – Junk. D. mends and maintains on fair days, so reads only junk!

('So what D'you want, – a well read husband, or an engine that works!')

This is easy-care sailing with twin headsails. Look, no hands! day after day. (plenty roll, though)

DAY 19: Fish, at last! large tuna. A fighter, blood everywhere. Felt faint. Death-blow technique needs improving. But wonderful to taste fresh food!

Veggie basket has 12 onions (sprouting) and half a cabbage (shrivelled). Last night had vegetable dream again. But so far, no signs of scurvy!

Both getting weary of sea, sky, sea, & more sky – & rolling, rolling, rolling every second of every minute of every hour......ROLL ON THE MARQUESAS !

Twenty-nine days – 2,900 miles. Tomorrow we should see land, all being well. It has been a classic trade wind passage; no really bad weather, but a boisterous wind at times and big following seas. There have been days of tedium and discomfort, and there have been days (and the odd night) of magic when I could have sailed off into eternity. Nothing, neither the good nor the bad, lasts for ever. We are weary, salty and tired of a diet which seems, to us spoiled Westerners, bland and monotonous. We are ready to laugh and talk with other people and sip chilled beer. But most of all, we are excited and curious about the islands ahead.

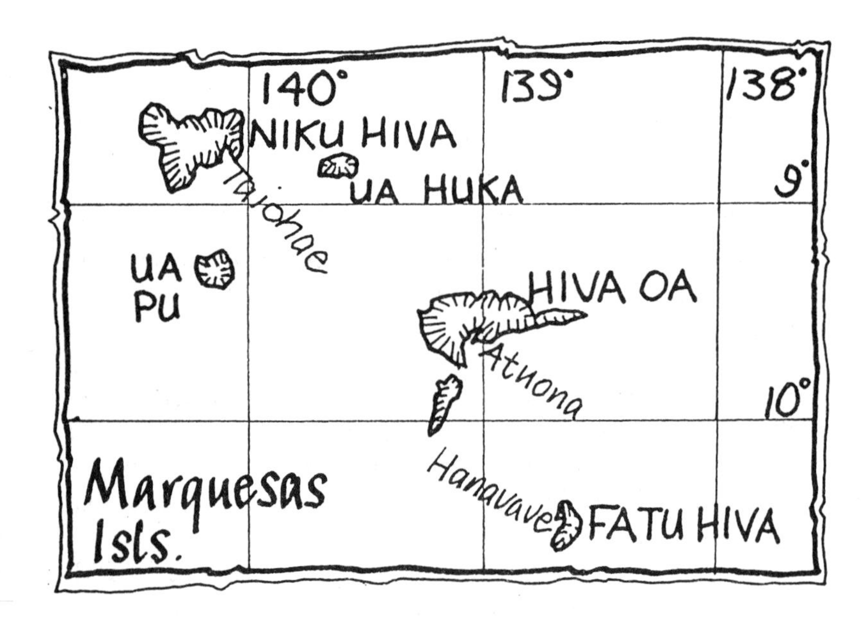
140°
139°
138°
NIKU HIVA
Taiohae
UA HUKA
9°
UA
PU
HIVA OA
Atuona
10°
Hanavave
FATU HIVA
Marquesas
Isls.

5

Gauguin's 'Savage Paradise'

> The first experience can never be repeated. The first love, the first sunrise, the first South Sea island, are memories apart, and touched a virginity of sense.
>
> Robert Louis Stevenson, on sighting the Marquesas.

We saw it first as a little smudge on the horizon, around noon, on the 28th day out from the Galapagos, 4,100 miles from Panama.

'There it is, Hiva Oa, as and when predicted,' said the master navigator. The student navigator was impressed, not by the master's proficiency which I took for granted now, but that we could see land thirty miles away. Unlike many previous landfalls, it wasn't hiding in the haze, to show up only at the last nerve-wrought moment.

And yet, I thought, how odd that such a striking landfall was missed by so many of the early navigators. In the wake of Magellan (who missed just about everything in the Pacific) came the Spanish and Dutch, up from Cape Horn en route for the Orient. For several centuries they passed just south of the Marquesas, unaware of their existence, even though the Spaniard Mendana had stumbled across them in 1595.

We rolled along through the afternoon and the smudge grew into mountains, their tops swallowed by the clouds. I honed up on the Discovery Of The Marquesas and by tea-time I was ready to scatter the seeds of freshly gleaned knowledge. Beside me was virgin ground, a truly vacant plot. He was busy unlashing the anchor ties.

'Did you know that when Mendana first saw the Marquesas he thought they were the Solomon Islands?'

'Oh yes?' said David, meaning not that he knew, but that he knew there was more to come; by the bookful.

'Yes. He was leading an expedition to find some islands that he'd come across thirty years before in the Western Pacific. He was convinced they must be the outliers to those fabulous lands of Solomon that were a current obsession with the Spaniards. When, six weeks out from Peru, the Marquesas hove into sight, the ship's company overlooked the fact that it was 4,500 miles premature and burst into a Te Deum. They were into their third incantation of gratitude before it dawned on Mendana that the natives who rowed out to meet them were not the black, fuzzy-haired Melanesians he'd seen before. These were light-skinned and handsome – so handsome that his pilot, Quiros, said it grieved him to think of their souls going to perdition.

'I bet he helped a few on their way,' said David. 'Could you pull on this line for a minute.'

I pulled and continued.

'About two hundred in two weeks, they reckoned. Mendana claimed the land for Spain and the souls for God and named the four islands he saw after his benefactor the Marquesa de Mendoza, the Viceroy of Peru. Then he sailed on for another 4,500 scurvy-ridden miles until he came to more recognizable islands. For another two centuries the Marquesas lay blissfully untouched by Europeans.'

'Okay, you can let go,' said David. 'Just tie it off at that.'

I drew breath for a few seconds.

'The next visitor was Captain Cook who came and stayed only to fix their position. He sailed off to Tahiti after four days, without knowing about the other clump of islands about a day's sail away to the north. It was an American ship that 'discovered' them, fourteen years later. From then on the Americans took a close interest in the islands, seeing possibilities of another Hawaii, no doubt. A U.S. Naval Captain actually annexed them in 1813. Intrepid souls from The London Missionary Society made several attempts to win converts, all of them unsuccessful. Finally, in 1842, the French, by then well-established in Tahiti, pre-empted everyone else's designs by running up the flag and installing a garrison and some zealous priests.'

'Watch it, your foot's in the way.' David was loosening the ties on the dinghy cover. Automatically I began undoing the ones on my side. There was barely a falter in my flow. The habits of lecturing die hard.

'But this made little impression on the natives. The islands were too isolated to administer properly. The hub of things in the South Pacific was 800 miles downwind at Tahiti, the model for the Myth of Paradise.'

David was starting to fiddle with the outboard motor so I knew for certain that I was addressing a reduced audience. However I had to tell him about the painter Gauguin.

'That was the Myth that lured Gauguin to Tahiti – twice. And when the disillusionment became unbearable, his last retreat was to the Marquesas. He saw them as "the last savage Paradise"'.

David looked up from the outboard motor and scanned ahead at the darkening crags and peaks of Hiva Oa.

'Not too savage, I hope,' he said. Maybe he'd been listening after all.

Savage or otherwise, we were at the portals of Paradise and they lay wide open before us.

But we tripped over a nasty step on the threshold. We were bowling along on curling seas before a healthy trade wind. Night was darkening the eastern sky and in the west the fair-weather clouds held the last rays of sunset, like pink powder-puffs across the horizon. The oncoming night promised brilliant moonlight. The coast of Hiva Oa was steep-to with no outlying dangers between us and the anchorage.

'I know we have a rule about not entering strange anchorages at night,' said David. 'According to the chart there's a light at the entrance to the bay.' I didn't fully share his confidence but the imminent prospect of an unbroken night's sleep was too much to resist, so we sailed on, under a rising moon, into the slot between Hiva Oa and two islands to the south.

Everything looked fine and I sat my watch, relaxed and unconcerned; until I happened to look behind. Enormous black clouds towered above, more massing with every minute. I oathed and woke David. He'd just got to the cockpit when, with a horrible hissing, the wind and rain ripped across the water and tore into us. *Moongazer*, with twin jibs still up, reared ahead like a demented racehorse. We clawed the sails down and it felt like being in a barrel at the foot of a waterfall. Suddenly the tap was turned off and the wind vanished and we were left, slopping horribly on a confused swell. In the lull, the damp warm air brought wafts of scented blossom and wet earth.

But if that was a mother of squalls, the rest of the family was all lined up behind, raring to get at us. We spent the night alternately wallowing one minute, being pasted the next. Our tactics, such as they were, were to try and keep station but the emphasis changed depending who was on watch. David was anxious not to get swept past the islands. I was even more anxious not to pile up on them. I was sure I could hear surf pounding on cliffs, all around us, or so it seemed.

We greeted a grey daybreak, wearily and gratefully. Hiva Oa was on our starboard bow, more or less where we'd last seen it. It was a breathtaking, tangled knot of mountains, ridges and ravines, carpeted to the top in jungle green. Precipitous cliffs plunged straight into the sea; no coral reefs and blue lagoons on this South Sea island. We sailed on towards the great sweep of Traitors' Bay, a spectacular dead-end where the ocean piled up in an explosion of surf. Spray and mist filled the air and carried with it the fragrance of wet greenery. With only a small jib set, and with the surf booming in our ears, we surged into the bay. The opening in the cliffs appeared to our right and we turned and shot into it. There, in the relative calm of Tahauku Bay, lay five yachts, including *Lord Jim*, rolling lazily at anchor. After four weeks of slewing down the swells we were almost at rest again. The banging-of-the-head-on-the-brick-wall had stopped and the moment was pure joy.

Before we could savour the moment to its fill we had first to anchor, a tricky operation in the restricted space. A bit of swell was running in the inlet, bouncing off its rocky sides, while, from the opposite direction, the wind flowed down over the mountains. Most of the yachts were anchored bow and stern in an attempt to keep their bows facing the swell. Half an hour later we were similarly anchored (more or less) and just about to reward our labours with a stiff drink, when our VHF radio crackled into life.

'Allo, *Moongazer*, this eez *Lord Jim*. Perhaps you would like to come and take an 'ot shower ? '

All thoughts of collapsing vanished. For two months we hadn't had one shower, let alone an 'ot one.

'What a nice idea, *Lord Jim*,' we replied in our British way. 'Thank you. We'll be right over as soon as we launch the dinghy.' The dinghy, a sturdy plastic affair weighing about fifty kilos, stowed neatly on the coachroof under the boom. We would launch it by hoisting it up on the main halyard, over the guardrail and lowering it under control down to the water. This was a simple operation when the boat was motionless, but like all tasks on the boat, its difficulty compounded in geometric proportion to the motion. Now the boat was rocking gently and while David worked the halyard winch I had the job of discouraging the dinghy's natural inclination to act as a giant pendulum. In spite of my struggles it bumped its way down the hull and landed with a splash in the green murky water.

Lord Jim was only a short row away and when we arrived at its high steel topsides we were given a hand up by two young Englishmen, who turned out to be the skipper and first mate. Inside the spacious wheelhouse was the French owner, M. Nouveaux, who greeted us, pleasantly, but a little as he might greet the friends of his children. A Canadian girl, Yvonne, showed us to the showers. 'I do the housework, and keep the ship tidy,' she told us.

'No cooking?' we asked.

'No, no, there's a qualified chef for that.' She handed us each a large pristine bath towel, a completely different species from the thin tired things we had brought with us. 'You'll find one shower up forward and one here amidships. There are hot and cold taps each for sea water and fresh water. We're full to the brim now, so go ahead and use as much as you like!'

Sweet words to a sailor – like being handed a blank cheque. My shower cabin was festooned with pipes and taps and I tried them all, just to savour the experience of having water run at the touch of a tap. I preened and luxuriated in my sudsy steamy cubicle. Cleopatra up to her neck in asses' milk couldn't have had more pleasure. I dried off among the fluffy folds of the bath towel and thrilled again to the feel of clean clothes on clean skin. Within minutes my T-shirt was damp and bonded to my back with perspiration.

Back in the wheelhouse among the banks of electronic goodies and radio telephones M. Nouveaux was entertaining a slim, dark-bearded Frenchman.

'That's Alain Colais,' the mate told me 'He's just come off that navy boat from Papeete, and he's waiting for *Club Mediterranee* to arrive. Then he'll be skippering it while it does charter work around Tahiti.'

The French make folk-heroes of their distinguished yachtsmen and Alain Colais had entered the ranks. Quiet and intense, he moved with surprising ease considering he had virtually no ankle joint in his left leg. It was crushed in the bight of an anchor-chain the previous year, just before the start of the single-handed trans-Atlantic race. He saw it as no reason to drop out of the race.

Sadly his ankle didn't trouble him for long; a year after we saw him he took part in another trans-Atlantic race and disappeared without trace.

Madame Nouveaux appeared and she was, as I expected, slim and attractive and wore a very carefully acquired sun-tan; every visible inch, and more, done to a turn and not overweathered. I took a sneaking pleasure in noting that she looked very bored.

The crew were eager for some British company and we retired to the aft deck to sip beer; beer that wasn't warm and fizzy like ours, but ice-cold. We all drank to the absent member of the crew, the engineer. He was down in the engine room wrestling with the refrigeration.

The talk drifted over me. Exhaustion and exhilaration were battling for my body. My mind was reeling from the impact of the scenery. From both sides of our rocky inlet rose cliffs which merged on upwards into mountain ridges. Everywhere dense greenery ran riot, a jungle slashed by brilliant light and jet black shade. It was the same stunning backdrop that Robert Louis Stevenson described as '...huge gorges sinking into shadow, huge tortuous buttresses edged with sun.' The most thrilling sight of all was the stand of coconut palms at the head of the bay. The crowns, waving in the wind like glossy green pom-poms, were borne thirty to fifty metres high on trunks, slender, elegant and gently curved. These were the palm trees of my childhood imaginings, of treasure islands and shipwrecked sailors.

Suddenly I was flipped back into conscious mode. The yacht anchored closest to the head of the bay was lurching with that jerky motion that comes from hitting the bottom. There was no one on board. We had seen the owners set off for the village .

'That boat needs help, – fast,' said *Lord Jim*'s skipper and as he spoke there was a flurry to action stations. We gathered spare anchors and ropes and set off in our dinghies to the stricken yacht. People from the other yachts were already on the scene, struggling to lay out a kedge. The tide was falling and with every lift of the swell the yacht bounced harder on the rocky bottom. It was a handsome varnished hull – but it wouldn't be for long. It was all we could do to keep the bow of the boat facing the swell but we were losing the battle to get her afloat. Just as we were despairing, M. Nouveaux (who was watching the proceedings through binoculars) recalled his skipper by megaphone. The high-powered inflatable paused at *Lord Jim* for a few seconds and then shot off to the naval landing craft. We had forgotten it was anchored in the bay, unloading supplies (including a bulldozer) into perilously small boats.

Within minutes a launch swung down from the landing craft and came speeding to the rescue. 'Here come the cavalry,' said someone. Someone else hummed the *Marseillaise.* And when the launch revved its powerful engines and dragged the yacht out of the shallows to the safety of deep water we all cheered and shouted '*C'est magnifique, Vive la France!*'

The day was M. Nouveaux's. He stood quietly on his deck smiling and nodding to himself, satisfied with events. The captain of the landing craft was no doubt already pinning pips to a clean shirt in anticipation of dinner aboard *Lord Jim*. Somehow it had never occurred to any of us to ask the navy for help, and the boat was very nearly wrecked because of that. Maybe we were becoming too independent.

The next morning *Lord Jim* left for Tahiti. M. Nouveaux was in a hurry to be back in France. We were on the cliff-top road to the village when we saw the sleek black ketch slide out of the anchorage. The skipper was at the wheel and the mate was on the anchor winch. There was no sign of M. Nouveaux. He was probably on the phone to Paris.

'Off back to the *Bourse* to make another million,' said David.

I remembered that Gauguin had worked for a Paris stockbroker. Hiva Oa was his ultimate refuge from the *Bourse* and all it represented. But even in this isolated spot, at the beginning of the century, there was too much 'progress' for him.

'I wonder how much more it's changed,' I said as we trudged along the dirt road to the village. 'What would he disapprove of nowadays?'

'Us, most likely,' replied David.

Nothing is ever likely to change the wild splendour of Atuona valley. From the turn of the road we looked down on the village at the head of Traitor's Bay and saw it, looking much as Gauguin must have seen it. Hemmed in by the precipitous valley walls and separated from the beach by dense groves of glistening coconut palms, the boundaries of the village have had little room to grow. On the steep valley sides it was difficult to see where domestic gardens and wild jungle met. Everything was smothered in a riot of greenery and blossoms. Only the stone tower of the church pierced its way through.

The wide dusty road through the village was deserted in the noon-day sun. The smoke of cooking fires rose in the air. We walked along the edge of the road, grateful for the shade of the majestic old trees – breadfruit, mango, banyan – that lined every garden. Nestling under their shade were the smaller trees like the papaya, the citrus trees and the odd banana palm. Vines and creepers and huge-leaved plants ran riot; plants that I recognized, but only just, as the same species that, back home, we imprison in little pots and cause to die of shame.

This profusion of vegetation fortunately hid most of each house. Gauguin would have been dismayed to find that, for reasons of durability and status, bamboo and palm frond was Out and that plywood and corrugated iron was very much In. However, the basic plywood box varied, depending on the energy and imagination of its occupants.

But it was in their shaded gardens that most people did their living. Through the flaming hedges of hibiscus we caught intriguing glimpses of women cooking, chatting, combing each other's hair and of children playing. This was a big improvement on Gauguin's day when the Marquesans were doing more dying than living and children's laughter was a rare sound.

Gauguin wrote in his journal:

> Many things that are strange and picturesque existed here once, but there are no traces left of them today; everything has vanished. Day by day the race vanishes... The chicanery of the Administration, the irregularities of the mails, the taxes that crush the colony, render all trade impossible... There is nothing to say except to talk about women and sleep with them.

No islands in the South Pacific suffered the fatal impact of the White Man more disastrously than the Marquesas. Ironically their isolation from 'civilizing influences' and the forces of 'law and order' made them a haven for the unruly whaling fleets of the nineteenth century. At the peak of traffic in the 1850s the whalers came in their thousands, bringing the agents of destruction: disease, opium, alcohol and firearms. These, combined with the reckless and often fatalistic Marquesan spirit, almost succeeded in wiping out the entire race. It seemed to Robert Louis Stevenson when he visited the islands in the Yacht *Casco* in 1888 that some blame lay also with the over-enthusiasm of the missionaries. They had proscribed so many of the Marquesan's ancient pleasures as to make their life unliveable. Bit by bit as new customs were forced upon them 'the unaccustomed race died of pin pricks...the mild uncomplaining creatures yawn and wait for death...change of habit is bloodier than a bombardment.'

In the late eighteenth century it was estimated that there were about 50,000 to 100,000 inhabitants living in the valleys of the six main islands. A count in 1842 showed that the population had plummeted to just over 6,000 and by 1929 it was down to 2,000. On the eve of extinction, the medical benefits of the 20th century and the tireless efforts of a few more sensitive priests began to take effect and the population is at last on the increase. The census in 1977 put it at 5,419.

To our eyes the future generation looked well-assured. Every woman seemed surrounded by a tribe of children. Dusky wide-eyed fauns with brown lean bodies, they were the most beautiful little beings we had ever seen.

The mothers might have glided out of Gauguin's paintings. The same handsome broad faces with the enigmatic gaze; the long jet black hair with the flower behind the ear: and those wide unfettered feet, just as he used to draw them! He would have been heartened to see what they can wear as street clothes these days. He would still be able to say '…their unconstrained bodies undulate gracefully,' but long gone are the missionary-imposed, full-sleeved chemises of lace and muslin. The women we saw wore either shorts and sun tops or boldly patterned cotton wrap-arounds, called pareus, tucked in just above the breast and hanging to the knees or further.

During the next few weeks we also saw many of the women he did not chose to paint: the fat and the wrinkled and the toothless. But, we wondered, where were the famed Polynesian maidens? 'The free, pliant figures', such as the 'beauteous nymph Fayaway', described by Herman Melville in *Typee*.

That same question worried Gauguin when he arrived. Then, as now, the girls were at school. But in 1901 compulsory schooling for teenage girls was virtually unheard of. It was a last ditch attempt by the Sacred Heart Mission at Atuona to save not only souls but bodies, by physically keeping them out of 'harm's way', that is, out of the way of the likes of Gauguin. This was a major setback, as he had come to the Marquesas partly, as he put it, '...to find new models.' However, with the skill of the practised agitator he found a flaw in French law and set about informing parents of their rights. School attendance fell dramatically, while, to the fury of the Bishop, there was a rush of pupils eager to broaden their education at M. Gauguin's self-named 'House Of Pleasure'.

We found no trace of the ill-famed House. On the site a Chinese baker produced authentic French loaves from a huge stone oven.

Across the road a couple of the village stores had survived more or less intact, pickled in the odour of kerosene and candles and souring flour. Nowadays business revolved around the freezer and cold chests which kept alive the vital supplies of lollies, sticky drinks, and beer. The sale of beer

Gauguin would have regarded as a personal victory. He championed the traders' fight to sell alcohol to the natives; '...otherwise they hide in the mountains and make their own.'

Like Stevenson, Gauguin sought in Polynesia escape from the strictures of a Victorian bourgeois upbringing. Unlike Stevenson, who found his paradise in Samoa, Gauguin felt pursued and tormented by petty bureaucracy even in Hiva Oa. He poured his frustration into polemic writings attacking his favourite enemy, the *Gendarme*: '...rough, ignorant, venal and ferocious.'

Happily for us, the Frenchman who stamped our passports at the *Gendarmerie* was pleasant, helpful and quite mild. He was dressed comfortably for the office, in boxer shorts and T-shirt, the latter emblazoned with the motto *Gendarme National*. Like him, we left our sandals on the doorstep and went in barefoot.

On our way out of the village we turned off and sweated up the steep track to the Catholic graveyard. Small and simple and set amongst scenery of the wildest beauty, one would hope that here Gauguin had finally found peace. But I doubt it. He will still be warring with his neighbour. His stone slab gravestone shares the shade of a frangipani tree with the marble vault of his bitterest arch-enemy, Bishop Martin.

We walked back to the boat that first day along a road which had become muddy from heavy showers, and twice as long, with knapsacks that held only two sticks of French bread. The one thing that no local needed to buy was fresh produce. Shops were for imported luxuries like canned pilchards. It seemed on the return journey that the entire road was now overhung with huge mango trees. I tried not to look at the pendulous clumps of fruit which dangled above, but David, I noticed, was sizing up a likely bunch at arm's height.

'No,' I cautioned. 'Remember the notice in the *Gendarmerie*.'

A large notice by the desk reminded visitors that all the trees everywhere, no matter how remote, belonged to someone and that taking fruit would be regarded as theft. This was more like Eden than I'd bargained for.

However, when we reached the cover of the coconut grove near our dinghy we succumbed, like Adam and Eve, and helped ourselves to limes from a little bush by the path. It had already been picked clean on its pathward side but with a little effort and a lot of scratches we managed to half fill a knapsack. At any moment I expected the sky to open, a bolt of lightning to strike, or some such Forerunner of Banishment. So when, *whoosh*! something plummeted from the palm canopy far above our heads and landed with a thud near my feet, I leapt in the air. On the ground lay a coconut, its thick green husk bruised by the impact. It probably weighed about two kilos and it fell from a height of over thirty metres. From then on I was always a bit uneasy about walking through coconut groves. I kept my mien humble and my eyes heavenward.

Back on the anchorage, I began to cast a covetous eye on my neighbour's bananas. A huge stalk swung temptingly from the boom of a small sloop in front of us. Fortunately, before I could nurse felonious thoughts, the owners, an elderly American couple, invited us on board. Procuring fresh produce, they told us, was a matter of getting to know the locals and finding what they had to trade or sell. Some even just liked to give stuff away. 'But,' our friends reminded us, 'it does mean you have to be around for a week or so.'

Fortunately the generosity was infectious and our neighbours plied us with bananas, *pamplemousse* (a delicious kind of grapefruit) and breadfruit. But as we were short of time and our stops through the islands could only be brief I saw our place in the food chain staying somewhere at the bottom (or the top, depending on how you looked at it).

The other three American yachts in the anchorage had

all sailed straight from California and their owners seemed to be adapting well to their first sailing experiences. For one couple the achievement was particularly remarkable. We had been on their large, home-built trimaran chatting for about half an hour when the girl made some remark about not being able to see.

'You can't see at all?' we asked, astounded.

'Virtually nothing. I started to go blind while we were building the boat, but I was still able to help with some of it.'

'She did all the cooking during the crossing,' said her husband with justifiable pride.

'Well, I know the boat inside out. My main problem was boredom. Next time I'll take some weaving or something.'

Even in my wildest imaginings I'd never stopped to think what a sightless ocean passage must be like. I just knew that the darkest hours of the night were the most frightening.

The water in the anchorage was murky from the streams that ran off the mountains after each downpour but it was deliciously comfortable to swim in. 'Warm tea', was how David described it, but the temperature was just right for me. I happily spent a day scraping off the bunches of goose barnacles that hung in succulent profusion from the hull. It was only afterwards that I realised the fish that had come to nibble at the falling barnacle scrapings were tiny sharks.

The valley at the head of the bay ran up into the mountains and looked enticing. In Stevenson's time it supported a thriving copra plantation with railways, boathouses and warehouses. A few years previous to his visit, an American was cultivating cotton successfully until his enterprise was overwhelmed by a tidal wave. Before that, Stevenson tells us in his narrative, *In The South Seas*, 'it was a place choked with jungle, the debatable land and battle-ground of cannibals.'

We would have to leave it unexplored as time was snapping at our heels. On our day of departure we managed to buy a sack of *pamplemousse* from a nearby garden. We lugged it to the little stone jetty and as we struggled to get it on board our heaving dinghy we met Ozanne, a fine young specimen of Marquesan manhood. He was loading crates of beer into a little powerboat, the only one we had seen.

'You must come to my place,' he said. 'Hannamenu, a bay to the north. It is on your route. There are three American yachts there just now and we are having a party. You must come.'

So we went.

6

Polynesian Make-believe

We found the bay of Hannamenu on the north-west coast, a slot in gaunt cliffs of bare red rock. Three yachts lay quietly at anchor. We could see their dinghies drawn up on the beach at the head of the bay. From the valley behind, we could hear shouts and laughter – the uncommon sound of adults at play.

Eager to be part of it, we rowed the dinghy through a moderate surf and dragged it up the white sand beach. We walked through the sun-dappled vaults of a coconut grove and as it opened out to a grassy corral we saw the source of the voices. A game of volley ball was in full swing. This had to be Ozanne's place as Ozanne was the only Marquesan in sight. His house and outbuildings, the fenced-in paddocks, the generator shed, the little thatched guest house, the water piped in from a stream, all displayed a sophistication that surprised us in this isolated spot.

For the next few days we all played at being Polynesians. We cooked our fish in Ozanne's cooking shed and sat down to communal meals. We bathed and washed our clothes in a deep, shady pool which was fed by a sparkling cascade of mountain water. Only Tarzan and Jane were missing.

Ozanne was keen that we should play all the scenes. As we gathered around on our second morning, he announced: 'I have killed a wild pig. This afternoon we will cook it in the ground, and tonight we have a feast.'

At first light he had gone by horseback up to the plateau where cattle, pigs and goats ran wild. With his dogs he had hunted and killed a young boar and now he was busy preparing it for the oven. The preparations took all day and involved all of us. We gathered wood for the fire, picked breadfruit, bananas and limes. We split open coconuts and spent hours grating the meat and wringing it through the fibrous mat of the kernel. This extracted the rich cream, a basic ingredient for the sauces, and for the rum punch. The pig, wrapped in banana leaves, was cooked in the traditional way, in a pit covered with large flat stones on which the fire was laid. When we finally ate it, four hours later, it was tough and gamey and bore little resemblance to what I remembered as pork. But to our palates, starved of meat, it could have been *filet mignon.*

Ozanne, with his gaily printed pareu and hibiscus in his hair, was playing make-believe just as much as we were. He should have been back at the family business in Atuona. Although only 28, he was already a father of six and his wife was in Tahiti expecting their seventh. His father had recently died and Ozanne was now playing head of the family. In the house were photographs of uncles, prosperous-looking types who lived in Tahiti, France and the U.S.A. There were more uncles in Atuona and it seemed that the little paradise in Hannamenu was now more a family holiday home.

'I could live here for ever,' Ozanne told us, 'but my children have to go to school; and my wife, she is only happy in Tahiti. Generations of my ancestors have lived in this valley. It is my true home.' Once, he told us, over 2,000 people lived there. The last permanent inhabitant died only a few years ago.

The main thoroughfare, a wide grassy road bordered by stone walls, was still visible. It ran from the beach through the heart of the valley and disappeared from sight in a tangle of trees and bushes. We wandered up inadvertantly in bare feet, not meaning to go far. But the surface, though overgrown, was compact and smooth, having been trodden down for centuries by thousands of pairs of broad bare feet, and we were able to walk comfortably, almost to the head of the valley. The old fruit trees, the limes and mangoes, were being suffocated by the undergrowth and the higher valley had become a jumble of regenerated forest that echoed to the crow of wild cockerel.

We discovered that the forest had grown over and around great platforms of stone blocks, the traditional *pae-pae* on which the natives built their houses. We could see the boundaries of former gardens and breadfruit plantations still neatly walled, block upon block.

Most impressive of all were the huge terraces and viaduct-like structures. 'This,' I told David knowledgeably, 'was probably a *marae*, a temple site. We're probably standing on the sacrificial altar.'

We felt as Herman Melville did when he stumbled upon similar but even more immense works in the valley of the Taipivai. We speculated that they were, as he put it: '...doubtless the work of an extinct and forgotten race.'

It would have been romantic to think so, but later I began to learn that Melville was keener on literary effect than on accuracy. It's possible he was misled by his captors as to the age of the structures, but also he was anxious not to contradict the very myth his writings helped to create: that the Polynesians were not only fun-loving but indolent and quite incapable of such feats of engineering and organised labour. The people who built these structures were vigorous and organised, as it seems the Marquesans were in the sixteenth and seventeenth centuries. Recent archaeological surveys in Melville's Typee Valley have shown that the terraces and platforms were constructed in various stages during this period.

The Marquesans were also enthusiastic fighters and each valley existed in a continual state of feuding with the next. Up on the hilltop ridges we could see traces of earthworks and fortifications. Later, when I had more access to books, I learned that this would have been a temple stronghold, one of the taboo 'High Places' guarded by the Demon *Po*, where particularly gruesome sacrifices were carried out. Prisoners were almost always used as sacrifices to maintain the powers of chiefly ancestors and the baked remains were served up to the chiefs and nobles. If enemies from the next valley were in short supply there was always some unfortunate from within the clan who could be deemed to have broken one of the many taboos which governed their lives. The temple high place was normally taboo to all but priests and selected custodians. The site was tended carefully and only the banyan tree was allowed to shade the terraces. For sacrificial ceremonies the whole clan was assembled and everyone took their appointed place below the highest platform. There, in full regalia, were arrayed the priests, chiefs, dancers and drummers, and of course, the unfortunate human offerings. They were often hung live from a gibbet by a cord knotted around their hair and passed through their scalps. There they swung while dancers, heavily tattooed and smeared with saffron, writhed to the throbbing drum beat, and priests conducted the sacrifice in piecemeal fashion, part by part. At the neighbouring island of Tahuata, Captain Cook observed these high strongholds with his telescope but with characteristic wisdom he would not allow any of his men to go near them.

It was in those pre-Colonial days that Ozanne felt he should have been born. Then, he told us, he would have lived as a true Marquesan. He didn't consider that he might also have died like one. At least he was aware and proud of his peoples' past. Most young islanders that we subsequently met in the Pacific were desperate only for the glitter of the twentieth century. They wanted cassette players, motor bikes and to go to America.

We left Ozanne as we had found him, playing volleyball. For us it had been a tantalizing taste of paradise, three fleeting days of lotus-eating. Yes, we said, we would come back again and stay longer. We meant it. It was another two years before we were in a position to carry out our promise, and when we tried to, we learned what we already suspected: one should never go chasing rainbows in the same place twice.

OZANNE

7

To Ua Pu For A Ukulele. Notes from the log.

June 3rd: Sailed overnight for Ua Pu. Dawn spectacle of spires and pinnacles.

'The place persists in a dark corner of our memories like a piece of the scenery of nightmares.' – R.L.Stevenson.

Anchored in Baie Hakahetau (we hope!)

Pilot book: 'A plantation of coconut palms with some huts fronting the beach are also good landmarks.' – But this applies to every bay in the Islands.

June 4th: Found the Ukulele Maker; he is also the shopkeeper. Spoke only Marquesan so children translated into French: 'I have never been to school, but I have 11 children.'

Ukulele will take 2 days.

June 6th: Ukulele ready – carved from single piece of hardwood. He starts to discuss price – only after 2 hours, and 8 rounds of beer.

Later: U.M., carrying lantern, accompanies us back to our boat – to demonstrate ukulele and drink whisky.

How do we get him back on shore in one piece?

Pilot Book: '...landing is difficult on account of the swell and a beach of large boulders.'

Much Later: U.M. safely on shore – still singing.

June 7th: Sailed at first light for Nuku Hiva.

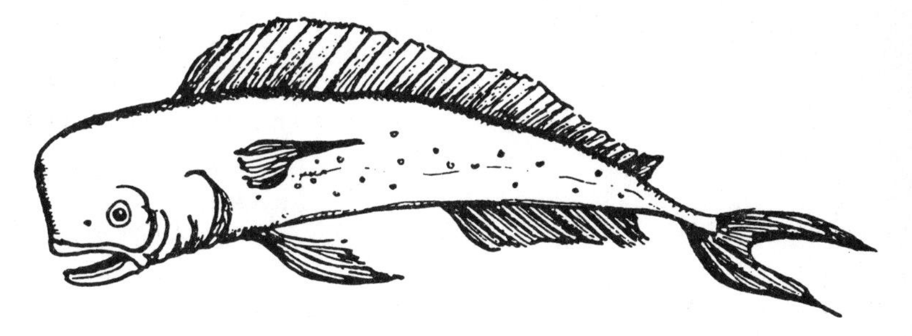

DORADO OR DOLPHIN FISH

8

Imperfect Paradise

We sailed all morning, hard on the wind, towards Taiohae Bay on the island of Nuku Hiva. The chart showed three large deep bays on the southern coast, but for a long time we looked ahead at a seemingly unbroken wall of cliffs. Shafts of light from the squally tropical sky played like a restless kaleidoscope on the rugged promontories, and we gave up guessing where our slot might be. And then, when we were almost up to the cliffs, they opened out and we were staring into the great mountain-girt amphitheatre that is Taiohae Bay.

But as we chugged in towards the anchorage in a corner of the bay, David's attention seemed more on the water ahead than the splendour above. I could swear there was a hint of expectation on his face. He'd been like that ever since I'd read a scene from *Typee* to him: the bit where Melville, on board a whaling ship, describes his arrival in the same bay:

> We were still some distance from the beach... when we sailed right into the midst of these swimming nymphs, and they boarded us at every quarter; ...they clung dripping with the brine and glowing from the bath, their jet-black tresses streaming over their shoulders and half enveloping their otherwise naked forms.

'You're 140 years too late,' I told him.

'Perhaps it's just as well,' he replied, still looking.

When, in 1842, Melville sailed in, the anchorage was buzzing not only with whalers but the warships of the French Admiral, Dupetit Thouars. He had just annexed the islands and was putting on a powerful show to impress the chiefs.

Now, a dozen yachts lay meekly at anchor, looking lost in the huge bay. There was little sign of life from the village, strung thinly along the shoreside road. A few mopeds and a jeep whirred past, the sound only just audible above the soft beat of the surf. A light swell seeped in from the ocean, breaking on the dark sand beach with the relentless regularity of a ticking clock.

On the eastern flank of the bay a ruined fort frowned down on us. Beneath it, near the water's edge and amid gardens of vivid blossom, stood a fine colonial-style house with wide verandahs. From a flagpole on the terrace fluttered the French *Tricolore*. We could see another *Tricolore*, high above a group of buildings near the village. There was no doubt that this was the capital of the Marquesas and that France was in charge. For us, it was our last hope of reprovisioning before the passage to Hawaii.

Fresh food, or how to get it, was becoming my number one obsession. The imminent prospect of a 2,000 mile ocean passage to windward didn't in itself excite me, but the further thought of being without the solace of tasty morsels filled me with gloom.

'You'll go bananas when you see Louise's garden,' our Australian friends on the next boat told us. 'She grows all sorts of stuff, just for yachties. But it's a bit of a hot hoof to get there.' We'd have willingly crawled over burning coals.

But first we had to present our passports at the *Gendarmerie.* We left the dinghy by the stone dock, a welcome change from having to brave the surf and drag the dinghy up beaches. On the dock I saw what someone had described excitedly as 'the shower': a tap projecting out at head height from a dank slimy shed. Still, it was fresh running water. We walked for a few minutes along the hot tarmac road, lined with hibiscus and flame trees, towards the tall white flagpole until we came to a cluster of old and new official-looking buildings. The oldest, a fine stone building with louvred shutters and a whiff of the French Foreign Legion about it, was the *Gendarmerie*. Passports stamped, we moved on to the Post Office, a pleasant, sensitively designed new bungalow. We fingered our bundle of mail excitedly, for it was our first mail stop since Panama, and stuffed it in the knapsack to savour at leisure. For most yachtfolk, reading letters from home was a time of great delight. We were always hungry for details of life back home, however trivial. We relished accounts of humdrum normality, something our friends found difficult to appreciate. 'Not much to to tell you,' they would write.

Business done, we made straight for Louise's garden. It was a long hot walk, but at the end of it there was no mistaking the lady or her garden. No-one else for hundreds (possibly thousands) of miles would be toiling in the sun among lettuces and tomatoes. There were rows of spring onions, radishes, cucumbers, and courgettes, all truly exotic to our eyes. It's the easy-care breadfruit, mangoes and papaya that are the boring, everyday fare.

Like children in a toy shop we wandered among the beds, picking what we wanted. Louise smiled happily as she pocketed the money. It was hard earned. Weeds grow here like rampaging triffids.

'Yes,' she told us, in good French. 'Everyone thinks I am crazy to work like this. But then they are envious when I go to America. I have been before and it was wonderful. So now I am making money to go again.'

Strange to think that most of her customers are doing the reverse!

Fruit and vegetables were our main concern as we had become quite used to doing without meat. I was beginning to notice, however, that we seemed only to be visited either by Feast or Famine. Right now it was Feast's turn.

On day number two, I was walking past the 'market' (a shed, usually empty, with wire grilles over the counters) when a wild-looking man rode up on a horse, dismounted and, accompanied by a cloud of flies, lugged a blood-soaked sack into the shed. Instantly a crowd of chattering women materialised and the man appeared at an opening with a rusty machete and a skinned cow. He proceeded to hack the beast to bits and after each hack, held up a chunk which was sold to whoever yelled the loudest.

That evening we invited friends over to share our prize. Roast wild cow and breadfruit chips, the nearest we could get to an English Dinner. Not such a treat, I thought as I chewed, and chewed, and discreetly deposited little lumps of fibre and gristle back on my plate.

'Boy, was that something else,' declared one of our guests, in what I could only imagine was ironic vein. But no, his plate was polished clean, and so was his wife's. She nodded in agreement. David's plate would have been clean even if I'd served up old deck shoes. I hadn't expected there to be such a booby prize, but it was a relief to know I was the only winner.

Feast next favoured us with the arrival of fresh fish. We knew it was coming when we saw a bevy of women gathering on the pebbly beach. I joined them, waiting at the water's edge while two paddlers in an outrigger canoe hung back until they found the right wave to bring them in. I was almost flattened by a herd of burly Polynesian ladies as they rushed past me, up to their waists in the water, and grabbed the best fish out of the canoe. Another canoe appeared and this time I was out in front with the best of them, but I grabbed my fish so hurriedly that some of the spines from its fins pricked my palm. It was only mildly irritating and I didn't think much more of it at the time.

Basic provisions like flour, canned butter and a sack of onions we bought at Maurice's store. There were two other stores, run by Chinese (the shopkeepers of the South Pacific) but the yachtfolk patronised Maurice's musty old place. This was a hangover from the days when his late father, Bob, was the white trader and the yachties' friend. Bob McKitterick was one of the old breed of seamen who jumped ship, turned trader and, with a native wife, lived out his days on the islands.

His son Maurice was a strange character with more of the Scots than Marquesan about him. Wrinkled and withdrawn, he suffered us hanging about his shop with a schoolmasterish scowl, which I reckoned concealed more approval than he would dream of showing. When I told him I was Scots, he lit up and burst into animated chat about some place near Inverness where he'd stayed in 1947. I had struck a chord and from then on he always greeted us warmly. There have been Scots in the islands well before McKitterick's time. Stevenson noticed a number during his visit: Mr Stewart from Fife, the plantation superintendent at Atuona, and at Taiohae the merchant clerks and 'The shrewd Scot who runs the cotton gin mill.' Possibly the Scots felt at home among the wild landscape and the abundant rain. Stevenson draws the parallel not only between the landscape of the Scottish Highlands and the Marquesas, but between the peoples. Both were fond of fighting but were now subjugated by an alien authority. Both had had their customs and costumes proscribed. 'Common to both races,' Stevenson wrote in 1888, 'are hospitality, tact, natural fine manners, and a touchy punctilio.'

Maurice's store was crammed with a jumble of boxes, bales, sacks and cartons, which we adjusted to our comfort while we sat around and sipped our daily extravagance of a cold beer. We chose not to sit outside under the palms by the shore – or anywhere else for that matter, for one tiny reason: the no-no fly, the Marquesas powerful anti-tourist weapon. These tiny black sandflies inhabit the beaches, rivers, water holes and other nice cool places where you'd like to sit. They seek out European skin, settle on it in their thousands, and munch away, often painlessly. Backs and feet are their speciality. Such a rude assault on our persons would come to our notice a few hours later, as we erupted in a mass of red spots. Each spot bore an itch that couldn't be ignored, and scratching became a way of life for all us visitors. But we had to scratch carefully. Broken skin could lead to serious infection which was difficult to heal in the moist tropic air. The arms and legs of many of the locals, both adults and children, were speckled with the bright red or purple stain of antiseptic on nasty ulcers.

Three days before we were due to leave I woke with an abnormally sore throat. It was different from the normal forerunner of 'flu and I could barely swallow my breakfast. I thumbed through our book on terrible tropical ills. I shut it quickly: I had already diagnosed two diseases and three kinds of poisoning. They all progressed to '... spasms, coma and death.'

'Well, if you're going to be struck down, at least there's a doctor here,' said David. 'You'd better go and make the most of him.'

I rowed in to the jetty and walked up the hill past the administrative buildings and the flapping flag. At the far end of the gardens I found the clinic, almost smothered by flaming blossoms of hibiscus and bougainvillia. On the cool verandah two dogs and a male nurse dozed.

I eventually found the doctor in a small room at the end of the building. He greeted me brightly, delighted to have a patient. He was young, seconded from the French army and dressed in a white T-shirt and tiny white shorts. His nurse was chic and elegant in that maddening way that French women have, even in the midst of the jungle. She lolled back on a chair, her long tanned legs on the table, smoking, and flicking the ash with great expertise across the room and out through louvred windows.

The doctor examined me carefully with his little hammer and flashed his torch into my eyes. 'Have you had any wounds,' he asked. I told him about the prick from the fish spines. He examined me all over again. Then he straightened up and said gravely, in English, 'either eet ees nozing important or eet ees very serious.'

Well, at least we were both thinking along the same lines. 'Come back immediately if the symptoms get worse,' was his parting shot.

For the rest of the day I kept a close watch on my condition, checking for signs of spasms or coma. As I woke up alive the next day, and with a much-eased throat, I had to conclude that I'd caught 'nozing important'. It probably was a reaction to some venom in the fish spines; a mild dose but a lesson enough to be more careful.

For me at least, Gauguin's notion of these islands as a 'savage paradise' was still holding good.

9

Playmates

One of the things that made paradise so tolerable was having playmates. Some of the yachts in Taiohae Bay we had met before, as far back as the Canary Islands. Most were new to us, from the west coast of the U.S.A. and they and their boats seemed neat and shiny and bright-eyed.

The British presence was maintained by three red ensigns (all pale pink by now) but it was thin on numbers, as our co-patriots were both singlehanders.

Long-term singlehanders plough a hard furrow and must surely have some character traits in common. Whatever these are, they're well hidden, for we found that rugged individualism comes in all guises. The Englishmen in the anchorage were a good example.

Ian, from Battersea (once upon a time), was sailing round the world in a scruffy looking boat he'd built, or more precisely, half-built, in Cape Town after a previous circumnavigation. He lurched through life, balancing chronic lack of money and planning against a big heart and surprising staying power. Like many singlehanders he yearned for the Right Lady to share his adventures, and though he knew that the stark, unfinished interior of his boat was an adventure most girls could do without, he never gave up hoping.

His fortunes at that moment were looking up. There was

in the anchorage that even rarer species, the singlehanded woman, from France, and the pair of them had got together.

In total contrast was Tom Blackwell, on his immaculate 17 metre ketch, *Islander*. Tom was lean and spry, in his 70s, with a boyish shock of white hair. We had met him in the Canaries and learned that he was on his third singlehanded circumnavigation on *Islander*. Built in 1937 and cared for meticulously, she was a classic wooden boat and the love of his life.

Tom was shy at initiating contact but he always seemed pleased when visitors arrived, as they often did, to admire his boat. He loved to show them round, particularly the engine room, which was something of a shrine. It had formerly been an aft stateroom but now it was entirely given over to a large glittering engine, festooned with gleaming copper pipes.

Tom's attention to his personal needs was more frugal. The galley was stark and simple with space for one set of dishes of the kind I remembered from childhood camping trips: white enamel with spidery cracks round the chips.

Across from the galley was a narrow wooden bunk, the only one on board. The saloon looked untouched since the 1930s. There were rows of books in faded bindings, and the table was covered with a cloth of green baize. Nor had he made any concessions to modern easy-care cruising. He still used the original paraffin navigation lights. Every night at sea, he'd fill and trim the heavy copper lanterns and raise them in position with a block and tackle. Inevitably there were dicey moments. On his second circumnavigation he arrived in Nuku Hiva with a broken mast and a hernia.

'But I had a rather wonderful four weeks in the little hospital. These people almost smothered me with kindness,' he told us in his clipped, top-drawer English that seemed at variance with the heavy tattoos on both arms. They were the only hint of what we later learned was a colourful past. He had been a racing driver and a fighter pilot and had only just survived crash-landing his plane on an aircraft carrier. The effects of his head injuries left him unable to cope with alcohol, which after a struggle he managed to give up. We had guessed he was 'on the wagon', as he would excuse himself from any invitation to Happy Hour drinks. 'That's when I wash down the deck,' he would say. So every evening as the sun sank below the horizon and cockpits stirred with the murmur of voices and the clink of glasses, Tom could be seen, determinedly scrubbing the life out of his teak-planked deck.

He planned to go quickly across the Pacific to Australia.

'There's nothing else in the Pacific like the Marquesas,' he told us one evening when we'd managed to winkle him onto *Moongazer* for supper. 'I'm going on to see a friend who lives near the Great Barrier Reef. Perhaps I'll spend Christmas there.'

We learned much later that he did spend Christmas there: his last Christmas. On his way back to England he died in hospital in Durban, South Africa.

Four years after his death we were there, and we dined at the Point Yacht Club, in the newly remodelled *Islander* Room. The renovation was Tom's last bequest to a club where he found friendship and hospitality. His memorial hangs on the long wall of the club dining room – the heavy wooden boom from his beloved *Islander*.

On our third day at Taiohae Bay, siesta-time was stirred by a new voice crackling over the VHF radio (kept on standby as an anchorage telephone).

'Nuku Hiva Harbour Control.'

It was unmistakably an American female voice: one whose owner was under a misconception about the Marquesas.

No-one answered: we were all waiting to hear what she would say next.

'Do you read me, Nuka Hiva. This is the yacht *Old*

Gold. I'm about four miles off. I think I'm going to make it before dark.'

'Oh-ho', we said. 'A single lady.' Eventually a German yacht with a powerful transmitter took her call and answered questions about the customs and harbour.

Just before dusk a little black sloop motored in and we were surprised to see three men in the cockpit.

'Maybe it's not the same boat,' said David, sensibly.

'Or maybe one of them's got a high-pitched voice,' I said, suddenly realising my life lacked gossip.

It turned out that there was a lady owner of the voice but she was below, saving herself for a suitable entrance. She made it next morning at Maurice's when we were gathered for our daily sup and chat. The conversation faltered when she teetered in on gilt high heels, all frothy blonde and flashing jewelry. We exchange pleasantries, mesmerised by the jumbo eyelashes and the glitzy sunspecs. Where, on a narrow-beamed 10 metre boat, shared with three men, did she stow it all? And how did she keep white pants so perfect? Not a speck of mould or rust; not a crease or crinkle.

Her entourage, hovering in the background, was less memorable. A son and a friend of his and a tall, thin, dispirited-looking soul who was introduced as 'Paul, my navigator.'

We were left in no doubt as to the ownership of the boat.

'My divorce settlement. I was damned if my ex was going to get the boat as well.'

Things were not going well on board. It had taken them 45 days from California, and they'd run out of water after the first ten.

'I just told the boys they'd have to learn to catch rainwater, and to stop showering every day.'

It wasn't clear whether they had really meant come to

the Marquesas, but they weren't staying.

'Not much of a place,' she said to me. 'I hope to God Tahiti's an improvement.'

Later, I reflected how much we were physically becoming part of that identifiable 'yachtie' group. The new arrival wouldn't have rated a second glance at a poolside soiree on her home patch in L.A. It was just that here, she'd wandered into the wrong party.

But it was something to talk about and a welcome change from the Josh and Nancy show, which was getting repetitive. Josh and Nancy were an Australian couple with whom we'd had some memorable moments in the West Indies. They could be engaging company, but their considerable energies were largely devoted to maintaining a state of marital war. The war would smoulder along, stoked by campaigns of mutual taunting, until it erupted into a violent physical battle. Then there would follow a period of passionate reconciliation. Josh, the master of the savage verbal swipe, seemed to come off worse in the physical engagements. 'Look at the bitch's handiwork,' he had said to us one day, displaying some large scars on prominent parts of his person.

They seemed to be operating just now in low-key guerilla skirmishes, and so far the anchorage was happily ignorant of their taste for open battle. I wondered how their poor crew was faring. An unsuspecting young German ('Another bleeding Kraut,' Nancy told me) had joined them in Panama and paid over $900 for the adventure of sailing to Tahiti with them. I had heard that he had already asked the *Gendarme* if he could change to another boat, but so far no-one needed extra crew. So, for the present all was quiet aboard the *Joncy* (I kid you not. The derivation of the boat's name took weeks to dawn on me!) but to those who knew them there were signs that they were gearing up for battle again.

Ian was about to have a birthday and Nancy threw her energies into organising a party. She ordered a pig, hired the village shelter, and extracted payment from us all, except Tom ('Barbecues aren't quite my thing') plus promises from every yacht to prepare a dish.

It was also a farewell party as a number of us would be leaving the next day, we for Hawaii and the others for Tahiti. It wasn't by coincidence that they were leaving together. In a few days they would have the comfort of a full moon as they passed through the yacht-snaring atolls of the Tuamotu Archipelago.

I didn't feel at all ready to leave. It had been a strenuous two and a half weeks; rowing through surf, dragging the dinghy up beaches, walking in the heat with heavy knapsacks, hauling the dinghy on board, taking down and putting up the sun awning, anchoring and re-anchoring. I longed just to sit around for a bit, or go snorkelling in the clearer water at the mouth of the bay, or exploring round the village. I'd like to have visited the wood-carver, or to have gone to a church service. After a rest I'd like to have hiked with David up the mountain road to the high plateau or taken the track over the ridge to Typee Valley. There was the north coast of the island still to see, where Stevenson first anchored: 'Of the beauties of Anaho, books might be written.' But if we stayed now we might not get to Canada before October.

'So which do you prefer?' asked David, knowing the answer, 'The autumn gales in the North Pacific?'

'I think it's finally dawning on me that there really is no such thing as a simple life,' I said by way of reply. David smiled.

'Only because we always manage to complicate it.'

Our penultimate day at Taiohae Bay was a long one. We finished preparing *Moongazer* for what might be a wet windward passage. David cut extra vent holes in the deck and, having no dorado boxes to hand, used lengths of plastic drainpipe to keep the openings high and dry. We caulked and sealed round hatches and windows and anywhere else we thought that spray might find its way in. We stowed our wash tubs and water carriers and dismantled the awning. I baked bread and cake and sticky goodies and wrapped them up in foil. Then I made up a dish for the party. I felt nervous about the party. All day Nancy had bustled around in an orgy of organising, and I couldn't see Josh taking this show of strength meekly.

The evening started well except for a slight hiccup when Josh, sitting stewing on a wall on the edge of things, suddenly addressed the startled assembly on the demerits of being married to Nancy. Then he keeled over, and to everyone's relief, passed out. The party hummed along and some young Marquesans with guitars joined us. We ate, drank, sang and danced and forgot all about crossing oceans.

At some late hour when David and I were about to leave it to the hard-core revellers, Josh woke up. Nancy's carousing came to an abrupt halt and they engaged battle, she defending herself with a practised vigour. It was an embarrassing spectacle and the American assembly, all earnest respectable souls, were especially shocked. The Marquesans, I noticed, seemed quite unconcerned. The antics of drunken sailors was something several generations of them were used to. Except that in the past the sailors were from ships.

Next morning everyone on the *Joncy* was up preparing for departure as if nothing had happened. *Old Gold*'s glitzy lady paid us a visit to buy some charts. Her evening too had been eventful. Her 'navigator', no doubt emboldened by Josh's example, had told his captain what he thought of her.

'Well, I can tell you, he's navigator no longer,' she hissed at us.

'I think these are the ones you need.' David tried to

direct her attention to the charts. Unsuccessfully.

'...as I told the boys, you've just gotta feel sorry for the guy.'

We nodded in heartfelt agreement.

'You'll want the plan for the pass at Papeete as well,' persisted David.

'We couldn't leave him behind in a dump like this, so I've stripped him of his duties and he'll travel as non-active crew to Tahiti. Then it's goodbye.'

She stopped for a few seconds while David pointed out where Tahiti was. He cautioned her about the Tuamotus.

'Wow! No kidding! Well, if that creep can learn to navigate, and he wasn't so hot either...'

When finally David rolled up the charts and mentioned the going 'yachtie' price, she gave an imperious wave of her hand.

'How if I just send over for a couple of bottles of champagne instead?'

'Too kind,' we murmured. 'But we'll just settle for boring old cash.'

Around noon the first flotilla set off. *Old Gold* led, with *Joncy* behind, towing the engineless Ian. All was back to normal on *Joncy*. Josh was at the wheel, the daughter was hauling up the anchor, the skinny German was feeding the chain down the hawsepipe and Nancy was centre deck, bellowing orders to everybody.

We watched them chug past, and out of our lives – we thought. They continued on their own colourful ways across the Pacific and several years later, each one crossed our path again!

The bay was now left to the curious-minded – those who planned to spend some time exploring the Marquesas. There were three yachts from San Francisco and one from Seattle. Already their owners seemed to have accumulated an astounding amount of information. This was the first trip for all of them but they could chat with ease about the South Pacific and all facets of ocean cruising. Their information systems back home obviously operated on a wholly different scale from ours. Their boats were already kitted out with all sorts of little details that add to the comforts (or rather, minimise the discomforts) of tropical sailing. We were still struggling along in the School Of Experience.

They were pleasant folk, not pushy with their knowledge but they dispensed it in such a way that we found ourselves listening attentively. Even as travellers, they had arrived primed with information on the islands.

'You didn't find the stone *tikis* on Hiva Oa?' they enquired.

'What *tikis*?'

'You didn't go to Fatu Hiva!....My God, they missed Fatu Hiva.'

'Then you haven't read Heyerdahl's book?'

'You mean *The Kon Tiki*,' I said, hoping for *some* marks.

'No, no, *Fatu Hiva*. What set him off on the whole *Kon Tiki* thing.'

We were definitely bottom of the class.

'But why the rush?' they asked. 'It takes time to soak this place up.'

'We'd love to stay, but we have to be up in Canada before the Autumn gales.' I explained.

'Canada? What for?'

'The winter', we replied and they, all refugees from the cold, stared blankly, silenced for the moment by polite restraint. But only for the moment.

'So you'll be going to Hawaii – have you read Michener?'

'Um, you mean...' I was feeling my way.

'*Hawaii*, of course (dummy). You want to read it on the passage. We've got a copy on board; I'll give it you before you leave,' said a generous soul.

They were taking our education in hand. We had entered Uncle Sam's orbit: we were being sucked into the great maw of the U.S.A. From now on, whether we liked it or not, our operations would be influenced by the American way of doing things; as long as we had the energy to roll with it.

So, clutching our 'could do better' reports we sailed out of Taiohae Bay into the snare of our old enemy – the capricious demon of the squalls. Our last look before we were enveloped in sheets of rain and lightning was of the wild northern coast; of Stevenson's 'strange, austere and feathered mountains.' We were playing the last scene in King Lear.

We had come to these islands as sailors, preoccupied with the demands of the boat and our bodily needs. We had run slap into a culture (such as remained) and a landscape that was outside our Western experience. It was my first South Sea island and I was smitten. I had come under the spell of the dark, menacing mountains; the deserted valleys; the fecund jungle and the profusion of its blossoms; the swaying, soaring coconut palms; the swift, savage squalls; the moist fragrance of the night air; the heart-beat of the surf; the quiet dignity of the golden-skinned people. They had all, as Stevenson put it: '...touched a virginity of sense'. It had been a brief encounter but a powerful one for both of us. We had sipped from the cup that nourishes travellers and keeps them wandering. We knew then, as we tore into the black night, leaving the lightning-lit sky astern, that wherever else our wanderings took us we would have to return.

10

Into The Trade Winds -- And Through The Doldrums

> ....oceans, where the soul of the world has plenty of room to turn over with a mighty sigh. Joseph Conrad

We had crossed the Atlantic and half the Pacific, running always before the trade wind. Downhill sailing, we called it. These great winds of the tropical ocean blow for at least six months of the year from east to west, steadily and often strongly. Our trade winds had swung around from north-east through to south-east and they brought with them big following seas which carried us along. I had watched these seas, day upon day, come curling up under our stern and wondered how it would be to take them nose-on. Now, en route to Hawaii, we would find out.

For 2,100 miles we would be heading north, across the climatic zones. We would leave the southern hemisphere on the south-east trades and creep through the doldrums until we found the north-easterlies. From then on it would be a hard, wet, slog to Hawaii, but as long as we held our easting, not an impossible one. That, at any rate was The Word, according to the *Pacific Islands Pilot Volume III.*

But winds have little regard for pilot books and we left the southern hemisphere close-hauled to a fresh north-easterly. With rare consideration, it brought a gentle and regular sea, and for seven days, heeling under full sail, we scudded along to the steady rhythm of the waves. By day the sea sparkled under a cloudless sky: at night it glittered under a full fat moon. Dolphins kept company with us for hours at a time, diving and leaping with the bow wave. In the cabin we could hear their happy squeaks transmitted through the hull. At night they made underwater trails of disturbed phosphorescence, streaking alongside like luminous torpedoes. Day after day *Moongazer* creamed along. The gurgle of foam along the hull and the humming in the rigging were the music of happiness. David's little pencil crosses marched across the chart; noon to noon, 130 miles. The Southern Cross dropped lower in the night sky. To the rhythm of the twelve-hour day we read, cooked and did chores. And while the round melon moon rose up behind the port hand rigging and slid down the other side, we slept fitfully and dreamed. It was ocean sailing at its best, a gift from the gods, and we knew it.

We also knew that in this life there is no such thing as a completely free gift and by the fifth day I was becoming uneasy.

'You'll see,' I said to David, 'there'll be a price to pay for this.'

But when, on the seventh day, we felt the wind slipping from us and saw, massed on the horizon, billowing mushrooms of grey cumulus, I felt no satisfaction, only depression. We were sailing into the doldrums, that great band of climatic no-man's-land where the trade winds of the two hemispheres merge into a mouthful known as the Inter-tropical Convergence Zone. More descriptive is its less used name – the Equatorial Trough. In the eastern Pacific this lies not on the equator but north of it, by anything up to ten degrees.

Daybreak on the eighth day found us heaving on a grey, glassy ocean. The sails slatted back and forth with a resounding crack as we rolled on the swell. We dropped them and rolled even more. Up went the mainsail again, sheeted tight in an attempt to dampen the motion. We lay on our bunks, poaching in perspiration, reading and trying to ignore our lack of progress – like turning on the car radio in a traffic jam. This was a traffic jam that could go on for days, or even weeks. There were those same bitterly teasing moments of raised hopes when it looked like the show was once more on the move and we sprang to action. Ha! Ha! Fooled again!

On the third day of wallowing, the god of winds answered our prayers – with a malicious twist. The day dawned dismally and almost immediately we were hit by a snarling squall. *Moongazer*, still wearing her scant but squall-proof nightdress of staysail and mizzen, responded sluggishly.

'No point in doing anything,' said David. 'It'll be over in ten minutes.' An hour later it was still with us.

'Beginning to outstay its welcome,' I said as we peered out of the cabin window into sheets of rain.

'I suppose,' replied David, 'we should make the most of it and get some more sail on.'

'Like, "lie back and enjoy it"…' I muttered to myself, as I fumbled unfamiliarly with a mildewed rain jacket. Tropical rain was usually a welcome coolant but this stuff looked chilly.

We raised the working jib and a reefed main, and felt *Moongazer* pick up her skirts and break into a trot. Albert, the self-steering gear, moved the tiller more confidently. We were respectably under way again. After a last look round at the dismal scene we retired, dripping, to add more moisture to the clammy cabin.

It was a day for a good thick book, so I climbed into my bunk with James Michener's *Hawaii*, so recently thrust upon us for our self-education. After a few pages I was no longer lying on my sticky towel-lined bunk, my head propped on cushions to keep it still, my foot braced against the bulkhead. I had forgottten my gloom, my anxieties about what might lie in store, the uncertainties, the tedium of our diet. I was thrilling to the real terror of lying frightened and soaked on the heaving deck of one of the great Polynesian sailing canoes. I was in the women's hut which gave some protection from the sun, but not from the seas that frequently broke across the stern. The slaves in each hull baled continously to keep us afloat, and when there was no wind they paddled until they dropped from thirst and exhaustion. We were all suffering terribly from thirst as rainwater is difficult to catch and store. I could hear the pigs squealing and the dogs whimpering. The farmers are actually more expendable than the animals. We women (there are twelve of us, and thirty-eight men) are way down in the pecking order for food. Half a stick of dried breadfruit today. The king gets the first of the fish that's caught. Right now he's with his chiefs in the other hut, the temple. They don't tell us but it's obvious they don't know any more where we are. For five days a west wind took us in a storm and we saw no stars. Last night the cloud parted and showed our stars to be much further away than they'd expected. We know from the tales of our ancestors that canoes have crossed these seas and that there are islands to the west of our Bora-Bora. We were heading towards these islands, but now it seems that we are being swept away to the north. We have done something to offend the great gods of the ocean and we are frightened.

An invocation of the twentieth-century kind brought me back to *Moongazer*.

'My God! Listen to it!' I heard David say. 'D'you think it's getting worse?' We were slewing and surging down a heaving sea. Rain was hammering on the cabin roof. A reply seemed redundant. Shortly we would be enveloped in the twelve-hour tropical night.

'Perhaps we should set the storm jib for the night,'

David said, in that casual I-don't-want-to-alarm-you voice which always sends my heart bounding out of its box. Storm jib! The very name shrivelled the inside of my mouth.

'Right now it's not that bad,' he continued, 'but you can bet there's a bombardment planned for 3 a.m.'.

I struggled into my oilskins in silence, a sure sign that I'm taking things seriously. Not since leaving Europe had we worn oilskin trousers. Then, they always kept company with thick socks and rubber boots; now, the pvc on bare legs felt odd, and the hem chafed the top of my feet. We buckled on our safety harnesses. I felt like a commando dressing for combat. David was the platoon commander, explaining quietly what we had to do. At the door he paused and nodded to me to follow. It was like hearing the bugle call to 'go over the top'. We tumbled out into a battlefield of rain, spray and surging seas. I was amazed at how a few centimetres of plywood could insulate us so totally from such chaos. Our snug and orderly cabin had belonged to another world. *Moongazer* was slewing erratically as she surged down the waves. 'We'll drop the main,' David shouted. 'We're going too fast.' He wiped the face of the wind-speed dial. 'It's only a good gale. Forty knots worth,' he yelled. I was almost disappointed, and at the same time alarmed.

'You mean it could get worse?'

'Your guess is as good as mine,' he shouted back, with unusual conviction.

We clipped our harness lines to the steel safety wire which ran the length of the deck and proceeded with our mainsail-dropping drill. We subdued the billowing folds of wet slippery terylene and David went forward to do battle with the jib. I disconnected the self-steering gear and took the tiller, the idea being that I would keep the boat steadier for David, working out on the bowsprit. I watched the foam-streaked waves come snarling towards the stern. I held the tiller steady, and as the boat rose, I let it give for a few seconds and then, as the wave surged under us, I brought the helm over, keeping the speed up and presenting the stern ready for the next wave. The steering gear had made it look deceptively effortless. What it lacked in brain, it more than made up for in brawn. After five minutes I was exhausted.

Reliable self-steering gears have only been on the scene for the last thirty years or so, and I reflected for a moment on all those pioneers who hand-steered their small boats around the world. I remembered Eric Hiscock's description in *Around The World In Wanderer III* of the agonies of a sleep-deprived Pacific crossing. He would wake from being off-watch to find his wife slumped asleep in the cockpit, her hand still on the tiller keeping *Wanderer* on course.

A yell from the bow directed my concentration to the steering. I had let the swell slew us sideways, almost broaching: a dangerous position, stopped broadside to the seas. David was perched on the pulpit, over the bowsprit, using both arms to stifle the flailing jib. Dry-mouthed, I concentrated only partially on my task. I tried to rehearse mentally how I would react if David went overboard. Would I be quick enough to throw him the dan buoy? Or stay cool enough not to fumble the release catches, or screw-up on dropping the sails, starting the engine, keeping the jib sheets free of the propeller? And then how much progress would the boat make back against the seas? I froze, even at the thought of it. Fear of inadequacy, in all life's situations, is perhaps the most debilitating fear of all.

A far-away shout came from the bows: 'Get ready to sheet-in!' David had hanked on the storm jib and was moving down the deck to hoist it. My heart beat settled again and I braced myself for action. The tiny jib went up well under control and I cleated it off and got both hands back on the tiller. If I concentrated very hard I found I could steer with relatively less effort on the tiller, but after a few minutes my mind would wander off and let brawn take over. The grey, foam-flecked world around me felt depressing, and I would rather not have had to look at it. There was nothing seriously frightening about the scene. (We were to see much worse in later travels.) But with every backward glance I felt a pang of gloom. It was the reverse side of seeing a beautiful landscape and feeling that stab of joy. The waves rolling towards us were hoary and greybearded and reminded me of Joseph Conrad's words: 'For it is a gale of wind that makes the sea look old.'

David joined me in the cockpit and we put Albert back on steering duty. Then, satisfied that *Moongazer* was managing well on her own, we piled back into the cabin. 'Mission accomplished!' I declared and peeled off my sodden oilskins. David stood, motionless, listening. Was it imagination, or was the wind easing? We looked at each other and then out of the window. Incredibly, the sky was a shade lighter, with pinkish tinges from a reflected sunset. For the first time that day we both smiled.

The wind continued to drop and stars sallied forth from behind sluggish clouds. After supper we went on deck to put up more sail. As surely as we hoisted the mainsail the last puff of wind drifted away. We were back to wallow and slop. I looked up to the heavens. 'Ha! Ha! Very funny.'

'So?' teased David, 'what would you rather have?'

I threw him a dark look. 'Now don't *you* start!'

Fortunately he laughed. It was wry and it was dry, but at least it was laughter, our sole weapon against Them Up There.

Next day we were greeted with all the dreary signs of still being in the doldrums. 'So what was yesterday all about?' I asked an empty cabin. David had removed himself to the cockpit when he saw me bear down upon the austere blue covers of *Pacific Islands Pilot Volume III.* I opened it and went straight to the page that was on my mind. It was headed:

'Tropical Depressions and Hurricanes.' A little map with arrows showed hurricane tracks in past years. They sprouted mostly out of Mexico, some running up the U.S. coast and some running out to sea, trailing off inconclusively to the east of us. But one snaked on out past Hawaii and several sprouted from the islands themselves. I picked up the book and climbed purposefully into the cockpit. At least I would be heard if not listened to.

'Have you seen this?' I asked accusingly and without waiting for a reply continued, 'It says: "Tropical storms are liable to occur…"'

David was ready with an unconvincing show of having studied the information. 'And it also says they are very rare around here. The barograph will soon let you know if there's a depression coming. Yesterday's action was probably just a tropical wave.'

'Well, I don't like the way those tracks run out in this direction and end so vaguely.'

'Look,' said David, his patience thinning, 'there's as much chance of us running into a hurricane as getting struck by lightning. So put it out your mind.'

It just happened that being struck by lightning rated high on my list of possible disasters, but I shut the book and my mouth and resolved never to mention the word 'hurricane' again – well, at least not for the next few days.

Those days followed one upon the other, essentially the same; varying only in detail. We inched our way mostly forward, sometimes sailing in the squalls, sometimes under engine. The fuel tanks held about 300 litres of diesel but we used it sparingly on the ocean. We might need engine power more seriously if any difficulties arose when closing land.

We were into our seventh day in the doldrums, and I had almost finished *Hawaii*, when a whisper of wind from the north-east stole through the rigging. We pretended not to notice. Off and on during the night it tested us, but finally, finding no fun in teasing, it decided to stay. As if to make up for the deviances of its fellows, this wind was straightforward and uncompromising. We sailed northward, hard against it for six days, keeping just east of the longitude of Hawaii. We daren't ease off toward the Hawaian islands in case we were pushed downwind of them. I couldn't bear to think about beating back.

We had expected this part of the trip to be wet and uncomfortable and for once we were right. *Moongazer* pounded along in a cross swell. Wind-driven waves slapped the bow, sending continual bursts of spray across the deck and cockpit. Life in the cabin, with closed vents and windows, was tedious and clammy. But, at least we were, as David so eloquently put it, 'Bloody moving'.

In that last week we covered twice the distance of the two previous weeks. From time to time the sun popped out from an otherwise leaden sky and triggered a feverish dash to the deck by David with sextant in hand. Even half a sun sight was worth hundreds of inspired guesses as to where we were. On the 20th day we felt confident enough about our position to fall off the wind and head north-west to the Big Island of Hawaii.

'It seems we've traded the relief of coming off the wind with having to roll in a beam sea,' I whinged.

'Listen!' said David, removing the earphones that he seems symbiotically attached to at sea. 'It's Radio Hilo, from the Big Island.'

My spirits soared. We listened entranced to the adverts. McDonalds were having an opening somewhere, with free hamburgers. 'Free hamburgers,' I murmured, trance-like. Already I was there, anywhere but in the hot, sticky switchback of a cabin sweating over the 130th way to camouflage corned beef. David cut in on my reveries. 'Around midnight we should pick up the lighthouse. 'Flashing, six seconds', the Lights book says.'

Like hamburgers, we hadn't seen a lighthouse since Panama. My eyes would be glued to the horizon. I wasn't so sure about David. His attitude to landfalls was a little more relaxed. 'I'll take the watch around then,' I said.

'As you like,' he replied with a flicker of a smirk. 'We might still be further off than I've reckoned. Don't worry if it doesn't show up.'

Right on schedule I saw, as we rose on the swell, the tell-tale sweeps of light in the far sky. I climbed on the cabin top and counted them. One every six seconds. It was a quiet moment of great relief and satisfaction.

By daybreak we should have been gazing at volcano slopes, 4,000 metres high. Instead, a morose ribbon of coastline lowered beneath the cloud. We headed, by instinct rather than calculation, to where we hoped lay Hilo, the capital and port of entry. We were making good progress when, at just fifteen sea-miles off, the wind vanished, sucked by the mountains, and we were left to roll horribly in the large swell. We nimbly switched our allegiance to the god of engines and worshipped him nervously as we chugged slowly toward the end of our penance. By mid-afternoon we rounded the massive breakwater and gained the promised land, the flat water of Hilo harbour.

2,100 sea-miles had taken twenty-one days. Seven were magic, seven were doldrums and seven were in the north-east trades. O, venerable gods of the wind and sea, perhaps after all there is method in your mischief!

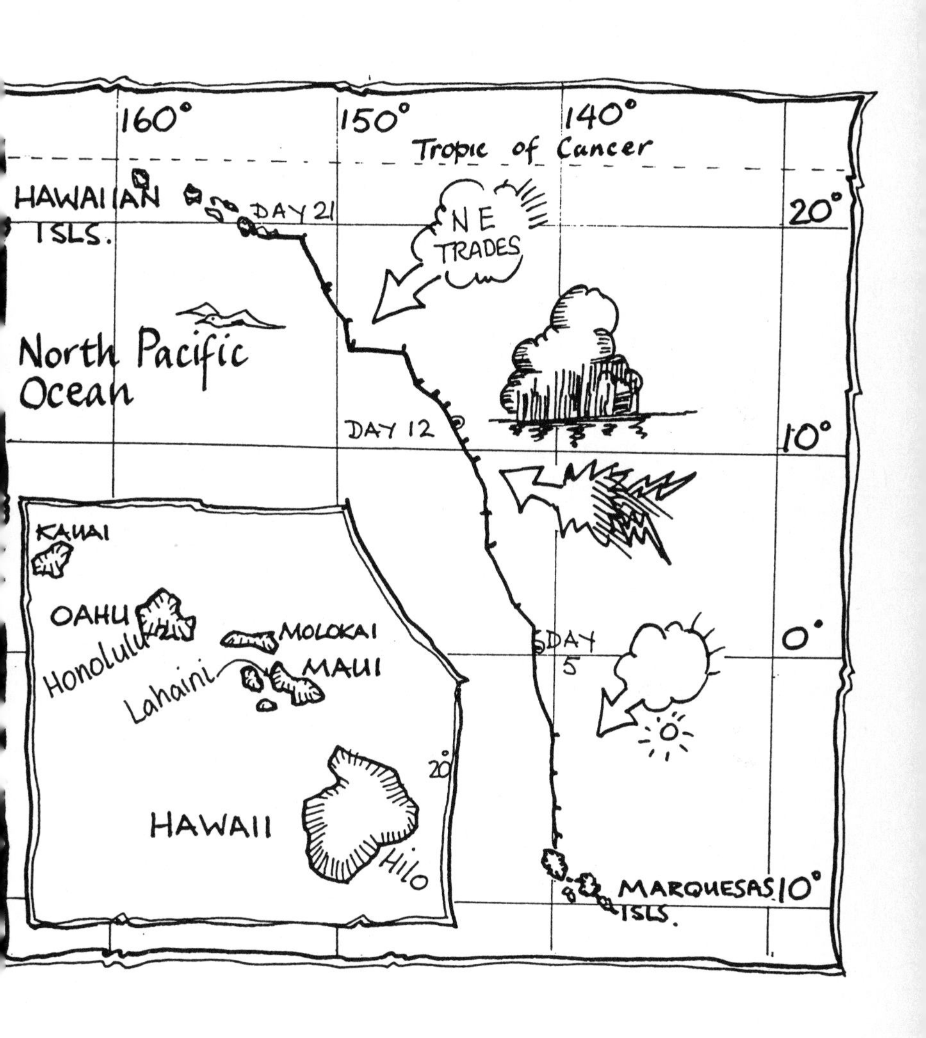
160°
150°
140°
Tropic of Cancer
HAWAIIAN ISLS.
DAY 21
NE TRADES
20°
North Pacific Ocean
DAY 12
10°
KAUAI
OAHU
Honolulu
MOLOKAI
MAUI
Lahaini
DAY 5
0°
20°
HAWAII
Hilo
MARQUESAS ISLS.
10°

11

Re-entry Rituals

When Captain Cook sailed into the North Pacific in 1778, he expected a tedious but uneventful haul to North America. Instead, he made one of the most surprising discoveries of his career – the Islands of Hawaii.

He had assumed that if there had been any land in these parts the Spaniards, or their predators, would have found it long before.

For two hundred years successive Manila galleons had lumbered back and forth across the Pacific between Mexico and the Phillipines. The journey back to Acapulco was made along latitude 30 degrees, not high enough for consistent westerly winds, and the voyage took at least seven to eight months. Countless men died of scurvy and starvation not knowing that halfway across, just to the south, lay these bountiful and welcoming islands.

Cook stopped briefly at the northern islands of Kauai and Niihau. He was on his way to look for the fabled North-West Passage, the much dreamed-of route into the Atlantic. He took his ships to four degrees north of the Arctic circle before turning south, back to the islands for a well-needed rest. Even then, he spent fifty days coasting down the chain looking for an anchorage. He battled with gales, headwinds and contrary currents to reach the western side of

'Owyee' where, finally, he found a suitable anchorage, for the last time in his life.

This was the fateful Kealakekua Bay, the site of the principal settlement. The native population saw Cook's arrival there, not as the coincidence it was, but as part of The Grand Design. They turned out in their thousands to accord the Aliens from Another World a tumultuous welcome.

The High Priests and Official Welcomers led Cook and his officers off to the sacred temples for what a young lieutenant described in his journal as: 'A long and rather tiresome ceremony at whose objects and meaning we could only guess.'

Now, 200 years later, our arrival at Hilo, the island's Port of Entry, raised only a faint flicker of interest among the seasoned loafers on the dockside. They were evidently inured to the antics of crews trying to back their yachts stern-to the dock. They gazed impassively as *Moongazer* zig-zagged into a tight slot while I rushed frenetically from one side to another, fending off between the huge flared bows of a Coastguard cutter and the projecting hardware of a rugged steel yacht.

Several grey hairs later we were close enough to the quay to throw ropes to willing helpers and to recognise our official welcomer. He was a custodian of the rituals, clad in the priestly robes of the U.S. Customs. Almost before we had tied up he scrambled aboard eagerly and introduced himself. He was newly posted to Hawaii, it was his first sea port, and today was his first yacht. Wondering whether this was the good news or the bad news, we settled him and his briefcase down around the cabin table. Somehow we both instinctively shrank from offering him a drink. We had found that officials on board were normally not averse to a little drink and it helped to relax the proceedings. In remoter parts it seemed to be the major perk of the job and the paperwork could last as long as there was still whisky in the bottle. Now we took care to enter ports with all visible bottles never more than one third full.

Our customs man delved deep in his briefcase and brought out a huge mound of papers. We sat in silence while he rummaged through them, eventually selecting a long form which he handed David to complete. David scribbled for a few moments and then stopped.

'It says here, 'List any item on board purchased outside the U.S.A.',' he queried.

'Yeah, you just write down anything you've got on board that wasn't bought in the U.S.,' replied our man.

We both made an attempt at indulgent smiles. David persisted patiently.

'But we're a British boat.' Our man stared blankly.

'Uh? So?'

'You can't expect me to list everything on the whole boat,' continued David, notching the temperature up a few degrees. Our man picked up the form and re-read the instruction to us, with slow deliberate care as if we were five-year-olds learning English. Aliens from another world were evidently no longer anticipated. I stifled an impulse to stuff the form in his mouth. Instead, I cracked my face into what I hoped was a smile and said, 'It would take armfuls of paper to list everything. I'm sure this instruction isn't meant to apply to foreign boats.'

He wrinkled his brow and thrashed around in the archives of his briefcase. David eyed him with mounting irritation. I thought longingly of the bacon sandwich which was going to be my first heady taste of civilization. Suddenly our man looked up and the light of dawning spread across his face.

'A foreign boat?' he said thoughtfully. 'Yeah, right, I guess you oughta skip that one.'

The forms completed, he consulted his book of rituals.

'Now may I see your medical kit?' he asked. I groaned inwardly. In the words of Captain Cook's lieutenant, this was becoming a: '...long and rather tiresome ceremony, the object and meaning of which we could only guess.'

For the first time since leaving the U.K. we unearthed the plastic boxes which held our ill-assorted medical supplies. This was part of a medical kit originally intended for a twelve-man racing yacht which had backed out of a round-the-world race. We had stuffed it all away, to 'sort out later,' so we watched with curiosity while our man poked around, deeply puzzled. He paused for a moment to recount the twelve tubes of anti-fungal ointment, and threw us an anxious look over the 500 anal suppositories. When finally he came to the boxes crammed with disposable syringes and packs of needles, he pushed them nervously aside as if he might catch something. We too, were surprised to see so many syringes but his inquiring look elicited only bland and unhelpful stares. He looked around in desperation for some familiar ritual to perform. Finally he remembered the time-honoured ceremony of the Bonded Locker.

'Your duty free liquor, I'll have to seal it up.'

Not since leaving the U.K. had any official carried out this technically correct procedure, so this took us by surprise. The only alcohol outside the locker was the whisky and gin in the booze cupboard, both, by careful design, no more than a third full!

He took over an hour to wire-up and insert the seals. They were back at his office, so first he had to go and get them, and then he had to drill fresh holes because the old ones didn't fit. My desire for a bacon sandwich was taking a powerful hold, but we were his slaves until he handed us that most sacred relic, our cruising permit. When finally he did, we once more became masters of our own boat, and in the manner of hosts dealing politely with a guest who has outstayed his welcome, we ushered him onto the quay and handed him his briefcase. We watched him disappear into the canyons of containers which lined the dock. Then we closed the cabin door and made straight for the newly tagged locker. I held open the lid of its neighbour while David slid his hand in and around the corner and carefully brought out a gleaming bottle of duty-free Scotch. If the previous two hours was a run-in to the benefits of 'civilization', we were going to need it.

We sat in the cockpit, savouring our drinks and chatting with the couple on the yacht beside us. They were Californians returning from a year in the South Pacific.

'Thirty-two days from Bora Bora,' said the man through a bushy grey beard. 'A hard beat all the way – not to mention a hurricane.'

'Hurricane?' I asked, my eyes widening.

'Yeah, well, we got the tail end of it. You must have felt it too.'

I looked at David accusingly. He stared back, nonplussed. Our neighbour continued,

'Don't you guys listen to W.W.V. weather?'

We had tuned into the time signals every day but the weather for the Pacific was broadcast on a different frequency and we hadn't persevered to find it. We had grown used to being without weather forecasts.

'You oughta,' said greybeard. 'I'm telling you we wouldn't be here talking to you if we hadn't known about hurricane Emmy. We'd have run straight bang into the eye. As it was, I hung off and we only got roughed up a bit.'

'Well, now that you mention it...,' said David as if it had only just occurred to him.

I exchanged a glance of female solidarity with Greybeard's lady. David picked it up, sighed and smiled.

'Listen, the pilot book says that hurricanes in these parts are extremely rare. It'll be years before another one comes this way. So you can relax.'

I felt, just for a second, that he shouldn't have said that.

'We'll be leaving tomorrow for Oahu,' said Greybeard. 'They give you three free days here but it's not a place for yachts. There's no showers or facilities and the nearest grocery store's quite a way.'

We saw the grocery store long before we got to it. It was a supermarket the size of an airport terminal and just as confusing. We wandered, dazed and shivering in the air conditioning, among the dazzling aisles. Tier upon tier of competing products thrust themselves before us. This was a vaulted temple to the God of Superfluity. We were stunned into a paralysis of indecision. A brown loaf? But which of fifteen different kinds of brown loaf? A carton of milk? In which permutation of homogenized, sterilized, pasteurised, fat, thin, vitaminized...? Chubby arms shot past me with unerring aim for the target of their fancy. I picked things up and put them down a hundred times. It was easier with the fruit and vegetables. Within each glittering tier of perfect produce, every tomato, apple, artichoke or whatever, was a clone of its neighbour. Gone was the tedium of individual selection when faced with the tomato master race.

We wound our way back across the docklands with buzzing heads and sore feet, although the sights and sounds of traffic and people had left us strangely excited. Back on board, surrounded by mounds of unpacked groceries, I grilled and ate that bacon sandwich, the first for nine months. When people ask about the highlights of our trip I can still say with passion, 'a bacon sandwich in Hawaii.'

On our second day we took a bus up into the clouds to visit the rim of the Great Volcano. It was in one of its quieter moods, only rumbling and smoking. The Big Island itself is a collection of five volcanoes, and the most recent addition (only a million years ago) to a whole chain of lava domes formed on a huge fissure line running north west across the ocean floor; a floor that is 10,000 metres below the summit of the two highest peaks on the island. We gazed at the great lava lake, nearly three miles wide, in the caldera of Kilauea. In 1959 it erupted in spectacular fashion sending blazing cinders 700 metres into the sky and poured 160 million cubic yards of lava over the island's surface. Since then there have been a number of secondary eruptions and lava flows, and although no lives have been lost, settlements, roads and farmland have been engulfed by ash and lava.

But even among the cinders of the caldera we were amazed to see life already re-establishing itself. Ferns, mosses, and lichens sprouted from cracks and fissures, and further down the mountainside ravaged trees were sprouting new shoots. It was a hopeful reminder of the persistence of nature and its ability to survive and adapt. Only a million years ago the whole island was one great lava field, a most inhospitable surface for those spores, seeds, eggs and larvae which happened to make landfall. But they hung in, evolved and multiplied into numerous unique species. The human settlement has a similar parallel: a chance landfall late in the world's history and a subsequent fruitful colonization. Captain Cook noted on his arrival that he had never seen so many thousands gathered in one place. Since then, many of the indigenous species, just like the people, have been overwhelmed or cut down and replaced by specimens introduced from all parts the world. But Pele, the goddess of the volcano, still has the last word. Man, so far, can do nothing more than stand in awe at her incandescent power when she spews out the earth's interior and spills fiery rivers of lava down her slopes.

Without much respite we girded up our loins on the following day and set out for the overnight sail to the neighbouring island of Maui. It seemed churlish to leave the island without paying our respects to Cook's memorial at Kealakekua Bay, but it was on the other side of the island, well out of our way. I noted with sneaking satisfaction that Eric Hiscock, writing in *Sou'West in Wanderer IV*, was also put off from visiting '...that sad, historic spot.' The tumultuous welcome that had greeted Cook's arrival lasted just eighteen days, until he left to continue his Arctic survey. Three days out, his ships ran into heavy weather and the *Resolution's* foremast was seriously damaged. Reluctantly, Cook returned for repairs to Kealakekua Bay and found, perhaps not to his surprise, that the mood of the Hawaiians had changed. Within days the tense situation erupted into the debacle which left several Hawaiians, seamen, and Cook himself dead. By the age of fifty he had mapped the shores of the world and led his devoted men to its edges, beyond where any man had gone before. Now, just over 200 hundred years later, many of the charts we used were only slightly changed from his original surveys.

Leaving the island was as difficult as arriving had been. The onshore trade wind was being sucked up over the mountains leaving a windless void around the coast. The ocean rolled in, in huge glassy swells that exploded on the cliffs behind us. As R.L. Stevenson noted in that same spot: 'The windward shores are beaten by a monstrous surf'. (An observation which gives no hint of the fact that his father was the first man to measure the force of an ocean wave. The elder Stevenson, Thomas, invented the wave dynamometer and used it to study the seas which battered the shores of his native Scotland.)

By midnight we were roaring down the notorious Alenuihaha Channel with a handkerchief of sail up front and thirty knots of wind from behind. By dawn we were nearing the southern corner of Maui and looking forward to some respite in the island's lee.

No chance. Ten thousand feet of old volcanoes, slashed by canyons and ravines, played havoc with the wind. Marauding blasts attacked us from all directions and sudden calms left us flapping and dancing on confused waters. We alternately battled and crept up the west coast of the island, too tired to appreciate the magnificence of the terracotta mountains rising from patchwork fields of bright green sugar cane. I was also anxious about the anchorage. It was an open roadstead further up the coast and I couldn't see how it would be tenable.

When, finally, Lahaina Roadstead hove into sight we were pounding along, hard on the wind, spray flying from the bows. Incredibly, the yachts on the anchorage ahead lay serene and unruffled, as if we were seeing them through a glass barrier. It was an extraordinary patch of wind shadow, for which I gave grateful thanks when we eventually gained it and wearily dropped anchor.

'Here,' said David brightly, rallying the crew, 'there are no anchorage charges or time limit. We've a couple of weeks in hand, so now you can completely relax!'

For the second time in a few days, I felt he shouldn't have said that.

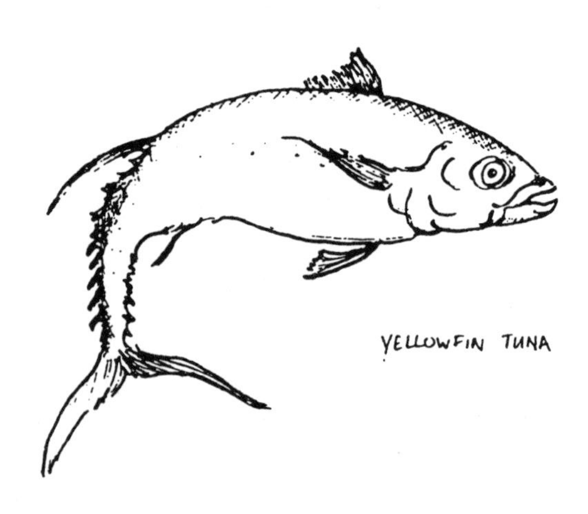

12

Hurricane In The Wind

One hundred and fifty years ago, Lahaina Roadstead was a wild, rumbustious anchorage, a favourite stop-over for the whaling fleets. The small settlement on the waterfront boomed into a boisterous town – much to the disapproval of the missionaries, then a powerful force in the islands. But by the 1870s both the whalers and missionaries had moved on and the little town was left to snooze under the candlenut trees. It quite enchanted the indomitable Isabella Bird Bishop, who visited the islands in 1873: 'A sweet soft breeze rustled through the palms, lazy ripples plashed lightly on the sand; humanity basked, flower-clad, in sunny indolence; everything was redundant, fervid, beautiful' she wrote to her sister, left behind to keep house in less fervid Edinburgh.

Now riding the tourist boom, it offered the Olde Tyme Whaling Town Experience. Tourists flocked from high-rise hotels tucked out of sight along the coast to mill among olde worlde shoppes crammed with imports from Taiwan and the Phillipines.

Out on the anchorage there were about twenty yachts, half of which had an air of permanent residency about them. A channel had been blasted through the fringing reef to allow a small boat harbour, but it was packed with craft, mostly with large, so-called yachts designed solely to take tourists round the bay on 'Sunset cruises with free *Mai Tai* cocktail'.

We planned just to potter around the boat doing light chores and socialising, before moving on to Honolulu on the neighbouring island of Oahu. There, we would prepare the boat for the next leg to Canada. Time was drawing in fast, if we wanted to beat the autumn gales of the North Pacific.

On the morning of our second day, life began to look quite good again. The sun shone from a trade wind sky of fluffy white clouds, and the breeze, in our sheltered spot, was kind and cooling. David was over on another boat fixing something and I was lazily pottering. 'Some light music,' I thought, and switched on the radio. A disc jockey was just signing off.

'Well, that's it, folks,' he breezed, 'Hurricane Fico is due to hit the Big Island, Tuesday; so just keep tuned to our updates. Take care and have a nice day.'

I could hardly believe what I was hearing. He said it so casually, as if the carnival was due to hit town. Swing-a-long music filled the cabin. Deaf to it, I sat down, stunned.

The news was getting around. Our neighbours, a skinny young couple with a baby rowed over.

'What you gonna do?' they asked, as if we had a wise old mariner's trick tucked up our kitbag.

'I don't know. The only decent harbours are in Oahu, but by the time you get there it might be too rough to get in. Then you really are in trouble.'

'Maybe the harbourmaster here will squeeze us all in.'

I looked at the low breakwater of the marina and pictured a monstrous tangle of yachts and docks, washed on to the highway behind. The alternative was to take your chance in the open sea.

David came back with some information on Fico. It was about 1,000 sea-miles south-east of us, travelling north-west at 25 knots, and packing 120 knot winds at its centre. A real smasher.

'Come on,' said David briskly, mustering the dispirited crew, 'We'll go ashore and see what the harbourmaster has to say and then we'll go to the supermarket. We've got a few hours to make a decision, so stop worrying about it for now.'

'STOP WORRYING!' I shrilled. 'For God's sake, there's a hurricane coming straight for us with winds of two hundred miles an hour, a warhead with our ticket on it. If I can't worry about that, what's left? Anyway, I'm not worried, just raving neurotic, and anyone who isn't is nuts!'

And with that I plonked myself at the bow of the dinghy. Not, I noticed, to much effect, as the outboard motor had beaten me (as it usually does) to winning David's full attention.

We found a small crowd buzzing round the harbourmaster's office. All sorts of speculations on what the hurricane might or might not do were flying around. The harbourmaster emerged from his office to give a soothing speech, especially directed to 'you folks out there,' (us on the anchorage). Before Fico hit he would open the harbour and pack us all in. There was a great murmur of relief and, glad of a chance to ignore reality, everyone dispersed slightly cheered.

I followed David round the supermarket, my misery mounting as I considered our plight. There was a hint of excitement in his step. I knew if left to himself he would choose to take his chance in the open sea. 'There'll be an almighty pile-up in the harbour,' he had said. His prime concern was *Moongazer*. It may sound crazy to think of risking one's life for a boat, but to cruising folk their boat is much more than just another possession. Joseph Conrad, reflecting on his life at sea, wrote eloquently about this relationship: 'The love that is given to ships is profoundly different from the love men feel for every other work of their hands...' He goes on to talk of the '...intimate equal fellowship of the ship and man, backing each other against the implacable… hostility of the waters.'

I shared this passion but not to the extent of laying my life on the line. I knew that if I were on my own I would have to abandon *Moongazer* to her fate and retreat to the concrete palisades of the Lahaina Hilton. But could I do that, I wondered, if David chose to head for the open sea? Singlehanded, his difficulties would be doubled. I trailed out of the supermarket in an agony of indecision. This was a day which I'd gladly have swopped for being back at the office.

On the anchorage, discussion was well ahead of action. We joined a group gathered on an immaculate 15 metre ketch belonging to Bob, an I.B.M. executive drop-out. Arrays of gadgets and an impressive filing system suggested he'd only swopped one office for another. Bob had been following the coastguard bulletins on VHF radio and had charted the hurricane's track. It looked like we were right in its path. I noticed that the radius of extreme winds was quite small and that at 150 sea miles from the eye the winds were only at gale force. Exactly where it struck was critical, even within forty or fifty miles, but that was something no one could predict as hurricanes can be wilfully erratic.

The four-thirty radio update brought a hush to the cabin. We scribbled down the facts and figures.

'It's slowing down!' said someone. 'That means it's changing course.'

'Yeah, right. Well that could be good news or bad news,' said Bob. 'But at least it's different news, and it gives us some more time.'

We arranged between us to monitor the bulletins through the night and to keep in VHF contact with each other. This was especially useful for the singlehanders. There is a comforting illusion of security in being a group in times like these. David is not so easily deluded.

'Having other people around,' he maintains, 'can't half screw things up.'

During the night *Moongazer* started to rock gently to a light swell, and Fico very slightly changed direction. By morning there was a chance it might just miss the islands. We held our breath and sat glued to the radio. The Islands were on Hurricane Alert and a High Surf warning had been issued for all coasts. The swell on its own wasn't dangerous, as long as we were well clear of the breakers. We re-anchored in deeper water and made the boat ready for sea in case we had to move quickly. We were still in the shelter of the mountain, although the trade wind had intensified to gale force and we could see, further along the coast, the dust whirling off the cliff-tops.

The swell, rolling in from the unusual direction of the south-west, built up quickly and by mid-day it was breaking across the marina entrance, effectively closing it. So much for the harbourmaster's plan of 'packing' us all in. Even retreating ashore by dinghy was no longer an open option. Neither was heading for the open sea, as there wouldn't be enough time to clear the islands. I was appalled at how quickly the choices had been cut off.

There was now nothing we could do but sit and wait and hope. With every hour Fico carried its fury another fifteen miles nearer. If it held its present course and didn't change, it would pass about 100 miles south of us, but no-one was taking bets on it.

It did change course again, but to everyone's monumental relief it tracked even further south of us, curving round the bottom of the islands before shooting off on its original north-westerly course. For several more days we kept a wary eye on it in case it sneaked back. I wondered how many yachts had been caught out at sea. A week earlier we would have met it, totally off guard, blissful in the knowledge that: 'Tropical storms are not frequent in this part of the Pacific, and hurricanes even less so.'

After a few more days the High Surf warning was withdrawn and we set off for Oahu. Between Waikiki Beach and downtown Honolulu thousands of masts bristling beneath towering apartment blocks led us to the great Ala Wai marina. We had come to this huge boat park because the Hawaii yacht club offered two weeks' free berthage to visiting yachts.

When Jack London arrived in the *Snark* in 1907 he sailed into Pearl Harbour, where a launch came out to meet him. In it were: '...members of the Hawaii Yacht Club come to greet us and make us welcome with true Hawaiian hospitality.' He wrote of a sweeping verandah, an avenue of royal palms and a spacious wonderful lawn.

Things had changed a bit. The lawns of Pearl Harbour were long gone and the Hawaii Yacht Club had moved to the marina. However, in relative terms, it did occupy one of the best sites. It boasted some palm trees and a tiny patch of garden, a great extravagance in these acres of concrete. The club building still had a verandah, though hardly 'sweeping', and it was crowded with members who greeted us and made us welcome with the same true Hawaiian hospitality. Visiting yachts were berthed bows-in round the garden with space for only about a dozen. We were lucky to have got in as our dwindling finances wouldn't otherwise have justified staying in the marina.

It was the perfect spot to prepare for a passage. By day we worked our way through the chores; in the evenings at the garden barbecues we relaxed, well-groomed and showered and enjoying the ice in our drinks. The other cruising yachtfolk were a mixture of those returning from a sojourn in the South Pacific and those just setting out. Most of the latter regarded the former rather wistfully but never the other way round. Those who were homeward bound, I felt, sometimes betrayed a hint of manic relief.

We became friendly with a couple who had just set out from San Diego. A former executive with a multi-national company, he had quit to run a pizza franchise with his wife. Now they were embarking on another adventure, and where it would lead they didn't know. His wife, a lady of great charm and character, confided to me one evening as we grilled the hamburgers:

'I don't know how we're going to get on. Dick has no patience. He's very easily frustrated. I don't know how much I can bear – I mean, of *him* not being able to bear it!'

(Several years later we ran into them in Tahiti. Much to their surprise they had got as far as Australia and had come back along the Roaring Forties. They had joined with pride the ranks of the happy returnees.)

We woke one morning to find a large well-built ferrocement ketch flying the Red Ensign and anchored rather cheekily in the turning basin where a dredger was working. It turned out to be owned by Mick, a Liverpudlian by birth and a rover by nature. He had chatted up the dredger skipper who had agreed to let him anchor (in breach of marina rules) in the basin. Mick had last lived in Seattle where he had built the boat. Across its stern was emblazoned *Bulawayo* and I asked if that was the boat's name or its Port of Registry.

'Its name,' he told me, 'is in honour of the town that saved my life.' As a mercenary in the Congo he had been on the run for weeks across central Africa and only just made it into the safety of Bulawayo. Now with his American lady he was set for the Pacific and 'all points west.' We said we'd probably see him along the way some day. We never did.

As we plodded through the chores we talked off and on about looking for someone to join us for the passage to Canada.

'This tropical sailing's made you soft,' said David.

'Right!' I replied. 'That's why I don't fancy the

prospect of sitting outside for three hours in cold wet gales. One more person means one less hour in the cold and a great improvement in my quality of life.'

We kept a watch on the yacht club notice board, but it was late in the season and most of the 'crew available' notices were of the sort: 'student seeks passage to the mainland, no exp. but quick learner.'

'Tough on everyone for the next four weeks if they learn quickly that they hate being at sea,' I said to David. 'And anyway we always said we'd never take on anyone we didn't know.' Brave words. I knew I would put up with almost anybody for an extra hour's sleep.

We made preparations for sea much as Cook, Vancouver and later generations of sea captains did. We caulked the leaky spots on the deck, stitched up worn seams on the sails, checked the rigging and provisioned up, as if we were going to the arctic. In the heyday of sailing ships and the China trade, thousands of ships used the islands for just such a a stop-over. But whatever else has changed in the last hundred years, the seasons run on inexorably, and like all those before us who were dependent on the wind and respected its power the timing of our departure was governed by the same rhythm of nature.

So, leaving the pleasures of the islands to the thousands of tourists swarming by the swimming pools, we filled out our clearance papers and gave the departure day. It passed in a blur of activity, as it always does. A hundred last-minute jobs, a hundred good-byes. We hated to leave, but we couldn't wait to get to sea. We pulled up our stern anchor and disengaged our bows from the palm trees and I finally accepted that there would be no superman crew member.

We went only as far as an anchorage along the coast, for a last quiet night and a good sleep. In the morning we performed the farewell ritual of scrubbing the bottom. We'd read somewhere that the spores of goose barnacles only form around coastal waters. Since we had started the routine of scrubbing immediately before leaving we no longer arrived, as we had done in the Marquesas, with a thick forest of barnacles dangling from the hull. Finally, just after 9 a.m. we cut our links with the world and set off out towards the Kauai Channel.

Around mid-day we saw a small motor-boat coming towards us. There was something odd about it. David picked up the binoculars and steadied himself against a stay.

'It's a yacht – with no mast!' he said. 'Just a little stub sticking up above the coachroof.'

As it drew nearer I realized it was one of our former neighbours at the yacht club.

'It's *Gypsy*! Remember the guy that had crew fly over from San Francisco? A father and son, they arrived just two days ago.'

We altered course to meet them and when we were within shouting distance I could see three glum looking people sitting in the cockpit.

'Lost it in a squall,' shouted the owner. 'Had to cut it away'.

We mouthed our commiserations and asked if he needed any help.

'No, the engine seems fine. We'll anchor at Pokai to-night and carry on back to Ala Wai to-morrow.'

We waved and turned to head off.

'Bet the crew are a bit pissed off,' remarked David. Just then there was a shout from *Gypsy*.

'Need any crew?'

We looked at each other inquiringly and quickly I held up one finger.

'We can only take one,' David answered.

The young lad immediately stood up.

'Guess that means me!' he exclaimed and disappeared below. By the time we had manoeuvred our stern near *Gypsy*'s bows the lad was on deck, his bag packed. With a quick, 'Bye Dad,' he scrambled on to *Moongazer*. His father stretched his arm out towards him.

'Bye Son. Happy Birthday next week!' he called, looking dazed by the swiftness of events.

As the boats drew apart I managed to stuff a scrap of paper in Dad's hand.

'Our names, us and the boat,' I shouted. 'We're headed for Victoria. About four weeks.'

He nodded. For some time he stood watching us as we, total strangers, sailed away with his teenage son.

Tall, lanky, curly-headed Jason. Here was my superman crew; to me, just as miraculous as the one who bursts out of phone boxes.

He was a dinghy-sailor and this was his first ocean passage. It was a rough initiation. We pounded to windward all night, through fierce thunder squalls. Jason, his face a pale shade of green, stood his watches like a mariner. He even managed a smile when he woke me for my watch at 3 a.m.

I watched the loom of the lights of Oahu fade into the black scudding clouds. 'Bye Bye Hawaii,' I whispered. My thoughts were interrupted by David. The new two hour watch had passed quickly. Together we sat in the darkness listening to the noise of wind and water. David spoke: 'I'm beginning to think we do have a Guy Up There on our side.'

'If we do,' I said, looking up at the cloud-torn ceiling, 'He likes his little tease along the way.'

Just then, as if in reply, the heavens opened. As we cowered from the bullets of rain there was a faint rumble, thunder perhaps. But it sounded to me more like a deep sonorous chuckle.

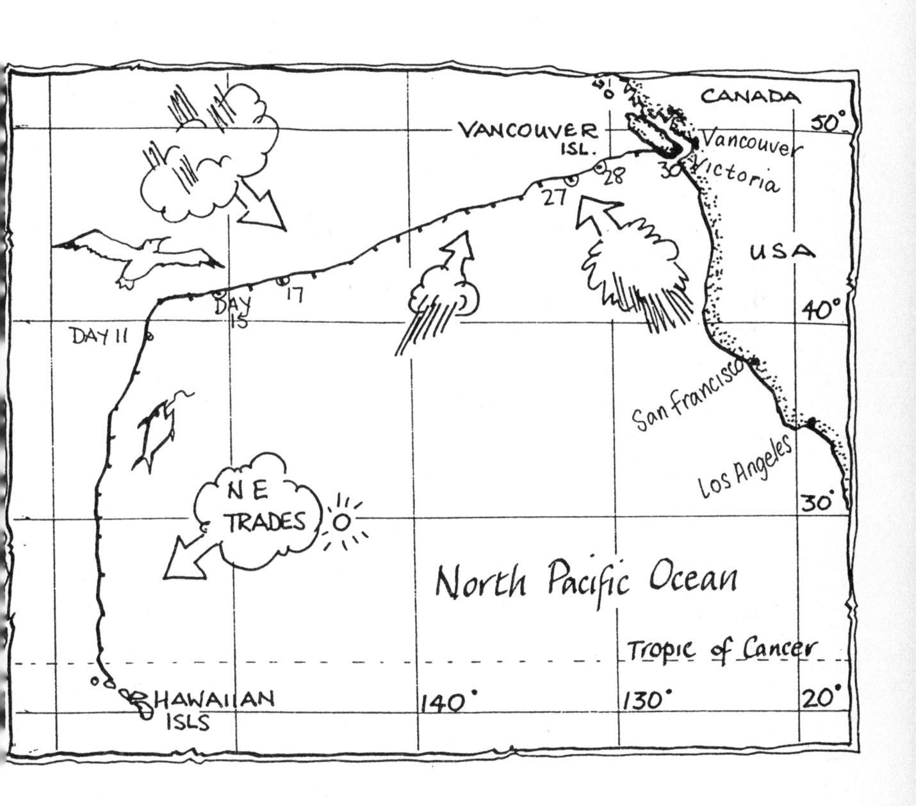
CANADA
VANCOUVER ISL.
Vancouver
Victoria
USA
50°
40°
30°
20°
DAY 11
DAY 15
17
27
28
30
San Francisco
Los Angeles
NE TRADES
North Pacific Ocean
Tropic of Cancer
HAWAIIAN ISLS
140°
130°

13

Good-bye To The Trade Winds -- Honolulu to Victoria

Four days now, still thrashing to windward as we expected. It's a horrible way to travel. Some of the seas come like sledgehammers, exploding cascades of sunlit spray over the deck; all the hatches and windows are shut. *Moongazer* is crashing along on her ear, with the lee rail not quite under. We are cautious with the amount of sail we're flying: the mizzen, a double-reefed main, the staysail and a small working jib. A larger headsail would power through the seas better, but at cost to our gear and nerves.

The barograph is slowly spiralling upwards. The sun shines from a brilliant sky. *Moongazer* climbs on a wave and we look down on magnificent battalions of white-crested seas, marching towards us. Soon we should get some respite in the variables. Even a calm would be welcome just now. We lie on our bunks, chatting, as our world heaves and slams and crashes around us.

Jason is taking it well. He'll be seventeen in a few days. He's a nice lad. Sails dinghies in San Francisco Bay. This is his first big boat trip. He came out with his father to help sail a friend's boat back to S.F. They were only one day out when the mast collapsed. I still can't quite believe he's real. Any moment I expect him to disappear in a puff of smoke. He tells us about his school, and about his summer job helping at children's camps, about his pick-up truck and its stereo system. He asks what kind of stereos English kids have in their cars. We learn from each other. David is teaching him to navigate. He uses the spare sextant, a cheapo plastic job which works fine. He's getting his sea legs back now and regaining his appetite. We've given him the jar of peanut butter. 'It's all yours to eat whenever you like. But remember, it's the only jar and there's no corner store.'

Nights are getting chillier. I see Jason shivering in the cockpit. Yes, he has a wool sweater in his bag but isn't keen to wear it. 'It prickles.' 'Try wearing it over a shirt.' 'Wow! That feels better.' I muse that the world may be divided into those that have never needed wool sweaters and those (like me) who can't imagine life without them.

We are making our average of 100 miles, noon to noon. Each degree higher in latitude takes us further from the risk of stray hurricanes. It also brings us nearer the gales. We listen to W.W.V. for their position, and their radii. They come across the North Pacific, mostly north of Vancouver Island, but some stray south and there's a chance that we'll meet one. For the present, we take one day at a time.

The log notes read:

DAY 11: Sea down, thank God! Relief from 10 days of bang, crash, wallop. Salt everywhere. We come to life again – do jobs, wash hair & selves – for last time on deck? Wind dropping – running out of the Trades? Barograph still going up, Pacific High must be near. Not too near, we hope.

Caught a tuna. Birds followed us all night. Skuas, or albatrosses with huge wing span.

DAY 15: Suddenly cold. On with the socks & sweaters. An odd muffled-up feeling. Dug out canned soups & steak & kidney pies!

Wind now from the N.W. Heeling to starboard – for the first time since the West Indies! The contents of the lockers slide and settle.

David tunes in to W.W.V. weather info. for the N. Pacific. Gales north of us. Skua follows now, night & day. A scavenger.

Dark, scowling cloudscapes. Wind up and down. Sails up and down. Barograph down. Rain & mist. Wind gusting 40 knots. D. washed in cockpit with HOT water. – M.& J. abstained.

DAY 17: Jason's 17th birthday. Promoted to mate (first class) at the Moongazer Academy of Navigation. Baked a cake. Found some small candles.

DAY 26: Nearing Vancouver island. Strong winds from S.E. pressing us too far north.

3.a.m. Fishing fleet ahead. Picked up Lennard Light. Turned south toward Cape Flattery. No signals coming up on R.D.F. Odd, as there are several strong stations around. Thick drizzle. I feel the presence of land hemming us in.

DAY 27: More muggy drizzle. Another yacht drifts into view. Amazingly we recognise it – met it in the West Indies!

We exchange chocolate and fish. They think they're 30 miles south of where we think we are. We go our separate ways. 2hrs. later: A yacht behind us, following.

An uneasy night.

DAY 28: Dawn; Vancouver Island shows itself – brilliantly.

I feel a prickle of tears at the sight – from relief at knowing where we are, and at the sheer stunning beauty of it.

Range upon range of mountains shimmer above a glassy sea.

We motor all day towards the straits of Juan de Fuca, which separate Vancouver Island from the U.S.A. We're heading for Neah Bay, a small fishing harbour on an Indian reservation at the mouth of the straits. Our final destination is the town of Victoria, one more day's journey on.

It has been a mixed passage: a bit of everything, with no really bad gale and no long calms. A sandwich of a pleasant few days between thick slabs of days best forgotten.

We make Neah bay before sunset and anchor beside yachts waiting for northerlies to take them down the coast to California. We finally switch off the engine and sit listening to the silence. Wood smoke rises from the pinetops in the still, mellow air of twilight. A kind soul rows out from one of the yachts with fresh blackberries. They smell of wet green earth; of crisp Autumn mornings. The three of us are excited, tired and stunned by fresh sensations. We are ready to collapse into deep sleep.

5 a.m.: we steal out of the harbour into the smoked glass waters of the straits. For hours we see only mountains and pinewoods – no smoke, boats, houses, docks. There is nothing to show that we are not the only humans left on earth. The early morning air is crisp and sparkling. Like powerful champagne, it hits senses starved of it far more than we knew. The fresh pungency of pinewoods is every bit as thrilling as the heavy fragrance of the tropics. It's a smell I used to dream of on heavy, doldrum days.

8 a.m.: There is something extraordinary in the distance, coming down the straits, very fast, towards us. I look through the binoculars. It's a huge craft of some sort, just above the surface of the water, throwing spray out to either side. It's not shaped like a boat. A spaceship? For a second the thought links up with the lack of signs of life. Then half a mile from us, it slows and settles in the water. A huge hovercraft. As it

passes we see the markings, *Boeing*, a reminder that just thirty or so miles off lies the city of Seattle and several million people.

We carry on along the straits in brilliant sunshine. On either side, the land looks wild and unmarked by man. We are starting to see small fishboats and the occasional pleasure craft. The current holds us up, running strongly round a rocky promontory. Eventually, in the late afternoon, we clear it and see the little town of Victoria ahead, its buildings glowing in the September sunshine. A yacht is coming out of the harbour. It's *Moonshadow* - friends met in Hawaii. There are shouts of happy recognition. We slide into the small municipal marina. Sailing people take our lines. Jason is beside himself with excitement. He's made his first ocean passage. We're pretty happy too. It's exactly a year to the day since we left England. I am overwhelmed by a warm feeling of having come home.

14

Winter Arrangements

From the first day of our arrival in British Columbia we revelled in the novelty of change. After a year in the tropics, my lungs tingled in the cool crisp air of Autumn mornings. We savoured the long mellow sunsets and slowly darkening sky. We went below to a heated cabin and lit the oil lamps. We drank hot chocolate and snuggled under warm covers on our bunk.

There was also something cosy about the town of Victoria, nestled in sheltered waters beneath the mountains of Vancouver Island.

'It's a wonderful country,' said our customs officer with a trace of mid-Europe in his accent. He took it for granted that we'd come to see the scenery.

'Don't rush it,' he said. 'There's a lot of country to see. When your permit expires you nip over to Washington State for a few days and then come back and re-enter.'

We would certainly do that. What we couldn't tell him was that we had reached that point in a sailor's life when the rattle of the piggy bank sounds thin and hollow. A few fistfuls of dollars would give it that heavy comfortable feel again, but the fresh stamps on our passports blinked out the words 'Employment Prohibited'. On the dock beside us, large notices warned of dire penalties for those caught working without a permit.

'You'll end up wanting to stay here permanently,' persisted our man, warming to his theme, and our whisky. 'Everybody does.'

'No,' said David firmly. 'When the spring comes we'll be off again to the South Pacific.'

In the event they were both wrong.

Our need to earn money was tempered only by our desire to ski during the coming winter, and on that first afternoon we hadn't the vaguest notion of how we might reconcile these seemingly opposing goals. What we didn't know was that we had already become members of an exclusive club: a sort of freemasonry of ocean travellers that stretched across the country.

A knock on the cabin roof next morning heralded the first signs. We were feeling a little bereft, having just seen Jason off on the ferry to Vancouver. He had to return to San Francisco, college and his family, who had 'lost' him for a month. On the dock was an old aquaintance now living in Victoria, who'd heard on the bush telegraph from Hawaii that we were on our way. That evening we dined with him and his wife in the baronial splendour of the Empress Hotel.

As the bush telegraph spread, invitations to dinner, baths and washing machines followed. Local information and advice started to shape our plans. We had first to get a car of some sort. Not in Victoria, where people cherish their cars like they do in Britain, but in Vancouver where they treat them more with American indifference.

We left *Moongazer* at the town dock under watchful eyes and took the ferry across the Gulf of Georgia to Vancouver. There we stayed with friends, on their boat in the downtown marina, and were introduced to the great North American Liveaboard Phenomena. Every morning, after an early rush to the showers, smartly dressed men and women of all ages emerged from boats of all ages and roared off in their cars towards the freeway traffic. Most had sold their houses and were saving up for The Big Trip. Some would eventually make it, but others had guessed that for them the preparations were probably the most enjoyable part.

Within a few days we'd found a modest car for a few hundred dollars, which seemed like a huge investment. It was over a year since we'd parted with so much money in one go. But it was a necessary investment. Without a car we couldn't hope to find a job and at the end of the season we would sell it for what it had cost.

The best skiing, it seemed, was in the Rocky Mountains and Calgary was mentioned as being a base where we would collect more local information. It was also the hometown of sailing friends who had said 'Come and see us. Bring a breath of salty air.'

From Calgary the trail led to Banff. There in the little tourist town among the mountains we renewed another sailing friendship, an English doctor who ran the clinic. Together we toasted the sailing life and looked out from his window on a stunning panorama of snow-capped mountains. The interior of his 'designer home' could also have been stunning but something was wrong.

'A nightmare,' he groaned. 'Six months ago the builder walked out on me. He left hundreds of unfinished and botched jobs. No-one's interested....' and he stopped, as if a brilliant idea had just struck him – at about the same time as it struck us.

'I know you can build boats,' he said to David. 'Can you build houses?'

'I can build anything,' said David, not sounding immodest.

And suddenly we knew where we would be living for the winter. There was even a self-contained flat in his basement.

'Take as long as you like, but finish it – *please*!'

The next day we put the icing on our arrangements by offering the manager of the ski area our services at weekends in return for a season's free ski pass. Business done, we started back towards the coast to deal with the problem of where to leave *Moongazer*.

There were plenty of marinas, at a price which would have gobbled up our winter earnings. David was sure that somewhere there had to be a sheltered spot where he could tie *Moongazer* to a pine tree and leave her for the winter. 'Not possible if it's within access to Vancouver or Victoria,' said everyone, including me – which only hardened David's determination. We had underestimated the power of the Brotherhood.

Halfway along the road to Vancouver, by the shores of Lake Okanogan, lived that couple who had so inspired us three years before in S.W. Ireland. It was our first contact with blue-water yachtfolk and those evenings we'd spent in the lamplit glow of their cabin, listening to travellers' tales, proved to be contagious. They had told us about the Eastern Mediterranean and I remember asking how long they had spent there. They looked at each other inquiringly.

'About a couple of years, I guess,' said Jim.

A couple of years! The words exploded in my brain. We were on the last week of our two week holiday. We were going to have to leave the next day, though the forecast was lousy. They were waiting, watching the barometer, until the depression had passed. What a glorious freedom, I had thought, most enviously.

They lived simply, had little money, but were millionaires in quality of life.

'So could you be, if you really wanted,' they had said.

I think it was from then on that David and I started to

talk about 'when we go', instead of 'if'.

Now, as disciples of their life-style, we were able to come back and thank them. They greeted us like long-lost friends and swept us into the warm embrace of their household. They lived in their beautiful self-built house like they did on their boat, on slender means, with charm and style.

'First a drink, and then a bath,' said Erica, offering the best of sailors' hospitality. And it was a bath like I have never had before or since. When I opened the bathroom door in the little guest house among the trees, I thought I'd got the wrong room. By the soft light of a table lamp, I saw an easy chair, magazines, rugs scattered on the pine floor, and along one wall, a fireplace, alive and crackling with blazing logs. At one end of the room was the bath, and at the other, framed by trees, a huge picture window. Looking out across the long sweep of Lake Okanogan, I soaked and preened in the hot sudsy water and reckoned that this was what the cruising life was all about. I didn't mean the bath. I meant knowing people like Jim and Erica.

Before we left next morning, Jim had come up with an idea for *Moongazer*'s winter quarters. The trail led us back to Vancouver Island, halfway up the east coast. There on a little island was the perfect lagoon, accessible only at high water and sheltered by belts of tall pines. Jim had given us the name of the owner, a former tugboatman and yachtie, and now the owner-driver of the island ferryboat. We took a ferry ride and introduced ourselves and before we got round to asking, Sandy had offered us the use of his lagoon.

By a coincidence that no longer staggered us, sailing friends had just rented a house not far from the island. 'Use our basement to store your gear,' they had said.

When we sailed *Moongazer* up from Victoria in early October the mountain-tops were already dusted with snow, and autumn was crispening into winter.

WANDERER IV

15

Heroes In The Flesh

In those first dizzy weeks of renewing old friendships and making new ones, we met, for the first time, two couples whom we felt we'd known for years.

On our bookshelves were a number of cruising narratives, well-thumbed and first read so long ago that their characters had become like the heroes of our childhood story books. Within two weeks of our arrival four of those characters had materialised from the mildewing pages into reality.

Not long after I had first met David and had become embroiled in boats I was aware that there was a way of doing things 'according to Eric Hiscock'. Although at that stage David owned nothing larger than a dinghy, the pride of his bookshelf was a volume entitled *Cruising Under Sail* by Eric Hiscock. First printed in 1950, and subsequently re-edited and reprinted, it was a reliable and comprehensive text-book which, even in the late 1960s, stood head and shoulders above the few others that were available. Our graduation to a small cruising yacht was marked by the acquisition of Hiscock's companion volume, *Voyaging Under Sail.* Then David, possibly to suggest that there was more to cruising than miserable nights in the Irish Sea, presented me with a copy of *Atlantic Cruise In Wanderer III*, an account of the Hiscocks' cruise to the Caribbean and the U.S.A.

I went on to read more about the wanderings of Eric and his wife Susan; their two circumnavigations in their well-loved sloop, *Wanderer III*, and later voyages and a circumnavigation in their Dutch-built 15-metre ketch, *Wanderer IV*. Up until then I had had the impression that ocean sailing was either for the wealthy in large yachts or eccentric adventurers. It was reassuring to learn that with careful planning and sensible sailing it was possible to circumnavigate without life-threatening drama. Here, too, was a woman who played an equal part and without making a fuss of the fact.

In 1952, when they left on their first circumnavigation, such yachtfolk were a rare breed and many of their anchorages were deserted, lonely spots. In 1976, in the Marquesas they met their old *Wanderer III* on its third circumnavigation. Eric wrote: '...when *Wanderer III* first sailed into Taiohae Bay twenty-one years before with Susan and me on board, she was the only yacht in the archipelago; on this occasion there were at least seventy-five yachts in the group.' The anchorages were filling up with a new generation, like us, of 'Hiscock's Children'. This added a not-unwelcome dimension to their cruising. Their first stop at the lonely Marquesas had been brief, and they 'did not care for them much'. In 1976 they '...met a wonderful crowd of voyagers... it was fun...'

Now, on Vancouver Island we heard that they had just sailed up from New Zealand, to 'see friends,' as Eric had put it, and were now ensconced for the winter in a little marina north of Victoria.

The Yacht Club community around Victoria was close-knit and at times gave the impression of having been transplanted straight from Southampton waters. This was the Hiscocks' old stamping ground and everyone seemed to know 'Eric and Susan' as old friends. It was inevitable that we would meet, which we did, early in the dinner party circuit, and they invited us to Sunday drinks aboard *Wanderer IV*.

We felt like pilgrims at the shrine. I remember now that we were among the first to arrive and the last to leave. Somehow I'd pictured them looking as they did in Eric's early photographs, so I was taken aback to see this elderly, almost frail couple, the sole crew of a large steel yacht. *Wanderer IV* was their home and a handsome one, but at over ten years of age she too was showing her wrinkles. It seemed, from the conversation of others that Susan was forever on her knees, chipping, sanding and patch-painting. It also seemed that in between she cooked, baked, navigated, sewed sails and looked after Eric. He told me, quite disarmingly, between puffs on his pipe, 'Yes, Susan does it while I just write about it.' Writing about it, well and often enough to make a living, was no mean feat in itself, especially for someone who was troubled for most of his life with poor eyesight.

At the parties Susan stayed quietly in the background while Eric was in the centre of things, where he was expected to be, as there was always a little group around him eager to elicit his opinion on something. When listening to Susan's conversation, I was struck by her power of understatement. Referring to a storm in an article by Eric entitled, 'Savage Force Eleven,' she said quietly that she found it, 'rather disagreeable'. Nor did I hear her even jokingly complain, as most of us do, about the rigours of the life or the occasional lapses of our spouses. She struck me as being one of a fast-disappearing breed of heroically uncomplaining women. Eric, I thought, and David readily agreed, was a singularly fortunate man. Not that he was unaware of it; he dedicated one of his books to 'Susan, seaman – navigator – wife.' Susan's contribution was acknowledged too, when they both received an M.B.E. in 1985 for services to yachting.

The Hiscocks were staying in a marina for the winter and at the first sign of spring would leave straight for Hawaii and New Zealand. In our relatively youthful ignorance we thought their sailing days must surely soon be coming to an end. We didn't know that they were actually in the throes of commissioning a new boat.

We saw them two years later in the Bay Of Islands in New Zealand where they were permanently based. Eric was by now in his early seventies and was having increasing difficulty with his eyesight. We saw them, rowing out to *Wanderer IV*, sitting side by side in the dinghy, each wielding an oar. In a yard nearby, their new boat, *Wanderer V* was nearing completion. We didn't intrude on them as we felt they had enough on their mind at that moment. However, two years after that, we ran into them again, cruising in Australia. They had just ironed out the wrinkles in their new boat, and seemed to have had a new lease of life. They were preparing to be off again, back to the South Pacific, a hard sail against the trade winds.

Their voyaging finally came to an end three years later with Eric's death in 1986, and Susan returned to live in the South of England near their old cruising haunts. Theirs was a remarkable cruising partnership. As Donald Holm wrote in *The Circumnavigators*, 'The Hiscocks did not go to sea to experience hair-raising adventures. All of their voyages were carefully planned and flawlessly executed... In their quiet and competent way... they came to epitomize, perhaps more than any yachtsmen in British history, the proper seagoing citizen.'

The other heroes of our bookshelves were by contrast, most unsuitable role models for ordinary yachtfolk. Miles and Beryl Smeeton courted adventure in wild places, and had a talent for survival when it threatened to overwhelm them.

Of English origin, they had made their home in Western Canada and had already become part of the legendary folklore. Throughout his warm and witty writings, Miles reveals that being married to the amazing Beryl was an adventure in itself.

She seemed to thrive on physical hardship, the tougher the better.

A taste for wild seas and freezing temperatures took them to the Southern Ocean, where, on their first attempt to round Cape Horn, their sturdy ketch, *Tzu Hang,* was pitchpoled by a giant wave. Beryl was tossed out of the cockpit and the boat was all but torn apart. When it righted itself, Miles and his crew John Guzzwell found themselves in what had been the cabin, waist deep in water and gazing at the open sky. They were further stunned to see Beryl swimming over huge waves. Miles remembers that she looked unafraid and was still smiling. With a broken collar bone and a gashed head she made it back to the sinking hulk, where the two numbed men were preparing to meet their end. Almost her first words were, 'I know where the buckets are, I'll get them.' Galvanised out of their state of shock they baled for their lives. Hours later when Miles was too cold to lift the bucket properly she urged him on with a quip: 'this is survival training, you know'

The rest of the story is a classic in the annals of sailing. After John coolly and carefully sharpened his chisels among the chaos, they fashioned bits of the interior for a rudder and mast and sailed *Tzu Hang* back to Chile. There the Smeetons rebuilt her and set off for a second bash at rounding the Cape. Before they reached it, they were again rolled over and dismasted. And once more they limped back to Chile under a jury rig. This time they shipped *Tzu Hang* back to England for repairs.

For the next fifteen years they sailed many thousands of miles in high latitudes and stormy oceans, but they left Cape Horn alone. In his book, *Because the Horn is There,* Miles wrote that he thought *Tzu Hang* had done pretty well and he was quite prepared to leave it at that. But Beryl never let anything beat her and eventually she managed to entice Miles, as he put it, '...to swing once more on that rope of youthful enjoyment and adventure that had supported us through 30 years of excitment and vicissitudes...' They finally made it, round the Horn and into the Pacific.

On that passage, one incident in particular impressed me and I think of it whenever I find myself sinking into a lethargy of gloom at the sound of a rising gale. Just after rounding the Horn they ran into a gale. 'Since it was difficult enough to sleep,' Miles wrote, 'Beryl decided to employ her time more usefully.' By baking bread. Naturally Beryl didn't have a normal convenient oven. It was a folding contrivance which had to be assembled and wired onto the cooker. The baking took half the night but resulted in eight fresh brown loaves swinging from a hammock under the deckhead. As Miles said, 'No gale can stand up to this sort of thing...' and by midnight it had moderated.

Beryl had been luring Miles into adventures from the moment he first met her in India. He was then a young officer in the Green Howards and she the wife of his second-in-command. When he left to take up a home posting she persuaded him to forego the sea passage and travel overland – and then asked to accompany him.

They travelled through the Middle East, Turkey and the Balkans and fell in love. But Beryl's husband was a Brother Officer and a senior one at that, so they agreed to go their separate ways without contact for a year.

Beryl made several solo journeys during the next few years – through India, Persia, Russia, China and Burma, and somewhere along the line got divorced as well. She rode on horseback for 1,000 miles up the eastern side of the Patagonian Andes, but finally, on a pier at Cherbourg, met up with Miles again and decided to get married.

Honeymoon was a modest climbing in the Lake District, a warm-up for their trip a year later which took them to the Himalayas and the peak of Tirich Mir. There, with the help of four porters, one of whom was the young Sherpa Tensing, Beryl broke the women's altitude record.

A few months later the Second World War parted them again and took Miles to Western Desert and to Burma where he finished up as a Brigadier with a D.S.O. and a M.C. The end of the war saw them together again, with a four-year-old daughter, and the title, bought unseen in India, to a piece of island in British Columbia. So, with the fanciful notion of settling down they made their home in a wild and beautiful part of the world.

It was only then that their sailing adventures began. Knowing nothing about sailing they went to England and bought, by instinct, the superbly seaworthy *Tzu Hang* and sailed her back to Canada. They had originally intended it as a means of bringing money out of Britain. By the time they reached their little island in the Straits of Georgia they knew they had found a way of life that fed their hunger for challenge. In the nineteenth century, people like them were born to found empires. Empires now being out of fashion, sailing to wild places was the next best thing.

Now, many adventures later, they had moved from British Columbia and bought a game farm in Alberta where they bred endangered animals for the government. It lay between Calgary and Banff so I knew that sooner or later we were going to meet them. It was sooner. Halfway into our third dinner party in Victoria someone said, 'Calgary? You can't possibly go there without seeing Miles and B.' And so it was arranged.

We found the game farm nestling in the foothills between the Rockies and the Prairies, where the sky stretched off into infinity as it does at sea. The Smeetons looked as I imagined them, handsomely seasoned by travel, like old leather suitcases. Beryl bubbled with energy, always doing something while she talked. The interior of the house bore the unmistakable stamp of her creative carpentry. Barrels, packing cases and old ploughseats had been fashioned into chairs, with Beryl's total disregard for comfort. One concession to loafing, was an old bed which swung on chains from the ceiling in the upstairs sitting room. The dining table was an old cable drum, the seats were cut-down barrels. The door latches were hand carved and bound with leather thongs. No piece of scrap escaped her inventiveness. There was nothing coy and arty about it: it was all no-nonsense functional, like the pole up the middle of their spiral staircase.

We had just finished dinner in the upstairs living area and were going down to see something in the workshop. The stairs wound up into the sitting room and I noticed there was no rail round the outside. Before I could work out why, Beryl, in long skirt and bare feet and without a pause in her conversation, flung herself off the landing and slid down the pole. I instinctively knew one followed or one failed. I carried on into thin air and embraced the pole as if I did it every day. I made a respectable landing and David and Miles followed in quick succession. Throughout the manoeuvre, the exchange of talk had flowed without falter. In any other house this would seem like a gimmick, but here it was the solution to a problem. Miles suffered from arthritis in his knees which made walking downstairs painful. And, it appealed to Beryl as it was also the simplest and quickest way down.

Beryl was quick to sense that David was a handy man to have around and she lost no time in putting him to work. He was up next morning at five-thirty feeding moose and kit foxes. This species of little foxes had become extinct in Canada and these had been sent from Montana to see if they could be bred and re-introduced to the wild. There were two pairs and, believing that kit foxes mate for life, Beryl named one couple Nelson and Emma, and the other Napoleon and

Josephine. However, the foxes had their own ideas on this, and I woke in the morning to Beryl's piercing call: 'Napoleon! Emma! Breakfast!' and, a few minutes later, 'Nelson! Josephine!'.

In spite of their taste for hair-shirted living, the Smeetons had an enormous sense of fun. Their humour could be wickedly sophisticated or frivolously childlike. Adults who can put a sou'wester on their daughter's giant teddy bear, stick it in the cockpit with its paw tied to the tiller and retire below to watch the reaction of the crew of a passing freighter, surely stay young forever.

During the course of the winter we stayed with them a number of times, en route to Calgary for supplies. 'Come and break your journey here,' Miles had said. 'Beryl's got such a long list for David it'll take all winter to get through it.'

The rivers were swelling with melting snow when we paid our last visit. We knew they wouldn't be there. Someone's daughter from England, on her world travels, was minding the shop, feeding the animals and doing the annual houseclean. Miles and Beryl were on their way across Canada to Newfoundland where they were going to rejoin their old love, *Tzu Hang*. The new owner, Bob Nance, had crewed with them on their successful voyage round the Horn, and was now inviting them to sail with him to Europe. 'He'll be appalled when he sees what old crocks we've become,' Miles had said. The old crocks were trying to persuade Bob to make the passage via Greenland. He was opting for the slightly less rigorous route via Iceland. 'But we've been to Iceland,' Beryl told me by way of explanation.

It turned out to be Beryl's last voyage. The following Autumn, we heard, almost unbelievingly, that she had died, of cancer. We had no inkling that during the winter we had known her, and had been swept along by her exuberance with life, she was in remission, having done battle with the disease the previous year.

To us, she had seemed immortal and, in a way, she is. The void in Miles's life must have been immense, but he carried on with the farm and kept active with cross country skiing, ice yachting and flying. Beryl would be there in spirit, exhorting him, scolding him, and still amazing him.

I remember one day as we watched her in action, he turned to me and said slowly, with wonder in his voice, as if he were a newly-smitten suitor, 'you know, she really... is... *quite*... the most remarkable... person.'

16

Beyond Desolation Sound

'When the Spring comes we'll be off again to the South Pacific,' David had told the customs officer. But when our friend Brian arrived from England to sail with us part way across the Pacific we said to him, 'I'm glad to see you brought your oilskins and wellies. You'll be needing them.'

'Uh?' said Brian who had given up his job and was planning eventually to join his Australian girl friend in Sydney. David opened up a map of British Columbia.

'Look at this coastline!' Like a filligreed relic, bitten and etched by centuries of corrosion, it showed myriads of islands, channels and inlets. 'How could we pass this up?'

'Looks great.' said Brian. He has an easy way about him which always makes him welcome crew.

When the snow on the ski slopes turned to muddy porridge we packed up house and drove back to Vancouver Island to release *Moongazer* from her winter bonds. The ravages of weather had faded her good looks, so we sailed her over to the Big City for a light face lift.

In the watery heart of Vancouver, the Royal Vancouver Yacht Club had an out-station with a small dock for visiting yachts. There we could work on the boat, entertain friends, and enjoy the city – provided we could resist the all-pervading temptation, that is the essence of a city, to spend money. The yacht club charged a dock fee, but it was a modest one and we discovered there were advantages to being guests at a prestigious club. The swing lids of the huge garbage skips hid rich pickings. Boat owners were too lazy or workmen too well paid, to salvage the fittings from discarded gear. By the end of the week David had gleaned a tidy heap of stainless nuts, bolts jubilee clips and other trinkets. Some of the gear wasn't so bad either; we still use the aluminium barbecue and the tiller extension.

It was a week of heatwave and every evening, crews from luxury motor cruisers would leave cartons of empty beer bottles on the dock. The Canadian government, in an attempt to change just this attitude to waste, made the empties redeemable at the liquor stores. Now, in public places there was rarely a can or bottle to be seen. Not because some people no longer tossed their litter around but because there was a whole sub-culture who worked at rooting out everything with a cent on its head. We had no time to go rooting, but if bottles came our way... The proceeds were enough to supply the three of us with all the beer we needed for the week.

Among the handful of visitors at the dock was a small, timid-looking elderly couple with a Grand Banks motor cruiser, or what the North Americans call a trawler yacht. They had brought it up from California, which surprised us as the Washington-Oregon coast has a notorious reputation. It further surprised us to hear they were going to Alaska. 'Holiday?' I asked by way of conversation.

'Well, actually no,' said Debbie. 'It's work. Norm's a wildlife photographer and we're going up to do a film on brown bears, if we can get close enough to them that is.' Most people prefer to put a lot of distance between themselves and brown bears. However, Norm and Debbie had spent several summers nosing around the wilds of South East Alaska and knew the area well.

'I don't think we'll have time to get that far north,' David told them.

Norm blinked with concern through his granny glasses. 'You can't come this far and not go to the glaciers. Look there!' He pointed to some photographs on the cabin bulkhead, stunning shots of their boat against the green ice wall of a tidewater glacier. We stared at them and Brian and I in our British way, said 'Wow' and 'Gosh'. David didn't say a word but I knew that he was transposing *Moongazer* to those photographs and that our summer plans had just stretched another 500 miles.

Much of that month of May, it seemed, was spent in leave-taking. It is the traveller's lot to be always saying goodbye, but I had never said it so often, in such succession and with such a sense of loss.

Moongazer staggered a little more under our acquisitions of the winter-skis, boots and attendant paraphernalia, power tools and warm memories. We found a stowage place for everything and set off quietly up the beautiful Straits of Georgia one day in early June.

This broad stretch of water between Vancouver Island and the mainland runs north for about a hundred miles and is used by a procession of ferries, freighters, tugs, log booms, barges, fishing boats and pleasure craft. Before 1791, these waters knew only Indian canoes. The ocean coast of Vancouver Island had seen the arrival of the Spaniards in 1774, followed by Captain Cook four years later. The aftermath of Cook's visit triggered off a fierce trade with China in sea otter pelts and, by the time Vancouver arrived, British, Russian and American trading captains had an extensive knowledge of the whole coastal area.

What lay behind New Georgia, through the Straits of Juan de Fuca, no European chart maker really knew. Myths legends and rumours abounded and some were nourished into accepted fact. Early cartographers often exercised a colourful imagination when filling in the blanks on world maps. In the 16th century the stretch of water that separated Asia and North America appeared on an Italian map as the Straits of Anian. This was a convoluted derivation from Marco Polo's account of the Chinese province of Ania, separated by a salt water passage. By the early 18th century these straits had moved across into North America as an ill-defined scrawl running from the Pacific to Hudson's Bay. Speculations about an Atlantic-Pacific passage were given a boost by an article which appeared in an English magazine in 1708. It was a vivid account by an Admiral de Fonte, describing his passage between the two oceans. The tale was generally attributed to the imagination of the author of the magazine. Two other authors of the day, Swift and Defoe, were also suspected of having a hand in it. After a while the yarn began to take on the substance of fact and by the time the tales of the Greek pilot Juan de Fuca were added it was an established event. Certain navigators were even claiming to have travelled the passage. Eventually the Hudson's Bay company sent explorers to find the Atlantic opening and when they found only vast tracts of land they were accused of withholding the truth.

When Cook was dispatched to investigate from the Pacific there were already French and Spanish expeditions on the way. Cook's death brought a halt to the British efforts until ten years later, when a row with Spain developed over the seizure of two British trading ships at Nootka Sound in Vancouver Island, (or New Georgia, as it was then called). The subsequent Nootka Convention provided that Spain should hand back all lands claimed by the British, northward of California - a reflection on the changing balance of world power.

George Vancouver had sailed these waters with Captain Cook and had become an officer in his mould, a natural choice of leader for an expedition to take formal re-possession from the Spanish. He was appointed King's Commissioner and given command of the newly fitted *Discovery*, a sloop of 330 tons, just over thirty metres long, with a hand-picked complement of 100 officers and crew. She would be accompanied by the smaller, armed tender, *Chatham* manned by a crew of 45. Vancouver's secret orders were to explore the whole northwest coast of America, from latitude 30 degrees in California to 60 degrees in Alaska and to search thoroughly for a northwest passage.

When Vancouver arrived up from the South Pacific and brought his ships through the Straits of Juan de Fuca into what he named the Gulf of Georgia, he was sure he was the first European to do so. He worked his way up the mainland coast, coping with the caprices of weather and Indians, and using the ship's boats to probe the deep inlets. One day, as he returned from one of these long expeditions in the open yawl he was astonished to come across two small schooners flying the Spanish flag. They were the *Sutil* and *Mexicana* with their young captains Galiano and Valdes, part of a command detached to continue an expedition started the previous year. Whatever disappointment Vancouver may have felt at his pitch being queered, he took a liking to the Spaniards and they agreed to continue the explorations in company.

The Gulf of Georgia ended in a wall of mountains dissected by narrow channels, and there was great doubt about where they led. Valdes, who spoke the Indian languages fluently, said that the natives told him there was a way through to the ocean in the north. He also warned that native information could be notoriously unreliable. The mountainous area depressed Vancouver. It was a dark wet night when he drifted into it under the grip of strong currents and fickle winds. He noted in the log: '...we were driven about as it were blindfolded in this labyrinth until, towards midnight we were happily conducted towards the north side of an island in this supposed sound where we anchored, in company with the *Chatham* and the Spanish vessels…'

Later that day, after sending out exploration parties in the ships boats they were driven from their precarious anchorage by a fresh wind to a, 'more eligible anchorage, though in a situation equally dreary and unpleasant.' To Vancouver the fjord-like scenery promised only difficulties - lack of fresh food, hostile Indians and fierce currents. In this frame of mind he lumbered the area for posterity with the name of Desolation Sound.

After nine days, one of the exploratory boat parties returned with the cheering news that two of the channels led through to the ocean. The bad news was that there were several sets of rapids on the way and they had nearly come to grief in the narrow passage north of Desolation Sound. Vancouver decided therefore to work further west and take the broader channel which the Indians had shown them. This was the parting of the ways for the Spaniards who felt their small, ill-equipped ships would hold up the party.

For several days Vancouver studied the fierce tidal flow through the half-mile-wide bottleneck between the northern waters and the Gulf of Georgia. On a weak ebb he took his ships safely through, unaware that in the middle, just under the surface, lay a large twin-peaked rock. Ripple Rock, as it came to be known, claimed many subsequent boats and lives, until in 1958, it was blasted apart by a two and a half million pound explosive charge, making it, at the time, the world's biggest man-made non-atomic explosion.

For us, Desolation Sound looked much as Vancouver saw it, wreathed in cloud and rain-mist. It reminded us of the Western Isles of Scotland, a scene, not of desolation, but more of damp splendour. It was a fitting backdrop for the tales that had been impressed upon us, of wrecked boats and lost lives.

'We've got a choice, you know,' said David, 'between the Seymour Narrows and the Yucalta Rapids.'

'Like asking a condemned man if he prefers the guillotine or the gallows,' I replied. I looked at the sailing directions, 'Travelling north, one should meet the Yucalta Rapids at the end of the flood. Strong east winds against these waters can whip up incredible turbulence and even large trawlers have met with disaster.'

I read no further. 'Let's take the Narrows.'

'Don't forget,' said David, 'that all the commercial traffic goes that way.' I had visions of tugs and freighters and log booms all swirling around.

'Which would you prefer,' I asked Brian, 'to be sucked down by a whirlpool or mangled by a tug.'

'It's all the same to me,' replied Brian, and meant it.

I remembered that Peter Pye on *Moonraker* had ghosted through the Narrows on one of his engine's many 'off' days. They had been carried across the bows of a freighter and only just made it to safety before the tide flooded. The episode so impressed him that he added a footnote to his account in the *The Sea is for Sailing*. It advised having an adequate engine, 'Without this, it is a hazardous proceeding.'

In the end we chose the Yucalta Rapids. We arrived on a day especially picked for its neap tides and mid-day turn and found that the weather was also co-operating. With a couple of hours to spare we tied up at the congested docks of a game fishing resort just south of the rapids and, from the safety of a rocky headland, watched the flooding waters. They were like an angry swollen river rushing downhill. My heart missed a beat at the sight and I heard Brian whisper, 'Jeez-us!' making it sound more of a prayer.

The surface of the water flashed with hundreds of small herring fleeing from the snapping jaws of salmon. Eyeing the salmon from their tree-top perches, over a hundred bald eagles sat hunched, looking, I thought morosely, like vultures.

Back at the dock we asked the fish rangers about the exact timing of the tide-turn. There were actually three sets of turbulence to get through before the ebb gathered strength, so the timing was critical. A ranger looked down the channel and pointed to a single file of power cruisers and small fish boats coming our way. It was time to join them. 'Go for it', he shouted. 'Good luck!'

We pushed off in a nervous scramble leaving some of our paint on the dock side, and joined the line. We were moving at the last of the flood on the back eddies, just as the sailing directions instructed. I was reading them out, mainly for something to do. David was on the tiller, concentrating on the water ahead. His normal cheer-up-the-troops routine had lapsed. Brian, festooned with camera gear, was lining up shots.

Dry-mouthed I intoned from the book: 'Small whirls and upheavals which can swing a small boat 30 degrees to either side are quite normal in the hour before high slack.'

I looked down at the water around us. It was changing with every second, forming little swirlpools, ripples and overfalls. I didn't feel we were being slewed around but I could see the boats in front of us sliding from side to side. 'We're being pushed too,' said David, 'I can feel the pressure on the steering.'

The gap between us and the other boats widened as we followed them into the Gillard Passage. Being the only yacht that day, we had the smallest engine. It thumped away at the highest revs we dared allow it and each of us kept a nervous and, we thought, unnoticed, watch on gauges.

The waters were still bubbling and swirling as we moved down the Gillard passage. We hoped our timing was correct, for I read from the book: 'The flood current here runs to 10 knots and maintains considerable strength until very close to slack water.' I consulted the dog-eared sketch map. I was worried about Judd Island. There was a dangerous reef off its south-west side. I looked up to figure it out and found we were through the passage, heading swiftly toward the next set of rapids. The tide had turned and we were being borne by a gathering ebb. So much for high slack.

We whizzed past Dent island and ahead loomed a rocky hummock bristling with pine trees - Little Dent Island. Back to The Book:

> This current meets at right angles the flow from the Sonora Island side, with a large standing wave angling out from the lighthouse. Off the end of the wave a whirlpool forms, perhaps 30 feet in diameter, which moves down-current about 300 yards before disappearing and reforming at the wave.

No one said a word. David stared straight ahead, concentrating intensely on the steering. I couldn't bear to look. With every second I expected a giant whirlpool to open up before us. I couldn't see any boats in front of us. Maybe they'd all been gobbled by a vortex. Then I saw we were bowling along in normal flattish water. The passage opened out into a broad channel. Brian's camera clicked for the first time. Suddenly we all noticed how beautiful it was. The sun had come out, bringing life to the sombre fjord. To the north and to the east we could see the mountains of the interior, range upon range, their snow-capped peaks sparkling in the sun.

We stopped for the night in a small indent between steep wooded hills. At the turn of the century it had been a busy place, a stop for steamers on the logging camp run. Now there was only a small boat float and a cluster of what looked like derelict buildings. We tied up to the float in front of a number of small motor boats. They were going north on fishing trips, and were so loaded with lines, rods, nets, crab pots, and things unidentifiable, that I wondered that there were any fish left.

Our friends in Victoria reckoned that our crab catches

would be so abundant that we'd soon be sick of dressed crab. 'And as for salmon,' they had said, 'the water just glitters with them.'

On their advice we had bought an assortment of lures spinners and spoons, none of which we had the slightest experience of using. Our ocean fishing was fairly basic. A heavy line, a strong hook and some coloured rag seemed to work for tuna. Salmon were obviously smarter. Our crab trap seemed a better bet and that night we used it for the first time. Our neighbours on the dock gave us some fishy remains and lots of advice for setting it up. We were assured that, 'come morning, you'll have some real tasty eating in there.'

We ate our supper in the cockpit to enjoy the long still twilight and caught the strains of singing drifting from the shore. Curiosity overcoming tiredness, we wandered along the boardwalk to the old wooden shacks. They turned out not to be so derelict as distance had suggested. They were a homestead of some sort and the singing was coming from a substantial, well-kept log cabin. We opened the door into a smoke-filled room, packed with huge lusty, mostly bearded, men, all wearing checked shirts. For a moment I was transported back to the last century when the loggers gathered at the hotel in this spot, waiting for employment. In recent years a German couple had, with Teutonic zeal, resurrected the buildings and were running a thriving inn. Their customers still came literally from out of the woodwork - loggers from the camp further down the channel.

That night our cabin floor was bed for Steve, who was rowing to Alaska in an open skiff. There seemed to be a fashion for that at the moment as we had heard of other attempts in canoes and kayaks. Steve was a quiet determined American, a mountain climber, and doubtless he would get there.

Next morning found us with time to spare before we

attacked the next set of rapids. We had heard that high up on the forested hillside, was an abandoned gold mine, so with the exploring zeal of the foreigner we set off to look for it. The trail, through thick damp stands of spruce and cedar, rose nearly vertically in parts. We passed moss-covered stumps of huge trees once felled by hand, and saw the the notches made by the lumberjacks to hold their planks. We toiled upward, our zeal evaporating with our sweat until, just on the point of giving up, we found the rotting, overgrown relics of man's endeavour. Cabins, platforms, buggy rails, all once dragged up by hand, were collapsing down the cliffside. Only the tunnel, hewn out of the rock had resisted nature's deathgrip.

It says much for the power of gold fever that men were prepared to tackle such formidable obstacles and endure such hardships on the tenuous promise of perhaps only a few flakes of gold among the gravel on the beach. In the thirty years after the first strikes further north in the 1870s, almost every beach and stream, no matter how remote, had been investigated. The slightest trace of precious metal triggered off a frenzy of clearing and digging in the river valleys and adjacent hillsides to find the source lodes. By 1912 the fever had subsided and most of the small mines were worked out or were uneconomic and left to rot, like the one we had now found.

Such a decisive reclamation by nature reminded us that this land, north of Desolation Sound, was noticeably wilder and harsher. The ripples from the conurbations of Vancouver and Seattle petered out at the rapids and we were on the edge of a vast territory where even now the people who lived here had made a certain choice about their lives.

We had cast off from the dock and were motoring out into the channel when I noticed Brian leaning over the side, signalling frantically.

'We're dragging something!'

I slowed down and he hauled it up. It was the crab trap,

with something in it. We rushed to look. It was a very drowned dogfish.

The next set of rapids presented no problems. In the event, neither had the first ones but now we felt like old hands and I was even beginning to enjoy the excitement.

We anchored at night in dark, silent bays, the water stilled by huge sheltering cedars which swept down to the shore. Each morning we were up with the dawn to take the tide down Johnstone Straits. Now we were meeting with the commercial traffic coming up from the Seymour Narrows.

The straits separate Vancouver Island from the rest of the Province and run out north-westwards to the ocean. This was the discovery made by Johnstone, the master of the *Chatham*, that so cheered Vancouver. When Johnstone and his men rowed and sailed the little open yawl down the Straits they noticed that the Indians were not especially curious about them and that some carried muskets, a sign that contact with the fur traders had already spread from outside waters. Vancouver had to wait for nine anxious days in Desolation Sound before the yawl arrived back with the good news. He moved the ships up through the narrows, into the straits and worked slowly along the continental shoreline. He used the open boats to search out and survey every inlet and passage, some of which ran inland for as much as eighty miles. They worked through the whole month of July, dogged continually it seemed, by wind and rain.

For us, it was mid-June and the short term forecast looked good. Being of considerably softer stuff than Vancouver's men, we decided to give ourselves a few days rest half-way along the straits. We tied up to a rotting dock in a large and beautiful bay which had once seen the bustle of logging and fishing camps. Now the only sign of life was a steel schooner moored to a scow (a barge-like vessel usually used for mobile fish camps). We lazed, dug for clams, fished unsuccessfully, explored and saw a bear, or rather the disappearing back of one. David spent most of his time in the bilges fitting warning bells to the engine oil and temperature controls. He also adapted a smoke detector to hoot when it got wet, and placed it under the starter motor. We knew from experience that at the very sight of sea water, starter motors sicken and eventually die. We paid the engine every homage we knew, short of placing little bowls of food in front of it. For the next few months it would be our god.

We discovered that a family lived on the steel schooner and they invited us aboard one evening. They were the MacAllisters; Dad, very attractive Mum, even more attractive teenage daughters and teenage son. Another son was away, working on the fish boats up north. They had lived in the bay for some years. 'First we built the schooner,' Dad told us, 'Then we salvaged this old fish scow. We're building a little place on it - somewhere to live and keep the animals.' The 'little' place was a superb house of cedar logs. The greenhouse was bursting with vegetables, and a beautiful little byre housed goats and chickens. 'We're going to tow it with the schooner up north. I've got a timber claim on a little island out near the Dixon Entrance. It'll be for a few years, so we're going to need that greenhouse.' They had built a floating homestead, a complete little ecosystem that they could transport to the site of their choice, however remote and infertile.

We ploughed on down the choppy Straits, stopping for the night at settlements strung along Vancouver island, till we came to the last outpost, Port Hardy. There, at the government dock we discovered the manager was the girlfriend of an English yachtsman we'd met in Hawaii. Now they lived on his little boat, saving up for their next trip.

Port Hardy would be our last 'civilization' stop for some time so we made the most of its benefits. We shopped in the supermarket, ate ice cream, drank cold beer and went to the swimming pool for a final hot shower. We were ambling slowly back along the dock, arms full of shopping when we heard from somewhere deep among the power cruisers and fish boats the continous wail of a horn. 'Sounds like some poor sod's alarm's gone off,' said Brian, and we all smiled. As we got nearer *Moongazer* the hooting grew louder. We looked at each other and smartened our walk. *Moongazer* came into view and the hooting became strident. David dropped the groceries and sprinted to the boat. By the time we gathered up the bags and reached the cockpit, he was pumping vigorously. 'There was water nearly to the starter motor, just under the engine.' he puffed. 'I think the packing gland on the prop shaft's getting worn from all this motoring. I can still hear it dripping.'

It had been a couple of days since I last checked the bilges and I wouldn't have thought of it for another day or so. But for the new alarm the engine electrics would have been dead by morning. 'Paid for itself already!' said David with great satisfaction. (Everything on *Moongazer* has to justify its existence, crew included.)

The next part of the journey we hoped, would give the engine a rest. The established route to Alaska, known as the Inside passage, and once the main highway to the goldfields of the Yukon, runs northward through a long series of channels sheltered by the coastal islands. We planned to leave this for a time and strike out for a 150 mile sail into the North Pacific to the enigmatic Queen Charlotte Islands. None of our Canadian friends had ever visited them, or knew anyone that had. 'Great wilderness country,' they told us, 'if you're into rainforests.'

At the last little island opposite the northern tip of Vancouver Island we waited for the weather - for bad weather. We wanted the south-easterlies of a depression to blow us smartly across the Queen Charlotte Sound. It wasn't an area we would be keen to drift around in. To the north-east lay the rock-studded waters that so nearly claimed Vancouver's ships. Drifting in thick fog, the *Discovery* grounded and heeled over on the falling tide. Through the night and early morning the crews of both ships worked to unload the *Discovery*'s stores into the boats and prop up the hull with the dismantled spars and top-masts. The weather held and she floated free on the next tide. The stores were reloaded and the top-masts raised in time to catch a light breeze. By late afernoon it had died and the ships were once again drifting on the ebb-tide among the rocks. In the early evening the *Chatham* struck a hidden ledge. Another night of struggle ensued, even more anxiously, as a slight swell was causing the *Chatham* to pound on the rocks. By superb seamanship she was refloated on the tide with minimal damage. It took two more days before they could work their way out into open water and on to a safe anchorage. By then it was mid-August and Vancouver was noting the: 'inclemency of the weather' and the fact that he and his men were: 'excessively fatigued'. A fur trader had brought news from Nootka that the Spanish Commander there was waiting to begin negotiations on the sovereignty of the area. Also, his supply ship had arrived from Australia. He decided it was time to call a halt to the surveys of 1792 and turned his ships south to Nootka, before wintering eventually in Hawaii.

Our few days of waiting were spent in congenial company. On the island was a coastguard station, staffed by a handful of men and their families. One of the wives, it turned out, had been a pupil of my mother's in a little school in Scotland.

I woke one morning, only hours it seemed, after a night of merrymaking, to the sound of rain pattering on the deck. I looked out of the porthole to a dismal scene of dripping fir trees and struggled with a strong urge to snuggle back in my bunk. David was already up and bustling. 'Rise and shine,' he chirped. 'A light wind from the south. Porridge, everybody?'

We slipped past mist-enshrouded islands out into the Goletas Channel. Valdes and Galiano had called it *Salida de los goletas*, 'Schooner Exit', and it marked the completion of their explorations. As we chugged out past Point Mexicana, into the ocean swell, I thought of the hundreds of miles ahead of us. We were only just beginning.

17

Islands Of The Haida

'You don't think we've overshot?' asked David in a rare moment of doubt. The wind had blown from the south-east all night, gusting to gale force at times. We peered into the unremitting grey drizzle of early daylight. A cold prickle of unease spread down my spine.

'It worries me that we didn't pick up the light on the southernmost island,' I answered.

David studied the chart. 'We'll keep on this course till mid-morning,' he said, 'and if nothing shows up we'll have to think about what next.'

'Or carry on to Japan,' quipped Brian, winking at David.

An article on the Queen Charlotte Islands in *National Geographic* leads with: 'Few people have seen these misty, storm-lashed isles,' and if I'd read it then I would have added, 'but not for want of trying.' We leaned over the guardrails, straining and squinting at a horizon of clouds and rolling mists. We had no way of telling how far off the horizon was. Two miles or ten miles?

Around mid-morning our guardian angel, tired of teasing, rolled back the mist. It was only for a few minutes, but enough for us to catch the grey, washy outline of land. We headed resolutely towards it. A lone fishing boat hove into view, so we dropped sail and drifted until it came near enough for us to ask directions. It was a halibut boat with stacked coils of long-lines and bundles of glowing orange floats filling the little deck. The skipper came out of the wheelhouse to answer us. 'Yup. You're right on. That's Kunghit Island. Heater Harbour's round the third headland.'

We closed the land and glided into the bay on a falling wind. It died just as we reached the head and into its still, dark waters we dropped the anchor with a splash that sent the birds squawking from the trees and a little fur seal slithering from its siesta.

We rested for two days in that silent spot beside the huge cedars. Huge too, were the mosquitoes that attacked us as we came ashore, and stung derisively through coatings of repellant. Layers of clothing were no protection either and eventually we learned to endure them stoically. We wandered along the white pebbled foreshore and found only the slightest trace of man – mounds of old clam shells. The Haida Indians would have used the site for a summer camp. They would have fished and hunted and gathered roots and berries. The harvest would have been smoked, dried, or packed in oil and when the autumn gales came, carried back to the greater shelter of the winter village. Bare feet leave light footprints.

When we moved round the headland to the next anchorage we found the rusting iron bootprints of Industrial Man. Boilers, tanks, machinery and planks rotted in a grotesque jumble among the foxgloves and the alders. For thirty years, until 1939, this was a thriving whaling station employing around two hundred Japanese labourers. The islands were a convenient base for whalers intercepting the seasonal migrations of baleen whales (the toothless vegetarians like the humpback and the right whale) from the Arctic to California and Hawaii. Even before the outbreak of World War II and the subsequent internment of all Japanese in

Canada, the land-based stations were becoming uneconomic and the whales had been hunted almost to extinction.

We clambered past the rusty relics on the foreshore and, drawing back a curtain of bushes, stepped into the great cedar forest. We were met with the signs of more decay, but it was of the magnificent and regenerative kind. Like most people in the Western World, we had never seen a truly virgin forest before. Cedars which were saplings before Columbus began sailing, were now towering above us. Their branches formed a filigreed canopy which filtered shafts of sunlight like stained glass windows. The forest floor was lost deep below a tangle of fallen trees, blanketed with moss and bristling with new growth. This was nature's own cathedral with vast, vaulted aisles, naves, cloisters, sweeping arches and flying buttresses – far outmatching even the triumphs of Europe's medieval master builders. We moved among the shrouded roots and deadfalls and through piercing shafts of sunlight, awed into silence by a powerful force, an unseen presence almost. I felt too, that same sense of the insignificance of man that comes to me during the long nights at sea under the winking galaxies.

It seemed incredible to think that these stands of virgin cedar may not see the end of the century. We had heard that the big-name logging companies were well-established on the islands, working their way southward towards the last of the old forests. There is much controversy and protest, but while it rages at local, provincial and national level the loggers continue to cut and clear.

None are more torn by the controversy than the indigenous Haida Indians whose ancestors' lives were bound culturally and materially by the cedar. The Haida were the lords of the northwest coast; a vigorous and warlike people who raided and traded in their great dug-out canoes of red cedar. These canoes were often over thirty metres long with a beam of two or more metres. In the late 18th century one sailing ship captain, arriving in the islands, reported being surrounded by over 600 canoes. They were a people whose economy and culture were highly developed, much like the Polynesians. They suffered the impact of the White man in the same way – decimation by disease, alcohol and firearms. By the early 1900s every village had lost most of its inhabitants and had been abandoned. Nowadays the remnant population of around 1500 is clustered round two mission stations on Graham Island.

The whole of the North Pacific coast is rich with the sites of abandoned Indian villages but few traces remain. What vandals and academics haven't taken, nature has claimed. We read, by chance one day soon after we arrived, that: 'The... best preserved and loveliest of all the Haida villages... is on remote, unsheltered Anthony Island, the southwesternmost home of the fighting Haidas until abandoned in the 1880s.'

Anthony Island was only a few hours away from our anchorage at the whaling station, but to approach it and anchor we needed perfect weather. For most of the year the rock-strewn waters around it take the brunt of heavy seas and in winter the storms roar in with hurricane force.

On our second morning at the whaling station we woke to a brilliant, cloudless sunrise. The water was glassy calm. Shamelessly we shattered the stillness as *Moongazer*'s engine coughed into life and chugged out towards our island. Around us, little knobs of tufted islets shone like gems studded in a mirror of blue glass. To the west lay the open ocean, temporarily and deceptively subdued. We nosed *Moongazer* as close as we dared into the rocks around the island and left her dubiously anchored in the kelp. So thick was the kelp that the surface of the water looked like some aquatic field and we had to punt the dinghy through it to reach the shore.

We beached it on a slope of perfectly rounded pebbles, the size of dinner plates. Between us and the forest stood a tangled barrier of driftwood logs, twenty feet high. Our log-running-and-jumping act was becoming quite proficient, but this pitch exercised us more than most. David stopped frequently to poke among the debris trapped in the tangle. He held up a plastic bottle. 'The Japan current brings more than warm wet weather,' he remarked. We saw numerous plastic containers covered in Japanese writing, but none of the prized glass balls which everyone had told us to look out for.

We walked through chest-high grass by the edge of the forest until we came upon a small, sheltered bay, sweeping in a crescent of white sand. I felt, almost before I could take in the scene, that we were not alone. Then I saw them, strung along the grassy bluff above the foreshore, gazing out to sea, ignoring us. They were old and losing the fight with the elements. Some had already succumbed and lay in the undergrowth, split apart by tree roots. The others were already leaning towards their final resting place.

'But,' wrote Emily Carr, the painter who, fifty years ago, caught the spirit of these lands in words as well:

> ...no matter how drunken their tilt, the Haida poles never lost their dignity. They looked sadder perhaps, when they bowed forward and more stern when they tipped back. They were bleached to a pinkish silver colour and cracked by the sun, but nothing could make them mean or poor, because the Indians had put strong thought into them and had believed sincerely in what they were trying to express.

The carved, and once-painted, faces of the Eagles and the Ravens and the Wolves, embodying the family crests and stories, were still there, staring past us. The boxes on the top of the mortuary poles were open and empty. Once they would have held the remains of an important person. Behind the poles and almost swallowed by greenery were the rotting beams and door posts of the great wooden longhouses. Often 20 metres long, these were the Haida's winter quarters, where they lived, entertained, told tales and worked on their artifacts.

The anthropologist John Swanton has likened the Haida to the old Highland Scots. They were divided into some 17 clans and clan loyalty came first above all else. Their personal possessions were marked with the clan and family crests which denoted family connection, privilege and honour. Any infringement of copyright was an invitation to do battle. The preserved bounty of the summer's hunting and fishing allowed a large amount of time and energy in the winter for creative leisure. This abundance of fish, molluscs and marine game throughout the whole of the northwest coast enabled all the resident tribes to achieve a level of civilization uniquely sophisticated among the world's hunter-gatherers. They established a culture that for 9,000 or more years, worked in harmony with nature. The development of their artforms suggests they led lives that were rich and satisfying.

Brian was the first to break our preoccupied silence. 'I can't help feeling the Haidas had got it right.'

'Nature's favoured folk,' I said, 'like the Polynesians.'

'Until the white man came along and made sure it never happened again,' added David.

It was a depressing thought and we wandered quietly away from the silent witnesses of sorrow. We felt, among the beauty and the wildness, that it was a place, as Emily Carr put it, '...more poignantly desolate for having once known man.'

We didn't know it then, but wheels were grinding on the international stage to make Anthony Island a UNESCO World Heritage Cultural Site. At least it will now be safe from the museum marauders. How the remains are to be preserved is in dispute. Many of the Haida at the mission settlements feel that the poles should not be kept alive by science but be allowed to return to the earth to die naturally, with dignity.

Such a well-timed day of perfect weather allowed us to tolerate, almost cheerfully, the wind and rain which dogged our progress for the next few weeks. We day-sailed up Moresby Island, anchoring in bays and inlets which all bore the scars of some failed economic enterprise. A copper mine, a logging camp, a Japanese cannery, a gold mine, a telegraph station, now only the haunt of bald eagles and black bears.

The weather worsened and a south-easterly gale was forecast, so we snuggled into a sheltered bay in company with some large halibut boats. David spent next morning chatting with the fishermen and returned, bouncy and bright-eyed.

'Anyone fancy a hot bath?'

Brian and I, roused from our reading, looked around. Mists, wetness and rusting fishboats were the general scene.

'Not a hot bath in a hundred miles,' replied Brian.

'Wrong!' said David. 'Just a dinghy ride away. That little island over there has a hotspring, so the fishermen tell me. They say there's a tub you can bathe in.' We looked at him sceptically, but for a hot bath we'd follow the slenderest trail.

Through driving rain and rough water we rowed the dinghy to a little rocky island. From the shore ran a trail to where we could see puffs of steam issuing from the bushes, and there we found an open-sided shack sheltering two cast-iron bathtubs. A pipe ran from the hillside continually feeding them with hot water. Further over among the rocks by the shore, stood a splendid enamel bath with curly feet, open to the sky. I made straight for it.

In record time I peeled off my oilskins, boots, sweaters and thermal underwear. I rolled them in a bundle and stuck it in a crevice, out of the rain. Then, before my goose pimples sprouted feathers, and, feeling like some goddess in a crazy bath-salts advert, I slid into the delicious, sulphurous warmth.

There I soaked for an hour with a vista before me, matched by no other bathroom in the world: sea, islands and mist-wreathed mountains and, high above, a bald eagle soaring against grey billowing clouds.

Back on board we spent the rest of the day in a glowing swoon of lethargy – almost as pleasant, but in no way as memorable, as that hot soak, *al fresco* in the curly-footed bath.

For much of the next two days we faced the rigour of the gale from the heated cabin of a fishing boat, drinking ice cold beer and eating steak. One of the fishermen presented us with a halibut, frozen stiff as a board, and huge, we thought. 'Nah, he's just a tiddler,' said the fisherman. 'A decent one comes in at 300lbs.'

'At three dollars a pound that's a lot of bucks,' said David.

'Yup, the money's not bad while the season lasts. But it's getting shorter and shorter. Everybody's on to it these days and the fish are sure harder to find.' It was a cry we were to hear echoed all over the world. But those who made it usually implied that depletion was someone else's fault.

On the dying breath of the gale we started north towards the main settlement, Queen Charlotte City, a few days' sail away. The wind now blew lightly from the west, rolling down off the mountains. The air was fresher and promising chinks of blue peeped from the cloud cover. By late afternoon the sun had struggled through, lighting up the dark mountainsides. Extensive areas, I began to notice, were an odd colour of light grey. 'A huge forest fire?' I asked David.

He shook his head grimly. 'No. That's what they call clear-cutting. It's modern logging, mechanized and fast; they can rip through a forest before the ink's dried on their permit.'

I'd read about it, but it was a shock to actually see it. As we came closer I could see hillsides with huge swathes shorn bare, like a skinhead haircut. Every slope seemed scarred by the zig-zag gash of a logging road. I was aghast that the logging had spread so far into what I knew was a proposed Wilderness Area. Nourished by its own success, it was like some rapacious disease in the final phase, searching out and devouring every last bit of venerable forest.

I heard Brian sighing softly. 'First,' he said, 'we did it to the people. Now we do it to the forest.'

We sailed on past bays choked with huge log booms and logging platforms. From one of the bays we saw a peculiar vessel chugging out into the Hecate Strait towards mainland Canada. It looked at first like two floating oil rigs. 'The *Haida Monarch*,' David informed us. 'The guide book says it's the world's largest self-loading, self-dumping, self-propelled log transporter. It can carry up to 3.5 million board feet of timber.'

Absorbed with our thoughts, we watched in silence as it disapeared into the distance with its irreplaceable cargo. I wondered how many trips it made each week. I also wondered how many other thousands of loaded-down ships had sailed off into the distance since the fateful day in 1787 when the first white man came ashore. It was Captain Dixon in the *Queen Charlotte* who had come to trade iron tools for sea otter skins. He sailed off, much satisfied, with a cargo of 1,821 pelts, 'many of them very fine.'

We anchored for the night in a bay surrounded by hills which bristled with rows of young second-growth conifers. This was tree farming; quick-growing timber which can be harvested in the foreseeable financial future.

Another day of favourable wind and flat water took us comfortably to the doorstep of Queen Charlotte City. The threshold was a shallow bar between Graham Island and a long sandspit which ran out from the northern tip of Moresby Island. We made the entrance on a rising tide and after an hour's sail up Skidegate Inlet, tied up beside some other cruising yachts at the town dock. It was a magnificent spot with sweeping vistas to the mountains of the west coast. Ahead, the narrow Skidegate Channel offered a passage through at high water. I remembered that Miles Smeeton had once anchored *Tzu Hang* at the entrance and thought the anchorage to be: '...one of the most beautiful that we had seen anywhere in the world.'

We turned our attention to the immediate foreground, the straggle of wooden buildings that was Queen Charlotte City. 'Obviously named in a short-lived burst of optimism.' remarked Brian.

'I have to admit I was hoping for a supermarket,' I said, 'but it looks like we've got more supplies than they have.'

'Well, you can't have wilderness and Woolworths at the same time,' reminded David.

'One day you will,' said Brian. 'There'll be a fenced-off area with a big notice "TO THE WILDERNESS – $100 PER CAR." '

'Maybe that's the only way there's going to be a wilderness left to visit,' I said. Something was getting to us.

Around the City dock there were signs that here at least progress was being quietly defied. So, too, was maintenance. Half the assortment of small fishing boats leaned perilously close to submergence. The lurching docks were stacked with junk, evidently serving as a back yard for a number of liveaboards – and for their numerous large dogs. Standing out smartly, were the big, deep sea trawlers belonging to the Haida families. Most of them lived a few miles along the coast by the old Skidegate mission, in what is now a thriving community.

The 'city' was full of life, like a Mexican or Greek village with people hanging around chatting. I was coming out of the Post Office when voices behind me said, 'Hello, sailor.' I turned in surprise to see a couple we had met on a yacht in Madiera. They were were staying for a few days with their friend, the town's young lawyer. We had planned a quiet evening, as we intended to be off at dawn next morning, but instead, we sat up late, discussing the problems of the islands. We were cheered by the optimism of the young lawyer. He saw public pressure and more widespread awareness beginning to have an effect at Federal level.

'Even the young Haida who work for the logging companies are beginning to realise that the end of the cedar is the end of the last link with their heritage,' he told us. 'Community leaders now see that there has to be a way for their people to exist in a relationship with the land without depleting it. If they can get everyone to take pride in it and feel a custodian of it, there's a chance. Tourism, fishing, hunting, logging even, can all be carried on, under control, if those involved are committed first to conservation.'

I hoped he was right. We talked on, of the problems elsewhere in the Pacific Northwest, where the Indians struggle to compete in the Western economic ball-game. Here at least they shared a sense of identity.

As we wound our way back to the boat in the early hours, I was heartened to see that the wind was blowing strongly. 'It could be too rough to go over the bar,' I said hopefully.

'We'll see.'

'Couldn't we stay just one more day?' I wheedled.

'If we do that we'll be here for ever…'

'And then we'll never get anywhere.' I finished this well-worn rejoinder of David's. This dialogue is a ritual of departure, which, even now we still perform. Deep down I know that David is right, and he knows he's right, so I don't push it too far. But now and then something works in my favour to hold us up. This time it was the weather. By morning the wind had reached gale force, but born of a high pressure system and bringing a sparkling sky.

We spent the precious day, each doing our thing. I sketched the fishing boats, Brian photographed them, and David worked on *Moongazer*. I could have spent a year of precious days in the Queen Charlotte Islands. Those west coast mountains beckoned seductively through the Skidegate Channel.

I was apprehensive about the journey ahead. We were going back among the inside passages to Alaska, back to strong tides and fickle winds. Parts of the chart looked like a navigator's nightmare. Once again we would have to endure the daily drone of the engine. There would be little time for resting if we were to get up to the glaciers by mid-August. By the end of that month we needed to be out of these waters, on our way to California, ahead of the September gales.

18

Ice In The Drinks At Last

'That Hecate Strait out there – one of the worst bits of water in the world.'

I added it to our ever-growing list of 'worst waters'.

'It's so shallow, see? When that sou'easter blows, them waves jist stand up on the bottom. Like walls, they are, ten feet high. And throwin' sand everywhere. Ah seen fishboats jist covered. One even got so full of the stuff it sank.'

I allowed for a little fisherman's licence in the description but I didn't dismiss it. I knew that the Pyes on *Moonraker* had run into a nasty gale and crossed the strait in extreme discomfort and nil visibility.

For us however, the Strait was on its very best behaviour. The high pressure system had moved in and we motored from Queen Charlotte City across all seventy, glassy-blue miles of it to the B.C. coast.

The visibility that day was astounding; none of us had ever seen anything like it. Islands and mountains filled our eastern horizon, running north and south into a luminous sky. Inland, to the north, a higher, ice-capped range glinted in the sun. Behind us, the Queen Charlotte Islands in a rare burst of immodesty, bared all their beautiful features to the cloudless sky. It was a day the old map makers would have dreamed of.

Following the great exploratory surveys of Cook and

Vancouver, generations of H.M. survey vessels worked these waters to fill in the details. The Hecate Strait takes its name from a survey ship, the *Hecate* which came this way in the years 1861-62. The name of its second master, Browning, was given to the entrance which led us between the coastal islands that brilliant evening. We motored up the Beaver Passage, a reminder of the *Hecate*'s successor, *H.M.S. Beaver*, and dropped anchor in Connis Bay. This, I was refreshed to read, was named after the captain's Skye terrier.

Even now, many of the details of the remoter waters are still sketchy, and silt bars and mud channels are continually changing. Because of the large area we had to cover, the scale of our charts made the finer detail difficult to read – and this serrated shoreline studded with rocks, islets and kelp beds was rich in detail. *Moongazer*'s entrance to almost every cove was accompanied by a ritual exchange between the crew.

'Watch that rock!'

'Rock? That's a dot above the 'i'.'

'Or it could be a bit of the fathom line.'

'There's something across this inlet.'

'I think it's a splodge in the print.'

'What if it's not?'

Sand banks and mud bars livened up the end of a weary day. 'Twenty feet, sixteen, sixteen, twelve, ten… For God's sake David, slow down!'

'I'm trying to find out where the bank is.'

'You'll have us on it in a minute. Chrissakes it's six feet!'

Where to drop the anchor was another conversation piece. Brian would be up on the bow, well out of the danger zone, with the anchor ready to go.

'O.K. Brian, now!'

'No, no, hold it! We're too near those rocks (or other sundry hazards). If the wind turns we'll swing on to them.'

'The wind's not going to turn.'

'Oh, for God's sake'... and so on.

Brian, of course, would have known not to drop the hook at first bidding. Some instinct told him which particular command to select, not because it was the most sensible or the most authorative, but because it would cause the least disharmony.

I had (and still have) strong feelings about where we should be anchored. I liked to feel snug but not closed in, and certainly not feet away from disaster should the anchor drag. On the other hand I felt uneasy if there was too much open water around. Arriving in an anchorage, I liked to sniff around, like an animal, before choosing the right spot to settle in. David preferred to get on with the job. Between these two modes of operation lay a minefield of one-sided compromises.

When we left Connis Bay next morning the tide was low, baring the bay's less attractive features of mud flats and kelp beds. They did not, I noted with disquiet, have much regard for our chart. We took the start of the flood tide north through the Ogden Channel to join one of the world's great waterways, the Alaska Marine Highway. The route, running for a thousand miles between Seattle and Skagway, threads through the almost interlocking pieces of the huge jigsaw of islands that lies between the Pacific Ocean and the high mountains of the mainland. As Vancouver discovered, these tideswept and often windless waters were almost impossible for sailing ships and it was the steamships, bringing gold prospectors, which effectively opened them to the world.

We hoped to make the town of Prince Rupert, forty-five miles away, before nightfall. The sun shone between scattered clouds and a light breeze from the north rippled the water. We motored easily through the ripples but we knew that if the wind increased, our speed would drop dramatically. That, coupled with an adverse tide could have us going backwards.

Ogden Channel led up past a junction of waterways into Arthur Passage. Small, hilly islands fronted larger, more mountainous islands, all thickly forested with spruce and hemlock. We kept mostly to mid-channel, well away from the rocky shorelines where dark, overhung waters were broken by waving fringes of kelp on submerged reefs.

We began to see the occasional large fishing boat, a purse seiner, drifting with its nets hanging from a large boom above the stern. Some distance off in an open skiff would be the net tender, waiting to close the net. It was easy to give a solitary seiner a wide berth but when several were operating in a tight space we would be forced to pass uncomfortably close.

The salmon were coming in from the ocean, gathering in the sounds and inlets for the last great swim of their lives. They were mature adults, fattened by a couple of years of ocean nourishment and now ready to travel upriver to spawn and then to die. By some process they would find the very river and even the branch of its tributary where they themselves were hatched. In the bonanza days of the early 1900s the canning companies built traps across the inlets and river mouths. Chinese labourers were brought in to work the canning machines and fortunes were made. In 1918, 3.4 million cases of salmon were packed by sixty-six canneries in Southeastern Alaska. But the disastrous season of 1921 put many of them out of business. Changing economic conditions, the development of refrigeration and powered fishing boats altered the size and siting of the processing plants. Conservationists were at work as early as 1895 to protect and preserve the salmon runs. Slowly they achieved successive restrictions on trapping, and the percentage of trap-caught fish diminished substantially, but the method was only completely outlawed in the late 1950s.

By late afternoon we had cleared the northern neck of Arthur Passage and were motoring into the low swell of open water. To the west, beyond a line of small islands lay the ocean and to the east, the shoals and sandbars at the mouth of the great Skeena River, winding down from the interior. Ahead, the chart showed a maze of rocks and islets but the main channel was well marked with navigation buoys. We worked our way slowly in the sloppy water with the tide against us, pushing us sideways. The light head wind was only an irritant but if it strengthened we would be in difficulty. Although the main navigation buoys had lights we had no desire to be caught out in the dark in such tricky waters. The engine had been thumping away steadily for eight hours, but for some reason I began to expect that every thump might be its last. I sat at the helm, cold and stiff, willing *Moongazer* on to sheltered waters.

Slowly I began to realise the landscape was moving past a little more quickly. The tide was slackening off and shelter was beckoning. Five more minutes and we had gained the flat water behind Digby Island. The open stretch was behind us and only an hour or so up the channel lay Prince Rupert. The crew noticeably relaxed. David unhanked our salmon trolling line and paid it out from the stern. Brian cracked one of his corny jokes. I groaned and unclamped my grip on the tiller. 'All yours,' I told him as I went down to put the kettle on. As an afterthought, in case the deck watch became too relaxed, I added, 'And watch those little fishboats.' I knew that this intended spur to vigilance ran the risk of being viewed as a nag but I felt it was worth making, as the almost invisible nets of these little boats were a real menace. They belonged to the gill-netters, the assorted one-man-and-a-boy outfits that were strung along the channel. Most were anchored and appeared deserted, which meant the crew was dozing. We would expect the net to be drifting downtide from the boat, buoyed with small white floats and marked at its end with a coloured buoy or flag, but there always seemed to be a variation on the theme to confuse us.

The channel to Prince Rupert looked solidly barred by nets. Bright orange markers bobbed on the water like a floating barrage of balloons. We zig-zagged our way around them, almost wrapping our own fishing line round our propeller shaft in the process. Some of the fishermen were bringing in their nets; curtains spangled with silver as the evening sunlight caught flashes of wriggling salmon. The days allowed for salmon fishing are regulated by the Fish and Game Department, so this day, with its added bonus of good weather was being squeezed to its utmost. As we rounded the northern shore of Kaien Island, we met more little boats, converging from other waterways, making for home. On the hillsides of the island we could see the white wooden houses of Prince Rupert, Canada's second largest west coast port, and the last town we would visit that was linked to the interior by road.

In 1905 Kaien Island, separated by a strip of water from the mainland, was chosen as the terminus for the Grand Trunk intercontinental railway and a townsite was laid out. Its name was chosen from among 12,000 entries to an open competition, and a $250 prize went to a Mrs Macdonald of Winnepeg.

Within minutes of tying up at the small boat docks we were surrounded by gill-net boats, rafted up, ten deep. Someone threw us a salmon and asked us over for a few beers after. But by the time we had cooked and eaten it we were spent. None of us even had the energy to go and tell our salmon provider. Oblivious to the noise of dragging fish boxes, generators, deck hoses and social revelry, we each fell on our bunks and into deep sleep.

We woke, as everyone in town except the dead, must do daily, to the clanking of the ice plant starting up and the hooter of the fish factory summoning the morning shift. Unlike most settlements which promised much at the turn of the century,

Prince Rupert seemed to be thriving. The deepwater dock was dwarfed by a bulk carrier from China, loading Prairie grain. Behind us a fleet of salmon trollers had come in during the night, dwarfing *Moongazer*'s mast with their high trolling arms, each pair stowed vertically and waving a little, like antennae.

The town was strung out along the waterside but as soon as we started walking anywhere we were given a lift by fishermen in clapped-out trucks. They were as varied as their boats. 'Well, I used to teach school in Vancouver,' our first driver told us. 'And maybe some day I'll go back. But right now this sure beats the classroom, and the bucks just keep pouring in – well, most times they do.' The really big money, it seemed, was earned by the herring fishermen who worked the dangerous outside waters in early spring. There was a long waiting list for herring licences.

Everyone remarked on the fine weather and warned us it wouldn't last. We needed it to cross the next few stretches of exposed water on our journey north, so we crammed our provisioning into one day and set off the next, with exit stamps in our passports and clearance papers for the U.S.A. We retraced our tracks down the channel, now almost unrecognisably free of gill-netters. At the southern end of Digby Island we turned and headed towards the maze of islets, rocks and submerged reefs which seemed to block the passage to the ocean.

It was here, at the end of his second summer, that Vancouver had the misfortune to be caught in a south-east gale. In the fading daylight and strengthening wind he tried desperately to get the anchors to hold. The ships were being steadily blown towards the rocks and there seemed no way out. Then out of the murk, there appeared like a miracle, a whaleboat crewed by white men. It signalled to the ships to follow, and led them through the islets to a safe harbour. There they were astonished to see another British vessel at anchor. This was the *Butterworth* with Captain Brown in command, trading in sea otter pelts.

He told Vancouver that the Indians had spoken of an inlet to the north-east which ran inland for nine leagues to navigable waters beyond. This was exciting news for Vancouver's men who stood to share the £20,000 reward to the first ship to find a north-west passage. They knew they were near the latitude where the Spanish charts showed a Strait of De Fonte. Unknown to Vancouver, a Spanish ship had been in these waters the previous year, on the same quest.

Vancouver had already explored many tantalisingly long inlets but none had sounded as promising as this one. He had the yawl loaded with supplies for a fortnight, 'being as much as they could possibly stow', and set out with the party up the narrow inlet which he named the Portland Canal. As they continued, his hopes rose, and he noted in his journal:

> The appearance of the country on the western side of this inlet left me in little doubt of its being the continent: and we departed in full expectation that, during this excursion we should finally determine the reality of the discoveries attributed to the labours of Admiral de Fonte.

Along the way they were harried by Indians different from any they had met before. These were dressed for battle, and the war canoes were steered by ugly old women with protruding lip ornaments. Some of the braves carried muskets, a sign of contact with the pelt traders. In one incident Vancouver had a narrow escape when a musket pointed at his chest failed to fire.

During all of these encounters Vancouver kept his cool as befitted a protege of Captain Cook. He had witnessed Cook's death in Hawaii, but had not allowed it to sour his attitude to natives, however threatening they might seem. Like Cook, he understood the ritual nature of hedge warfare and made his men hold fire in the face of frighteningly warlike displays. Vancouver's writings show a respect and sensitivity towards the Indians that was not generally shared, especially by seafarers, a particularly rascally bunch. He upheld the ideals of the Officer and Gentleman universally. His men were forbidden to remove anything from abandoned villages or to disturb burial tombs:

> Not from motives of superstition,.. but from a conviction that it was highly proper to restrain our curiosity, when it tended to no good purpose whatsoever... and might give umbrage and pain to friends of the deceased, should it be their custom to visit the repositories of their dead.

For almost a week Vancouver's party rowed on through the Portland Canal. With every further twist and bend, excitment rose. Then, suddenly, to their bitter disappointment, the Canal ended abrubtly in a small unnavigable river. Vancouver, exercising the control which had got him so far, remarks in his log on the abundant salmon and sea otters, before allowing himself a trace of sentiment: 'Mortified at having devoted so much time to so little purpose we made the best of our way back.'

We skirted to the inside of those reefs which so nearly claimed Vancouver's ships. Abeam lay the opening to Browns Passage, named in gratitude by Vancouver and now marked by two large navigation buoys. A breeze from the south-east had us eagerly hoisting sail, for the Chatham Strait ahead was broad and free of hidden hazards. Clouds were also moving up from the south, blocking out the blue above. We ran gently on, past fragmented islands and up the east coast of Dundas Island. Vancouver named this after a Scottish M.P. who, as treasurer of the navy, did much to improve the pay and conditions of seamen. Under a lifeless evening sky we rounded the northern tip of the island. Our anchorage was a dark inlet between the rocks, our last in Canadian waters.

At 4 a.m. precisely my dreams were invaded by the strident bleep of the radio alarm. The day ahead would be long and the tides were not co-operative. We struggled out of our bunks to greet a changed world, grey and dripping. There was a light, indecisive wind which felt as if it might just gather strength. We sailed out across what for the next month would be our last stretch of water open to the ocean. We stood watches, one to steer, one to navigate and look-out and one to keep dry and rested.

I thought, as I sipped my hot chocolate, of Vancouver trying to find a route for his lumbering ships, and of the hundreds of journeys in the open boats. To our east lay an area riddled with passages and inlets; the small boats surveyed every one, under harassment from Indians and bad weather. I wondered why people so quickly die of hypothermia these days. Vancouver's parties would have spent many nights in the open, sleeping soaked to the skin. One boat party was out for twenty-three days. The hard life took its toll in other ways. Vancouver, at thirty-six, was already suffering from tuberculosis.

I watched the ghostly headlands in front of us grow larger but no less ephemeral. Somewhere among them lay the U.S. border. 'I'm half expecting to see a chequered barrier,' I told the others. 'Or something to show that we're now entering Uncle Sam's benign embrace.' The scene remained an unremitting wash of grey.

The headlands began to close around us as we neared the entrance to the inside passages. A peculiar thumping sound came from somewhere up the channel. Anxiously, we scanned the water ahead. It grew louder, coming towards us alarmingly quickly. We peered intensely at the surface of the water, half-expecting a submarine to surface, before we realised with a jolt that the noise came from directly above. A helicopter, emblazoned with 'U.S. Coastguard', buzzed in under the cloud level, feet from our mast, it seemed to us. We waved nervously. Without recognition it turned and disappeared up the channel. David switched on the VHF radio which up till now had received such poor signals that we'd stopped using it. It cackled into life with a breezy, 'and here is your twenty-four-hour round-the-clock weather update.' Almost immediately, our attention was diverted by two large white leisure cruisers which burst out of the mist with a roar and swept by, rolling us heavily in their wash.

'There you are,' said Brian, 'Uncle Sam's benign embrace.'

Our wind veered around 360 degrees as the land closed in, so we dropped sail and became once more the slaves of the engine. We picked up the flashing light off Foggy Point, named by Vancouver on a day when he estimated the visibility to be down to fifty yards. We still had a lot to be thankful for, I reminded the others, who showed no sign of acknowledgement as we chugged our soggy way up the Revillagedo Channel. According to our chart, the islands on our port side were studded with mountains over a thousand metres high. All we could make out were darker patches in the murk, shadows of overhanging hemlock on the water. Some shadows had more substance and we only just managed to avoid the little hump of Spire Island in mid-channel, unlike the famous gold ship the *Portland* which piled straight into it one December night in 1905.

We continued on into the Tongass narrows, its steep sides swallowed in mist. Close by, but in hiding, was Ketchikan, the Salmon Capital of The World. We followed some fishing boats and tied up at what we hoped were the town docks. If they weren't, we were too tired to care.

In the sunshine next morning, Ketchikan looked better. A string of rickety wooden buildings leaned over the waterfront and the smell of wood rot hung in the air. The sunshine had flushed everyone out and the dock was busy with fishermen working on boats and nets. Many of the locals wore a kind of brown rubber boot we hadn't seen before. 'Ketchikan sneakers,' a character informed us.

'See that mountain up there,' he said, pointing to Deer Mountain rising steeply up behind the town. 'That there's the town barometer. When yeh can't see it, it's rainin', and when yeh can, then it's jist about to,' and he burst into a wheezy cackle.

'Ketchikan has an average rainfall of 150 inches,' We read from the guide book. It didn't appear to have deterred the invasion of gold prospectors, fur trappers, labourers, loggers, bootleggers and general scallywags that came this way a hundred years ago. A customs officer stationed on a neighbouring island reported in 1881 that 'there are in this area as God-abandoned, God-forsaken, desperate and rascally a set of wretches as can be found on earth. Their whole life is made up of fraud, deceit, lying and thieving and selling liquor to Indians...'

Our interest in Ketchikan was growing. Even as late as 1926, the *American Weekly* was reporting on 'Vice In Ketchikan'. It found evidence of considerable bootlegging and drug trafficking, and over two hundred prostitutes.

'Anything to get in out of the rain,' remarked Brian.

The town still had an air of the frontier about it. In this climate buildings deprived of care, even for a few years, quickly acquire a 'gold rush' look, now much prized by cruise tour operators. We watched a herd of cruise-ship passengers trooping behind their leader, dutifully noting the 'historic' buildings. Oblivious to them, the townsfolk strode about in their brown wellies or rumbled past in clapped-out cars, but otherwise looked neither God-abandoned nor God-forsaken. They looked more like refugees fled from the squeaky clean American Dream.

The good weather stayed with us and we left the little town with its tiers of pile houses and boardwalks gilded with the morning sunshine. We motored between the high wooded bluffs of the Tongass Narrows out into the wide blue reaches of the Clarence Strait. The scenery was becoming even more majestic, enhancing the feeling of travelling through drowned valleys at the foot of wooded mountains. We chugged past headlands, inlets, islets, all with a tale to tell of some pioneer's heroic survival or mysterious death. These were busy waters in the 1890s and 1900s, and the rocks snared many steamers and small boats. Nowadays the main means of transport is aircraft, and it is the misty mountainsides which claim lives.

The long twilight and short hours of darkness allowed

us to make up time lost through adverse currents. We were now in the middle of the jigsaw and the currents sluiced around from confusing directions. After ten hours of motoring we anchored for the night in Steamer Bay, south of a rocky point which claimed a ship, but not its passengers, in 1902.

Thirty miles north of us lay the tightest part of the jigsaw pieces, the twisting Wrangell Narrows. They were well buoyed and charted and used by cruise liners at high water, but for small boats the timing of the tides was critical. Half-way through the narrows they met, sometimes violently.

We took the last of the flood up in the late afternoon, weaving and twisting around the channel markers. Half-way through, amid a swirl of eddies, the flood became the ebb and carried us on northwards. We rounded the last bend between high bluffs and reeled before a dazzling vista of snow-capped mountains, their glaciers glinting in the evening sunlight.

At the mouth of the narrows lay the little town of Petersburg where we tied up for the night. It was founded in 1897 by Norwegians when they set up a canning factory, amid scenery which would have reminded them of home.

The cannery was still thriving and we were rudely wakened in the morning by its hooter, earlier than we would have liked. We used the extra time for a pre-breakfast nose-about. Petersburg's Norwegian heritage was unmistakable. The wooden houses with their floral-painted window shutters looked fresh from the fjords. Everything was spotless, even the townsfolk gleamed and shone. The fashion here was for white wellies, no doubt courtesy of the cannery, but it lent a further clinical touch to the Nordic atmosphere.

The sight of the snow-capped mountains spurred us on. We motored out into Frederick Sound, a wide, steep-sided fjord, fed on its mainland edge by waterfalls from the melting snow high above in the hanging valleys. Vancouver was less excited by the sight. He was into his third and last summer, having wintered again in Hawaii. From Hawaii he had sailed straight up to the Gulf of Alaska to sixty degrees north and had worked his way southward, filling in the last gaps in his survey. He noted, with a touch of weariness, that the Horn Cliffs which we found so spectacular: '... presented an uncommonly woefull appearance rising to a vast height and loaded with an immense quantity of ice and snow overhanging their base'.

He could never have imagined that only sixty years later the rush to exploit the resources of this new-found wilderness would be so great that even the ice above these cliffs was being shipped south to the booming new city of San Fransisco.

We began to see little icebergs, 'bergy bits', like lumps of white fondant. They became larger as we moved north and soon we were passing more menacing green glacier mints the size of *Moongazer*. They were fragments from the great terminal walls of the glaciers whose journey from the icefields ended at the water's edge. Almost every inlet that we passed had a glacier at its head. Our goal was to take *Moongazer* as close as we could to an ice wall, but there were only a few inlets whose headwaters were not silted with moraine. On local advice we had chosen a suitable specimen about two days' journey north of Petersburg.

As we came to the broad junction of Frederick Sound and Stephen Passage we saw our first whales. Two huge humpbacks burst out of the water and launched themselves skyward. They flopped back into the water with a resounding splatt, and with a great thrash of tails disappeared. Then they repeated the performance, over and over again. Sometimes they twisted around in the air, sometimes in unison, sometimes alternately. Whether this was some courtship dance or just an attempt to rid themselves of body parasites we didn't know, but we liked to think that they leapt in fun rather than frustration.

In the autumn, the waning hours of daylight would slow up the production of plankton, their main food supply, and they would be off, like all sensible mariners, to winter in the waters around Hawaii or Mexico. As an endangered species they no longer have to fear the whalers' grenade-tipped harpoons, only the indiscriminantly lethal drift nets which hang in the ocean like invisible curtains for distances of over thirty kilometres.

From the long reach of Stephens Passage came a stiff, cold breeze and we motored uncomfortably into the choppy water, hugging the shoreline of Admiralty Island for some shelter. Admiralty Island is a special wilderness with an old reputation for wild inhabitants. In the 1800s the Hootznahoo Indians were reportedly the first to learn the white man's secret of distilling rum from molasses. The home brew was known as 'Hootchenoo', later shortened to 'Hootch', or so the story goes. In 1879 the naturalist John Muir was paddling past the Indian settlement when he heard:

> ...a storm of strange howls, yells and screams rising from a base of gasping bellowing grunts and groans... Our guides quickly recognised this awful sound, if such stuff could be called sound, simply as the 'whiskey howl' and pushed quietly on ...the whole village was afire with bad whiskey. This was the first time in my life that I learned the meaning of the phrase 'a howling drunk'.

Now it hosts a large population of brown bears and more bald eagles than in all the other states put together. The coves and inlets on its shoreline beckoned seductively, but we had no time to spare for side trips.

We motored for another day up Stephens Passage, under broken blue skies until finally we came to the doorstep of our glacier, the mouth of Endicott Arm. The actual glacier, Dawes Glacier, was out of sight, fifteen miles up and round an elbow in the arm. However, just inside the entrance was a little cove, suitable (it said in the pilot book) for anchoring. The pilot also cautioned:

> Icebergs float out of Endicott and Tracy Arms creating significant hazards to navigation. The current swirls at the entrances are strong except for the hour before or after high water. Great care should be taken if there are large pieces of ice floating or grounded in the area.

We could see dozens of large pieces of ice; blue, white, green, some strangely sculpted as they melted. They were jumbled at the confluence of the inlets, like lumps of toffee in the neck of a jar. A couple were beached forlornly on the shore. The water was milky-green and thick with glacial sediment, and there was no way of telling where the shallows might be. The pilot book suggested: 'Since there is yet no detailed chart of these arms or their entrances, the U.S. Geological survey map sheets may prove helpful.'

In their absence we used instinct and the depth sounder. I kept my eyes glued to its scale as David steered slowly over the entrance shoals. We seemed to be steadily running out of water when suddenly the depth signal ran back and off the scale into unfathomable depths. We were over the sill, but among the icebergs.

David was bright-eyed with excitement; Brian was busy with his camera. I could only think of the accounts I had vividly absorbed of how bergs could suddenly roll over without warning, submerging their unlucky admirers in the icy waters.

'Not too near' fell, of course, on deaf ears. By the time we motored over to our anchorage I was nicely wound up. Once more we had to guess what lay beneath the opaque waters of the little cove. The chart was none too clear, especially as I had obliterated the more delicate detail with a sweaty fingerprint. A plunging depth sounder had sent us backing off several times, scattering the gulls with the roar of our engine.

'Why can't we drop the hook here?' I whined when we were some safe distance from the shore.

'Just you try getting the anchor up from seventy feet. Anyway we're right in line for the icebergs out here,' replied David. I hadn't thought of that. Another of those choices: be crushed by icebergs or be grounded by a mudbank.

'O.K. Further in. But slowly, *please*.'

We did eventually discover the profile of the bay; next morning at low water when we woke to face seagulls staring in at window level. They were lined up on a wall of mud, only metres away.

The day, by unspoken unanimous agreement, was to be a day of play. The glacier could wait and we would take our chance with the weather. Cool draughts of air from the glaciers across the arm sent us rummaging for thicker sweaters, but only of the type we would wear in a Scottish summer. We sat in the cockpit and ate breakfast and watched the salmon leap in bursts of spinning silver.

'Why haven't we managed to catch even one ?' I asked. 'I've been given loads of recipes.'

'Because we're lousy fishermen,' said Brian. 'There must be more to it than meets the eye.'

We had followed every scrap of advice, most of it conflicting. We had used this spinner, that spoon, assorted lures; we had trolled at four knots, two knots, six knots, in rain and sunshine, and still they had disdained our lure.

This morning David had a determined look in his eye. In tropical waters we had never gone short of reef fish and lobsters.

'Maybe you should put on your mask and go spearfishing,' I teased.

We spent the morning wandering on the grassy

foreshore of the cove. On the beach, a ten metre-high iceberg sat like some stranded leviathan, melting into a masterpiece of modern sculpture.

Like all the foreshores in Southeastern Alaska, this was squeezed between the forest and the water. The forest was mostly impenetrable, but we found a track along a river bank and followed it. We were looking out for relics of the large mineral workings which operated here between 1870 and 1903, but we found only a few rotten timbers among the chest-high grasses. It took a leap of imagination to see ten stamp-mills processing forty tons of rock a day, bringing it up through 1,000 metres of tunnel. Higher up the mountain, prospectors, returning disappointed from the Yukon, made some of the earliest gold finds of S.E Alaska.

Around noon we met up on the beach and David held up a salmon.

'Great!' I applauded, 'At last!' Then I noticed his spear gun.

'You speared it?' I asked, a shade appalled.

'From the river bank,' he said sheepishly. 'There were several, going up very slowly. I couldn't miss.'

'Looks a bit peculiar,' said Brian. 'I hope it's okay to eat.' It was no longer the sleek, silver specimen of the salt water. Since it entered the river it had stopped feeding, living off its body fats. Its skin was mottled and scabby and its upper jaw had become hook-shaped.

'The bears find them tasty enough,' I said. 'The river bank was littered with half-eaten remains.'

'Why only half-eaten?'

'We'll soon find out. Salmon special to-night!' I dumped our dubious prize in the dinghy and tried to avoid its baleful eye. I felt guilty that in the twilight of its life, after having survived enormous odds, we had denied it its final moment of glory. I would have felt worse had I known then, that of the 3,000 or so eggs laid by one female, only 300 survive as fry; of that 300 no more than four or five reach maturity, out of which two probably make it back to the spawning ground.

When cooked, the salmon was brown in colour, like trout and it tasted similar. We kept half for the next day's lunch, in an ice box packed with slivers of glacier iceberg. Had we been Tlingit Indians, great ceremony would have preceeded this first catch of the season. Only the chiefs would have been allowed to eat it and the bones returned carefully and with gratitude to the river. The salmon were regarded as a race of supernatural beings who dwelt in a great house under the sea. There the salmon-people took human form but when the time came for the salmon run they inhabited the bodies of fish and sacrificed themselves for the nourishment of the earth dwellers. Once dead, the spirit returned to the house beneath the sea. If all his bones were returned to the water the being could live again and make the trip next season. If any of the bones were missing, he might return deformed. It was important not to offend the salmon-people, and all the Indian groups of the Northwest had long lists of regulations and taboos referring to the maintenance of good relations. To the Tlingit the white man's method of fishing must have seemed extravagantly brutish.

That night the glacier reminded us of its presence. The ominous grindings and squeakings of ice upon ice woke us several times as the bergs collided in the current. Once there was a horrible rumble as one rolled over, sending a little wash some minutes later to splash against the hull. By the time dawn broke, we were already half awake.

We set off under an overcast sky and began the long haul up Endicott Arm. A light cool breeze met us, and as we motored into it I had the curious sensation that we were rising in altitude. The rocky bluffs became steeper and higher and bearded white with waterfalls from the melting snow above. The trees became scarcer, and the air colder and thinner. We rounded the last bend just as the clouds parted and suddenly, as if a switch had been pulled, sunlight poured over the fjord. It lit up the hundreds of little broken ice floes that lay ahead of us, fronting the great green wall of ice, pitted with crevices and moraine. Behind it, the glacier swept down from the mountains like some huge highway. We nosed *Moongazer* in among the floes, as close as we dared. A seal cub, dozing on a drifting slab, woke with a start and slithered into the water.

We had seen glaciers before; flown over them and skied down them. But there was something surreal about being beside one in a yacht – the same yacht that sails in coral waters and anchors under coconut palms. David manoeuvred *Moongazer* into a photogenic position while Brian and I, festooned with cameras, fussed around in the dinghy, taking once-in-a-lifetime shots.

This was *Moongazer*'s great moment, although I didn't recognise it at the time; only much later, when I saw that in all our photographs, we humans featured scarcely at all.

Eventually we turned around and nudged our way out of the ice to the sound of little chunks of ice clinking against the hull. A breeze sprang up and we sailed with it, back down the inlet to reach the anchorage in the glow of the northern twilight. I sat for a while in the cockpit after the others had turned in. I felt as if I'd just crossed an ocean, or climbed a mountain. We had been on the move almost every day for nearly two months, and finally we had achieved our goal. I felt much as if I had just seen that longed-for smudge of land on the ocean's horizon – pleasantly wearied and deeply satisfied, but aware that the journey was not yet over.

19

South to Sitka

Overnight our sights were set on a new objective – San Francisco, before the Autumn gales. It would take a week or more to work our way around the islands, out to the open sea. On the way was Juneau, the capital, a couple of days' journey to the north. There we could provision-up and prepare the boat. After that we needed some snug cove where we could rest for a few days.

We took our leave of an Endicott arm that was almost obliterated by a curtain of grey drizzle. We slid past mist-enshrouded icy shapes and into Stephens Passage. For two whole days we groped our way in soggy greyness up to Juneau. Mists swirled around the bluffs and drifted in ragged patches across the water. Nets, crabpots, fishing boats, ferries and cruise liner kept us constantly alert.

The cruise liner was a sleek and handsome vessel, much smaller than the wedding-cake varieties of the warmer waters. It came particularly close, possibly to give the passengers something to view. With our binoculars I could see a few brave souls huddled over the deck rail, peering down at us through *their* binoculars. The rest of the passengers were probably attending the daily 'enrichment lecture', or even watching a video of the scenic splendours now blotted by the murk. This was the weather that everyone had warned us about; Alaska's ever-present deterrent to a population explosion.

However it didn't seem to have dampened the growth of Juneau. Juneau was created the State Capital in 1959 and, in keeping with its new respectability, much of the old gold town was bulldozed out to make way for new businesslike blocks of official buildings. Now, with the advent of the cruise ships, developers were busy erecting Red Dog saloons and Panhandle Bars and wishing they could bulldoze the office blocks.

Our few days in town were busy. We stocked up, socialized, and enjoyed bath and dinner invitations. David pampered the engine and changed its oil. We had continually been at its mercy and it had never let us down, even in jest. I wondered how long it could sustain such faithfulness. I still nursed a nagging mistrust of boat engines, a legacy from our eventful early sailing days.

The realities of the impending ocean passage began to take up our thoughts. We decided we would head out from Sitka, about sixty miles further down the coast on Baranof Island.

'But first, a few days rest, away from town,' I reminded David.

'So long as we're in Sitka, ready to go, by August 22nd,' he conceded. 'Every day later – up goes the chance of being zapped by gales.'

For once I didn't argue. I remembered that Vancouver, on his second summer, stayed on into early September and experienced several fierce storms. The following summer, he left on August 22nd.

North of Juneau the channel opens out into the Lynn Canal, named by Vancouver after his birthplace, King's Lynn in Norfolk. It runs for about a hundred miles to end at Skagway, the terminus of the Inside Passage and the beginning, for the gold prospectors, of the Chilkoot trail. Pack-laden men queued in their thousands in the snow and ice to climb over the Chilkoot trail on their way to the Yukon.

We followed the Lynn canal only as far as the northern tip of Admiralty Island and reluctantly we turned at Point Retreat where one of Vancouver's survey parties had breakfasted after an all-night row to escape hostile Indians. *Moongazer*, for the first time in four months, was now heading south. That night we put into a small bay which, we had been told, was inhabited by a remarkable couple.

We would have guessed, anyway, that someone unusual lived there. The cluster of cabins did not, for once, look deserted and derelict. They were surrounded by a rare sight – mown grass and flower beds, and next to them a vegetable garden laid out with military precision.

Next morning we saw an elderly wiry figure in checked shirt and jeans struggling on the jetty with some timbers. We went to help and met Gunnar who shook hands with an iron grip for all his 79 years. 'From England, Heh?' he said, traces of Norwegian still in his accent. 'I was there once, before the war, on a whaling ship. Come! You will take some schnapps with me?'

We trooped into the large welcoming log cabin and met Lassy, his wife, a homely lady some fifteen years younger than Gunnar.

'I never thought I'd ever get married,' he told us, 'but at sixty I felt it was time to settle down, and now I've had nineteen happy years.'

'And so have I,' added Lassy. She bent to stoke the gleaming iron stove and the kettle on the top began to sing.

The house was handsomely furnished and almost everything we saw around us was made by Gunnar. He brought out a bottle of Scotch and poured a large measure for everyone except Lassy. This was obviously the 'schnapps'.

'Skol!' he said and poured the neat whisky down his throat.

'Skol!' we echoed and sipped gingerly at ours. It takes practice to down neat spirits at ten-thirty in the morning.

Lassy came to our rescue with coffee and fresh-baked scones. Then they took us to the outbuildings and into a bygone age. We saw the slaughter house and the meat room, with venison hanging from the rafters. Lassy showed us the cool room, dug out of the rock and lined with shelves and shelves of preserves. 'Come the fall and I'll have enough bottled fruit and vegetables to see us through the winter,' she told us. We saw the workshops, the engine shed, the boathouse, the gun room, and a little forge. There was even an authentic Nordic sauna with a woodburning stove and a steam-making system. Everything reeked of hard work and staying power. Lassy also found time to be a Weather Observer and radioed readings to the Met. station at Juneau eight times a day. 'I get up at five forty-five every morning, even in winter,' she told us. 'But twice a year we take a little holiday. We charter a plane and fly to Juneau for a few days, to shop and see friends.'

But it wouldn't be for much longer. Gunnar was having trouble with his eyesight and they felt it was time they moved nearer the medical facilities at Juneau. They had put the homestead on the market.

'All those folk who say they're dying to get away from it all and be self-sufficient – well they don't seem to mean this self-sufficient,' Lassy said. 'So far the only interest has been from folk who want it as a vacation retreat. We've spent half a lifetime building this up. I'd have thought someone would have leapt at the chance to take it over.'

They didn't seem to know they were the remnants of a near-vanished breed. Eighty years ago almost every cove and inlet in these waters was peopled with Gunnars and Lassys. Nowadays, just living in Juneau is pioneer life enough for most. Possibly, too, they were forgetting how much satisfaction sprang from the process of creating and developing the homestead. A ready-made outfit was unlikely to attract people like themselves, even if there were any left.

They came to visit in the evening and left us with fresh lettuce, strawberries, cans of deer stew and a message in our visitors' book from Lassy, for God to take care of us. No sailor could hope to leave harbour with more.

That night, as we slept, fingers of fog crept in from the ocean and we woke to a white and swirling world.

'It'll burn off when the sun gets up,' said David in one of his best-yet bursts of optimism. He saw no reason to hold back, although I had just re-iterated several. Our course headed westward toward the ocean, along the great arm of Icy Strait. In Vancouver's time, glaciers flowing from the Fairweather range spilled out into the strait causing his boat parties great problems. Since then the glaciers have retreated by as much as ninety kilometres, leaving the huge bay that now forms part of the 1.3 million hectares of Glacier Bay National Park. Of the cruise ships' many 'scheduled attactions' this was the highlight. Even in the 1880s passenger ships made trips to the ice walls which attracted people from all over the world – until one September in 1899 when a violent earthquake caused huge amounts of ice to calve off into the sea. The resulting jam of floating ice stretched for over sixteen kilometres.

We groped our way blindly along the strait, cocooned in a world of cotton wool. It showed not the slightest hint of 'burning off' so we crept round some rocks and dropped anchor to wait it out. Beneath the high range of glaciated mountains, we were in the frontline of the battle between the warm and cold systems. It was two days before the cold one finally triumphed. We woke, dazzled by cloudless, brilliant skies. From 5,000 metres above, Mt. Fairweather and its acolytes glittered down at us. We motored across to the small fishing settlement of Elfin Cove and tied up beside a yacht from Anchorage called *Permafrost*.

Here we played for a few blissful, sunny days and in the evenings, for the first time since the previous autumn, we fired up the cabin heater. The chilly draught wasn't only from the glaciers. The nights were drawing in and the air temperature was dropping. Summer was on its way out and we should take the hint.

The brilliant windless weather followed us south, past the islands of Chichagof and Yacobi, their names a reminder of the days when the Tsar's flag flew over all this area. The voyages of Bering and Chirikof in 1741 were followed by an invasion of Russian fur trading companies, first to the Aleutians where they decimated the animal and human population, and then inland and down the coast. Their monopoly came to an end in 1778 after Captain Cook's visit, when some of his men discovered on the journey home how much the Chinese were prepared to pay for sea otter pelts. They returned soon after as traders, with ships of their own. The Americans followed. For them the trade was particularly lucrative as they suffered no monopolistic restrictions. The loser was the sea otter.

The Indians were also keen traders and they organised mass hunts. The highly intelligent mammals put up ferocious fights (they often tore the harpoons out with their teeth) but the odds against them were too great. The hundred-mile offshore limit, decreed by Tsar Alexander I in 1821, was not only difficult to enforce, but too late. The otter population dwindled and trade fell off. The Chinese Mandarins turned their interest to sandalwood and the trading sloops went off to scour the South Sea Islands. The otters were finally made subject to a preservation order in 1911, when they were almost extinct. Now, to the annoyance of many fishermen, they are thriving once again. We saw them often; furry, entertaining little creatures who can put away 10 kilos of shellfish meat a day.

The Russians had dreamed of an extended empire stretching from the Aleutians to California. California was to be the granary of the new colony, and there was even an interest in Hawaii as a provisioning source. These ventures failed to materialise and the colony, half a world away from St. Petersburg, was persistently plagued by food shortages. In 1839 a pact was made with the Hudson's Bay Company to lease Russian holdings in exchange for produce from the Company's Oregon farms. As the influence of the HBC grew, Russian interest in its far-off dependency dwindled and by 1867 it was sold off to an unenthusiastic United States for 7.2 million dollars.

We continued south, down the narrow, heavily forested Lisianski inlet, and threaded our way nervously through a maze of rocks at its mouth. Before we realised it we were out in the ocean, where the North Pacific meets the Gulf of Alaska. It lay blue and unruffled before us, fooling those who might miss noting the huge baulks of flotsam thrown high up on the shores. We motored on, late into the evening. It was a almost a year to the day since we'd watched a western horizon aglow with sunset.

We beat the darkness into a wooded inlet and let the anchor go in waters of midnight blue. In the gathering damp of the dew we sat for a bit in the cockpit, savouring the sounds of silence, knowing that this would be our last solitary anchorage for many months.

By now we thought we must be inured to scenic splendour, but the journey south among the mountainous and wooded islands of old Russian Alaska left us reeling. We stopped finally at Sitka, set among an archipelago of tiny pine-clad islands.

Sitka, in the early 19th century was the New Archangel, the settlement which its founder, Alexander Baranof, dreamed would be the 'Paris' of The North, a colonial capital worthy of Imperial Russia. Baranof's zeal was unquenchable, even by the Tlingits who wiped out his first attempts at settlement. By 1808 the New Archangel was the capital of Russian America and the centre of its commerce. Senior officials and merchants were transporting the fine contents of their houses across Siberia and the Gulf of Alaska to lend some semblance of style to the town. But within fifty years its citizens had become the hungry inhabitants of a neglected backwater.

Sitka served us well during our last few days in Alaska. Here too, tourism had awakened the town to the value of its past. All things junk and genuine were credited with some Russian, Indian or pioneer connection. Genuine enough was the Alaska Pioneer's Home, built in the thirties for ageing pioneers. In the radical sixties a new wing was added – for lady pioneers.

Our attentions were less with Sitka's past and more with our immediate future. Ahead lay 1700 miles of North Pacific Ocean. I had heard enough scare stories to know it was a stretch of water we shouldn't hang about in. We needed to be sure of a good few days of northerlies to blow us quickly out of the higher latitudes.

For four days David rowed over to the airport and came back with a weather map. A small front was moving through and weakening the high pressure. On the fifth day he returned with a gleam in his eye. 'A big High is moving in. The met guys say go for it – it'll give northerlies for four or five days.'

The moment had finally arrived. My stomach muscles contracted by another notch, but like a well-trained soldier I busied myself with the jobs in hand. After supper we stowed everything movable and prepared the battle stations. The wind was already rising. At first light we slipped away from the dock and shot out of Sitka Harbour like a cork out of a bottle. For a moment, as we fell under the lee of Mount Edgecombe, *Moongazer* faltered. Then the wind came rushing in from behind and we were off again. We roared down the coast and I sat in the cockpit and took a long last look at Alaska.

I could see the southern tip of Baranof Island. Behind it, nestled Port Conclusion, where, after three summers, Vancouver finally completed his great survey. He had filled in the gaps between Cook's explorations in the north and his own, in the two previous seasons, in the south. Ahead, in the distance, lay Cape Decision, from where he sailed, convinced that there was no northwest passage south of that latitude. He was sure that when his reports were published '...there would no longer remain a doubt as to the extent or fallacy of the pretended discoveries said to have been made by De Fuca and de Fonte, de Fonta, or Fuentes.' It was Cook's unfinished business, completed by his former midshipman, in the same superbly competent way.

The white-flecked sea turned to brassy gold as the last humps of island slid astern. We lay off-watch in our bunks, enfeebled by this rough baptism. *Moongazer* romped on, rearing in joy like a racehorse freed from its pen. She was free of the twisting tide-swept channels, free of the dark tree-hung deeps, free of the engine, free of us. For the next three weeks it would be we who were her captives.

20.

Running (And Beating) Down To 'Frisco
Sitka to San Francisco

Two days out and 260 miles further south. The high pressure is still holding. Goodbye Alaska. This is a swift leave-taking. *Moongazer* is romping along among the foaming whitecaps. The wind is blowing thirty knots from a hard blue sky, shaping the sea to a dazzling pattern of white and indigo. The tiller sweeps back and forth, moved by an unseen helmsman. The air is charged with noise and movement. By contrast, the crew are slumped in lethargy; we eat, sleep, and keep desultory watches. But we are not unhappy. Every degree south lessens the risk of meeting gales. We are keeping well offshore, 200 miles or so, away from shipping and fishing boats – and the notorious Washington/Oregon coast. Tales abound of wrecked yachts on its shores. One look at the chart says enough for me. The harbours are on river estuaries running out to the ocean with shallow bars at their entrance. The rest of the coastline is wild and inhospitable, no place for a yacht hemmed in by gales. The best defence against a gale is sea room.

We lie in the cabin or, when we want a change of scene, hang on in the cockpit, hoping that this bumpy sleigh ride will last for another 1500 miles. (It didn't, of course) The log notes read:

AUG. 22nd, DAY 5: Sea easing. Wind dropping. A day of relief – for the body but not for the mind. Barograph is falling. Something is coming from the south.

DAY 6: It's here, from the south-east. Bang, crash, on the nose. Close hauled, just holding course. Not nice.

DAY 8: The Low is moving off. The sun is out and the crew revive. B. & D. shower in the cockpit. M.(less brave) does a flannel job. Clean clothes! Life looks good again.

DAY 9: Fresh northerly. Big sea building, rolling us southward. Good progress, but wearying motion.

DAY 13: Oh, no! afraid so. Pressure dropping, wind going round to south. Morale low.

DAY 14: Closing the Californian coast in thick drizzle.

Pick up the smudge of Cape Mendocino in the murk. Wind heading us. Change tack and head out to sea, clear of shipping lane and coastal traffic. Rising gale. Noise awful.

We sheet the mizzen and heave-to; then retire to bunk to read junk. No point in keeping look-out – vis. is nil.

DAY 16: All clear. Sunny northerly back again. New life in crew. Full main up and going like a train – Blowing down to 'Frisco. (But I worry about a foggy landfall).

DAY 17: 5a.m. – picked up Pt. Reyes light. Relief!

Brilliant day. Surfing down the seas, main and jib boomed out, steering carefully. White-crested glittering sea.

We carry on, flying goose-winged, surging towards the threshold of the Golden Gate. The spans of the great bridge soar high ahead. David, at the helm can't relax his concentration for a look. We have joined the late afternoon traffic, a fleet of small sport fishers, on its way back to the bay. We're close to the gaunt cliffs of the northern shore, in the deepwater channel, all moving in a tight cluster, surfing down the steep swells. We surge under the northern span of the bridge – a thrilling moment. I can see the city ahead, shimmering in the hills. The water flattens out and we follow a line of boats across the bay to the town marina. Yachts, power cruisers, fishboats, and ferries are criss-crossing from all directions. The noise and bustle fuels our exhilaration. We are laughing and chatting at the tops of our voices. Is this the same crew of a week ago? What week ago?

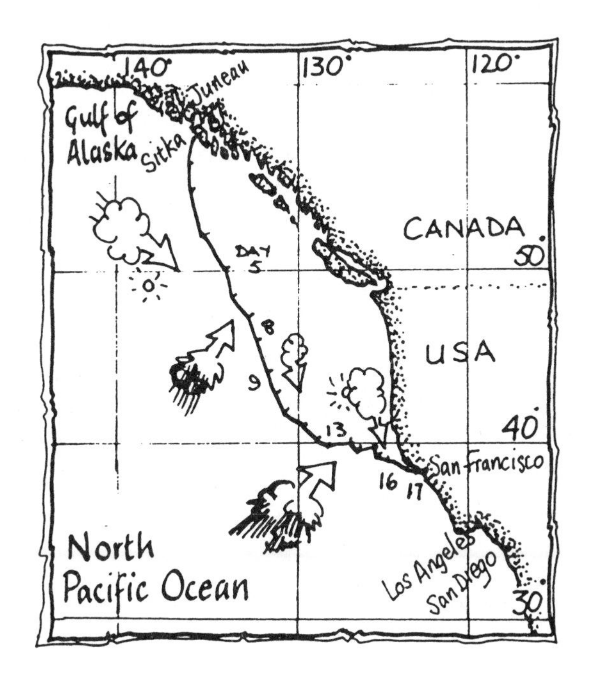

21

Urban Adaptation

'Sedate and exclusive' was how someone had described the Saint Francis Yacht Club.

'For a hot shower,' I had replied, 'I can cope with anything.'

But when we found the club, superbly sited on the fringes of the Town Marina and the Golden Gate Park, it looked exclusive certainly, but not a bit sedate. Swarming all over the club docks were dozens of finely-tuned and weathered young he-men. The focus of the fuss was a number of fat, sleek, racing boats, some of which we'd seen before in Hawaii. We had arrived in the middle of the Big Boat Race Series, an important international racing event. So much for our intention of berthing at the visitors' dock.

By an astonishing chance, the adjacent docks, owned by the City, had just been renovated and were vacant. We nosed in and tied up, light-headed by the excitement of arrival and the buzz around us. The pleasures of civilization now awaited, and for me the one most immediately desirable was that hot shower.

'It could just be,' David reminded us, 'that the yacht club's too busy to take more visitors. We'd better bring our own club membership cards.'

'I shouldn't think the Royal Anglesey is high on their

reciprocity list,' I said, sobered by this prospect. 'It might help if you two smartened up a bit – looked less wild and woolly.'

David responded by dragging a hand briefly over his tangled locks. Brian squinted into our tiny mirror and protested: 'But I *am* smartened up.'

As we trooped up past the gleaming race boats and through a car park stuffed with German and Italian hardware we grew more nervous about our reception. The club building, overlooking the bay, was modern, stylish and dauntingly smart. We stepped cautiously inside its elegant portals, and were at once sucked into a pandemonium born of on-going crew meetings, race committees and skippers' briefings, quite outclassing actual racing for noise and excitement. We found our way to the reception desk where, almost before David started to speak, a sleek and lively lady dazzled us with her smile, made out a temporary membership, and wished us a nice stay. Then she answered two of three ringing phones, simultaneously, it seemed, flashing her smile at the handsets as she spoke.

I went into my shower feeling worn and grimy and salt-roughened. I emerged, some thirty minutes later, pink and shining and squeaky-haired, the inhabitant of a new persona. Still slightly dazed, I came into the hall to find Happy Hour in full deafening swing. I caught a glimpse of David and Brian at the bar and squirmed towards them through a hot press of alligatored shirts and multi-pocketed shorts. With cold beers in hand we peeled off from the bar and retreated to the side lines, beside some urbane, straight-from-the-office types, displaced from their regular perches by the invasion.

David and Brian, in spite of a hair and beard trim, were quite obviously not racing crew, and ladies over twenty, like me, certainly weren't. The regulars, quick to sniff out novelty among the throng, engaged us with searching questions. 'Wow! No kidding? You *sailed*,....all the way from Alaska?'

That we'd sailed all the way from the U.K. didn't register. The Atlantic held little importance for West Coasters. Slowly we began to relax in the company of these pleasant people and let the city weave its spell. By late evening we were firmly in its grip, in an elegant gingerbread house overlooking the marina.

With senses keenly honed by deprivation, I sank into soft upholstery and savoured the pleasures of sophisticated living. We ate and drank well and laughed and talked in good company. The memory of tossing around in a dank cabin began to fade fast, leaving me slightly punch drunk by the rate of transition.

That night should have given me my first unbroken sleep for seventeen days, but I woke like clockwork at three a.m. and seven a.m., ready for my watch. By mid-morning I was ready more to snooze than to contribute to intelligent discussion about our plans for the next three months. That was the time allotted on our U.S. cruising permit which David had collected from the Customs' office first thing in the morning.

All three of us had visited San Francisco previously as tourists and enjoyed the city for its cosmopolitan sophistication. Now, if we were careful, we could stay for longer, renewing old friendships, buying bits for the boat, and enjoying the city, but this time it would be in spite of its sophistication. From now until we left California our main challenge would be to control our expenditure. This would be as easy as resisting the forces of nature; nowhere on earth is there a system more dedicated to encourage spending than in California.

Boat owners are particularly fair game, as hundreds of thousands of pleasure craft pack the limited water space and each week thousands more roll off the production lines. Berthing space is at a high premium. A year's cruising budget could vanish in a couple of months if we used marinas mindlessly. Some municipal marinas were reasonably priced, but they were usually packed to capacity, especially where they allowed long term live-aboards. Anchoring in the few odd corners not taken up with development, we were warned, would be discouraged by the harbour police. No-one wanted a return of the floating squats of hippy days.

David was not for a minute put off by this unpromising information. In the absence of natural hazards it was something he could get his teeth into. We knew that many Californians were very successful at beating the system, but they paraded their success too conspicuously for our more low profile approach. Being part of a group is inevitable in California, but we had no desire to be hailed as practising Nirvana seekers, or even plain Yachtie Bums. To lessen the likelihood of misunderstanding we spent our first few weeks smartening up *Moongazer* with paint and varnish and, with bargain basement specials, did a passable job on ourselves.

Brian, who had expected by now to be near Australia, had a more acute cash problem. His funds needed an immediate injection, so he put the word around: carpentry, repairs, decorating...etc. The word spread, 'There's this kinda neat Brit – just sailed in...' and within a few days he was on his first job, fitting bathroom cupboards. He then moved on to greater things, building a patio and house-sitting, in classy Tiburon, across the bay.

We stayed on at the Town Marina for two weeks. The berthing fee rose progressively with each additional week, so we moved off across the bay to Berkeley. It was a day when the fog rolled in, bringing wet salt air from the ocean. Within fifteen minutes the temperature had dropped by twenty degrees and our visibility had closed to a boat-length. We were approaching Berkeley Marina at the time and we knew there were a number of hazards ahead. There was no let-up in the strength of the wind. We reduced sail immediately, but moving through the void, even at three knots, felt like being caught in a stream of fast traffic on a foggy motorway. Eventually we dropped all sail and motored behind a radar-equipped power boat which led us in to the marina.

Berkeley was a quiet and sober place, almost unrecognizable from the seething hotbed of dissension that existed during our visit in 1970. Those were the heady days of the full autumnal bloom of Flower Power. Since then the winds of change and hard-nosed commerce had swept through, clearing the good and the bad, and everyone was on-line again for the American Dream. But there were old survivors still lurking in odd corners around the bay and, we discovered, in Berkeley Marina.

At the invitation of a friend who was away sailing for a week we moved into his berth. On our first morning David went off to investigate the shops while I got on with painting the saloon ceiling. I was carefully cutting in the line along the beams when a loud rat-tat on the deck made me jump and smudge the line. Paint brush in hand and irritation on face, I stuck my head out the companionway. Leaning over our rail was a weedy, bearded man with granny specs and a greying pigtail.

'You're in my space,' he growled. 'Number 53.'

Maybe we had made a mistake with the berth numbers. 'My husband'll be back shortly. We can sort it out then.'

'Right now!' he demanded, 'Ah'm not gonna wait.' It was fighting talk, so I countered it with a patently insincere smile and said brightly, as I closed the cabin door, 'I'm sure my husband won't be long.'

Ten minutes later there was another rap on the hull. The pig-tailed hustler was back again. By this time I was fairly sure we had not made a mistake about the berth numbers.

'You owe me fifty bucks,' he demanded, but not very convincingly. I stared at him. Avoiding my eye, he continued 'For overnight use of the slip and the hassle you've caused me.'

His audacity was impressive, but I was more stung to think we looked like suitable suckers. I waved my paintbrush in front of his beard. 'You've picked the wrong folks for a rip-off. Next time try someone who can afford it, the place is full of them.' And with that I slammed the door.

He was nowhere to be seen when David returned. 'Well,' he said when I had finished my tale, 'I guess we don't look like yachtie bums any more.'

This mantle of respectability was even credible enough for our dock neighbour, whom we hardly knew, to give us the keys of his 'other' car. 'For as long as you like.' It turned out to be a Mercedes. We enjoyed the novelty of gliding along the five-lane freeways, listening to the stereo, playing with the electric windows, adjusting the seats and everything else that could be fiddled with.

'If we lived here on U.S. salaries we could have cars like this and a house overlooking the bay,' David remarked as we bowled along beside the sparkling shoreside. It was an image I held until rush hour when we streamed back over the Bay Bridge, packed five abreast. I looked at the faces in the cars all around me. I was slightly surprised, but gratified, to find I felt not the slightest tinge of longing to join them.

From Berkeley we moved around the bay to docks reputed on the grapevine to be reasonably priced or even, through occasional anomalies, to be free. Inevitably we met other cruising boats doing the same thing, mostly Canadian, bound for warmer waters. Some of the owners turned out to be ex-Brits, who suffered stirrings of nostalgia when they saw the Red Duster flying from our mizzen masthead. 'My God, the Menai Straits.' said a Welshman, his eyes glazing over at the Beaumaris registration on the stern of *Moongazer*. 'Where I learned to sail as a boy.'

At least he had learned to sail. A surprising number had

built or bought large boats without ever having sailed before. Few had ever been out of sheltered waters until the trip down the Washington-Oregon coast, and it had come as a rude baptism. However, everyone had told them the worst was now over, and as the mind has a wonderful way of filtering out the bad and highlighting the good there was now an air of bravura in the camp. The women were not so convinced, and I became a sounding board for anxieties whenever their husbands were out of earshot.

'What's it really like?'

'As a way of life, it's great!'

'I mean, being out on the ocean for weeks on end.'

I felt like a doctor who is being asked, 'will this hurt?' It probably would at times, but there seemed no good purpose in saying so. Also, I knew that it was almost impossible to predict who would take to it and who would give up. I had learned that, contrary to the oft-repeated strictures of my forefathers, soft living does not necessarily erode those sterling qualities of stamina and resilience.

Autumn, a pleasant time in San Francisco, was now drawing on, but the wind was blowing more often from the south. It was time to go. Brian was behind schedule with the patio, so we arranged to join up along the way. He came down to the boat to pick up some belongings in a new BMW. 'The runabout,' he told us. 'I'm not only a carpenter these days. I'm chauffeur, gardener, cook, butler – Mr Indispensable in fact. But I've given in my notice for the end of the month. They're a bit peeved. I don't think they really believed I'd move on'.

We spent our last few days swinging to a yacht club mooring at Sausalito, a Sausalito that had also changed since our last visit. Gone were the beads and bangles and flowing robes, the pyschedelia of colour and sound and the aromas of pot and incense. Apart from a few tawdry pockets of resistance, Sausalito was now bland and respectable for tourists with similar characteristics.

The yacht harbour, once a hang-out for old wooden boats, was now a self-conscious showground for immaculately restored classics. The house boat scene had shrunk to authorized designer-float dwellings. 'Squat city' a barely floating jumble of dereliction when we last saw it had disappeared, possibly to the bottom of the bay. One more phase in the short meteoric life of the bay had passed.

To me, schooled in the Old World experience of History's measured tread, it seemed incredible that less than 150 years ago this Mexican outpost was virtually deserted. When Richard Dana sailed in, in 1836 on the voyage which he immortalised in *Two Years Before The Mast*, he found, 'a magnificent bay of fertile wooded country.' On the hilltop was the crumbling old Spanish Presidio and near the shore, the Mission Dolores, deserted apart from a few Indians. The only other habitation was ...'a shanty of rough boards put up by a man named Richardson, doing a little trading between the vessels and the Indians.' This was to become San Francisco's 'first house'.

There was one other ship at anchor in the cove, a scruffy Russian brig from Sitka, loading tallow and grain, to take back to Alaska. Dana's ship stayed for a month, loading hides, and during that time he saw only a handful of Indians in the entire area. 'All around was the stillness of nature.' As his tall-masted ship floated out of the harbour with the tide, herds of deer came to the water's edge to gaze at the strange spectacle.

In 1859, eleven years after the first gold strike in Sacramento Valley, Dana returned. He arrived from the Isthmus of Panama in the steamship *Golden Gate*, crowded with passengers and brilliant with the lights of state rooms and saloons. He steamed past some of the greatest lighthouses in the world and into his old anchoring ground. Before him, covering the old valleys and the sand dunes, flickered the lights of a city of one hundred thousand inhabitants. The docks and wharves were packed with '.. thousand-ton clipper ships, more than London or Liverpool, sheltered that day.' Freighters and passenger carriers steamed to all corners of the bay and up the great tributaries to far inland cities. San Francisco had come of age. It had been through a season of '...heaven-defying crime, violence and blood,' but, now (in 1859) thanks to the Committee of Vigilantes it had been handed back to 'Soberness, Morality and Good Government.'

The gold rush established San Francisco as the great terminus where East met West. When Robert Louis Stevenson came overland on the emigrant train in 1878, the gold trail had moved further to the east but settlers were still streaming in from all over the world. Stevenson was excited by the cosmopolitan flavour. It was neither Anglo-Saxon nor American; there were more 'of the airs of Marseilles and of Peking'. In the harbour, among a forest of masts, Cape Horners loaded grain for Europe. Beside them, clippers from the Orient discharged treasures for the houses of the new rich. Extremes of wealth and poverty existed, often in the same street. Up on the hill, the rich dined under crystal chandeliers and waltzed to palm court orchestras; down at the dockside, the wrecks and derelicts of humanity sought oblivion in the opium dens, lying stacked one above the other, shelf upon shelf. The cellars of the docklands were, according to Stevenson, '... seats of unknown vices and cruelties, the prisons of unacknowledged slaves and the secret lazarettos of disease.'

Stevenson was uneasy about the city's phenomenal rise. With a rare burst of Scots foreboding, he wrote; 'Such swiftness of increase, as with an overgrown youth, suggests a corresponding swiftness of destruction.'

However, the great earthquake and fire of 1906 caused

only a falter in the irrepressible development of every hill and shore for miles around. But the economic importance of the city had declined with the demise of the sailing ships, and Stevenson knew, when he looked at the forest of spars of the full-rigged, deep-sea ships, that he was witnessing '...these merchant princes' in their finest, fading hour. There was no place on earth, Stevenson wrote of the bay, '...where the power and beauty of sea architecture can be so perfectly enjoyed as in this bay.'

During our stay I had seen only a handful of freighters, all bound for Oakland. San Diego and San Pedro seemed to have claimed most of the trade. The value of the bay lay now in its amenity value; to sail on and to look at, and to insulate the city from suburbia. The new wealth lay in the valleys south of the city, born not of gold nuggets, but of silica chips.

On a day when neither wind nor fog came rolling in from the sea, we cast off our mooring and motored out under the northern span of the Golden Gate Bridge. It took us four hours to reach the mouth of the bay. Dana's steamer took about the same time, but when he first sailed out under canvas in the *Alert*, the head tides, variable winds and sweeping currents made it a passage of two full days.

We motored and sailed in light winds, day-hopping down the coast to Monterey. This was the port where George Vancouver and his men had so enjoyed the hospitality of the Spanish governors. Forty years later, as a Mexican capital, Monterey's importance was less but Richard Dana, loading hides from the neighbouring *ranchos,* found it still, 'decidedly the pleasantest and most civilised place in California.'

California became part of the U.S.A. just days before the first gold strikes in Sacramento and from then on Monterey's fortunes slid further into decline. When Stevenson arrived to court Fanny Osbourne in 1878 it was little more than a 'bankrupt village' of adobe houses, still essentially charmingly and decorously Mexican. Stevenson saw signs of an impending but unwelcome revival. A huge hotel had sprung up by the railway and Monterey was being advertised in posters across the country as a resort for wealth and fashion. The charm and style of the little town was about to succumb before the 'Millionaire vulgarians of the Big Bonanza.'

Since then several generations of millionaires, not all of them vulgarian, had come and gone and Monterey was currently basking in its John Steinbeck connection. Cannery Row, when we had last seen it, had been a graveyard of derelict fish-canning plants, an evocative memorial to the shoals of sardines for which the local waters were once famous.

We anchored beside some other yachts just outside the crowded harbour and prepared to go ashore.

'I'll bet Cannery Row is smartened up for the tourists these days,' I said to David as we unlashed the dinghy. 'I can't imagine there's anything left that Steinbeck would recognise.'

But we were not to find out. We had just launched the dinghy, when the wind started to blow straight into the bay from the north. Not only was this going to make the anchorage uncomfortable but it was the wind we needed to take us south.

We up-anchored immediately and beat round a headland draped with basking sea-lions, as the wind gathered strength. It sent us roaring down the coast, past Hearst Castle, the rococo extravaganza of William Randolph Hearst, where we would have anchored in calmer weather. We tore on, all through the night, a few miles off the wild rocky coast of Big Sur.

Just after daybreak the wind began to drop. I came out into the cockpit, wakened by the change in the boat's motion. The air was wet and salty; the sky, a dull opaque white. The coastline looked blurred, half-screened by a haze of fine spray. I could just make out, looming high above the surrounding land, an extraordinary feature like a miniature model of a mountain peak.

'Morro Rock,' David informed me. 'At five hundred feet, it's the highest monolith in the world.' He left me pondering abstractedly on the meaning of 'monolith' and disappeared into the cabin to catch the weather update on the VHF radio.

A voice intoned from above the chart table: 'A depression moving north. Winds, south to south-east, twenty to twenty-five knots. Small craft warning in effect.'

I looked at David. 'Morro Bay?'

'There's nothing else south for over a hundred miles.'

One more night of northerly winds would have taken us right down to Southern California. Still, I was grateful that there was a harbour on hand at such a moment. Once the Southerly got up the entrance would be dangerous, especially when the tide turned on the ebb. Morro Bay was a river harbour with a narrow, south-facing entrance guarded by two long breakwaters. I was wary of these kinds of entrances, or more precisely the approach where the depth usually shoaled steeply over a sandbar. I had seen, from the safety of the land, such waters in strong onshore winds, whipped up into a white maelstrom of breaking seas. A yacht caught in breaking seas is in danger of being rolled or pitchpoled, which in shallow coastal waters, usually spells the end of the yacht and sometimes of its crew.

We turned and motored towards the great monolith. The wind had dropped completely although a swell was still running from the north. I comforted myself to think that its energy would be spent on the sheltering headland. But as we closed in to make our approach we seemed still to be rolling on the surge. Suddenly, I was aware of what looked like an unbroken line of surf across the mouth of the breakwaters. My heart took a bound and I looked at David. He seemed quite nonplussed. 'It'll be O.K. It's just the angle you're seeing it from,' he said, almost casually.

I waited, tense and silent as we surged inexorably towards what looked like certain doom. We were past the point of no return. The swells were carrying us higher and faster. It was critical to keep the stern face-on to them. A sideways broach at this point would mean disaster. Slowly a gap began to open up in the surf-line and I could see that David was right. The swells were attacking only the ends of the breakwater. The water in-between was flat and beckoning. We lined up for our approach, gunning the throttle up as high as we dared. The needle on the temperature dial flickered into the red and our speed notched up to six knots. It was only just enough to avoid faltering in the backwash of the troughs. With morbid fascination I watched the pent-up power of the ocean exploding on the rocks beside us. On the long beach to the south, a solitary surfer was riding just ahead of the breakers. Inch by inch the scene disappeared as the long dark arms of the breakwater enfolded us and drew us into safe water. We slowed the engine and I took the tiller to steer up the channel towards the town. I felt aged by the ordeal of the past twenty minutes. David, unlashing the dinghy, looked positively buoyant. He stopped and glanced back at the entrance. I could tell he was about to have a go at cheering me up. 'See?' he said, 'I told you it would be O.K.'

Later, someone showed me a photograph from a book of famous boating incidents. It showed a page-high explosion of foam. In the centre of it was a motor cruiser, slamming, almost vertically into a towering wall of breaking water. It was entitled 'A cruiser only just makes it out of Morro Bay.'

Morro Bay was a quiet low-key place with river moorings. We picked one up beside a number of other cruising boats, easily identified, as we were, by the clutter on their decks. For three days we sheltered companionably, and some of the friendships we made in that short time endured for several years as we continued to meet up across the Pacific.

At the first sign of clearing skies and northerly winds we slipped our mooring and set off down the channel. Half-way down, the U.S. Coastguard materialised in a small runabout and escorted us to the entrance. There they briskly wished us a nice day and headed back up the channel. The Southeaster had left some of its seas behind and we motored out into a short steep swell. For some reason I always felt more confident about leaving an entrance than approaching it. We plodded slowly out into the safety of open water and I saw behind us that three of the other cruising yachts had decided to follow.

That night was one of the blackest I have ever groped in. Black hissing seas reared up behind and carried us along. It was a wild sleigh ride into blackness, but a blackness alarmingly pierced with the innumerable lights of ships.

'Some bloody funny lights around,' said David when I came on watch. He pointed to a vertical row of lights about a quarter of a mile off our starboard beam. 'That should be a tug with a tow, but I don't see any tow. It's been running parallel with us all night.'

I watched the lights uneasily for the next few hours. Slowly they pulled ahead, and, crossing our bows in the distance, gradually disappeared. Several times I thought of altering course to let the vessel pass more quickly out of my line of worry, but each time I would have had to gybe the jib.

The VHF radio crackled away all night with traffic, weather forecasts, and coastguard announcements. Streaks of dawn were lightening the landward sky when I caught the tail-end of one announcement. 'Navigational warning number three-four-six: Tug with two tows proceeding south. Navigation lights on first barge non-operational. Repeat: navigation....'

A cold prickle of horror, mixed with reprieve, stole

through me. I remembered there had been a red light far behind us. A fishing boat, I had assumed. In fact, it had been the second barge. The darkness beside us had contained the first barge, and the whole lot was strung together with thousands of feet of towing hawsers. But for the angle of the wind, I would have altered course, straight into a silent, invisible and horribly lethal snare.

The last sherds of night were enough to keep the light at Point Conception still occulting, and give us a position. Point Conception has been lumbered over the years with many sub-titles (the Cape Horn of the Pacific, we were warned) and it marks the north-south divide of California. Even Dana found this. He noted that northward of the Point the country was well-wooded and watered, while southward there was 'very little wood and the country has a naked, level appearance..'

Before we could get a twentieth-century view down the Santa Barbara Channel, past the oil platforms, the wind vanished and our world was obliterated by dense, wet fog.

22

Tupperware Tinseltowns

> The first impression which California had made on us was very disagreeable – the open roadstead of Santa Barbara; anchoring three miles from the shore; running out to sea before every South-easter; landing in a high surf; with a dark looking little town a mile from the beach; not a sound to be heard, nor anything to be seen, but Kanakas, hides, and tallow bags.

So wrote Richard Dana in 1836.

The silent landing where Dana loaded hides and tallow bags was now a yacht harbour so packed that to ensure a space residents of Santa Barbara have to have their name down at birth.

The town was no longer brown, but pastel coloured, an impeccable confection of neo-Spanish colonial, holding aloof from the great ooze of Los Angeles.

We dropped anchor, in solitary splendour, just off the entrance to the yacht harbour. 'Santa Barbara may have changed, but the Sou'easters can still blow,' I reminded David. 'What then?'

'We move in to the harbour.' He replied, meaning, then we pay.

We had come to Santa Barbara particularly to renew some sailing friendships, so our first act ashore was to call up on the phone. From that moment on we were pitched into social overdrive and held there till we left California.

A whirl of dinners, roast-outs, swim-ins, jacuzzi dips, and old-fashioned booze-ups on *Moongazer* sent us spinning, and there was always a car thrown in. Each time we expected to be our last car loan, and we spent what spare time we could steal whizzing around a tangle of freeways to discount warehouses and damaged goods markets.

For our next stop we decided to strike at the nautical heartland of L.A. – Marina Del Rey. 'Oh no!' said our friends, cocooned in the cosy chic of Santa Barbara. 'It's Tupperware city. It's gross.'

'The Biggest Yacht Marina in the World,' I reminded them. 'We can't pass that up. It would be like not going to Disneyland.' (We'd done that on the previous visit, thank heavens.)

So we motored over to the Channel Islands and down towards L.A. There was no mistaking where it lay. Under where the ribbon of orange smudge which hung above the land deepened to rust-brown. The Sunday Afternoon Drift was drawing to a close and we joined a long line of boats waiting to go up the marina entrance channel. The yachts in front and behind looked like they'd come fresh from a boat show. *Moongazer*, in spite of our efforts, looked like a tinker's caravan.

'What bugs me,' I said to David, 'is that I mind.'

At the end of the mile-long entrance channel, a space-age control tower hove into view, bristling with aerials and scanners. Nestling at its base was a row of high speed police boats. Further on, a lightless, old-style lighthouse warned that we were heading for Ye New England Fishing Village. We passed a pier of clapboard houses with palm trees peeping from behind the rooftops. The palm trees belonged to the Bali Hai Eatery, or possibly to the El Torito. Palm trees and ethnic eating stretched off into infinity. 'Marina Del Rey,' boasts its blurb, 'offers more restaurant seats in one square mile than most anyplace else in the world.'

Yachts? Before us lay over 8,000, in nineteen different marinas. We slunk past the municipal dock, reputed to cost thirty dollars a night. 'Go for the yacht clubs,' people had told us. 'Flashy, but friendly.'

In the falling dusk the marina dissolved in a blaze of lights, melting into the backdrop of condominiums, airport and freeways. A cruising police boat, equipped to repel an invasion, spotted us dithering, and with blue lights flashing escorted us to the California Yacht Club. We had hoped to slip in quietly.

Next morning we awoke to find ourselves in Ghost City. The playground was empty save for cleaners and deliverymen. But for all their lack of humans the docks were not silent. The boats around us were wired and plugged to life-support systems. Deepfreezes gurgled and hissed, bilge pumps spewed and spluttered, and telephones rang from muffled depths. Dusk fell like a giant switch and triggered off 8,000 photosensitive cells. All over the marina, cabin windows twinkled with light.

Our yacht club was a palace of swimming pools, saunas, lawns and tennis courts and, most important for us, three nights free berthage. When that was up, we moved over to the Del Rey Yacht Club, an even glitzier affair. They put us in their prime spot, below the front balcony, flanked by two huge ocean-going motor yachts.

On Friday afternoon we heard stirrings of human life. Squads of teenagers came to clean the boats. The cruiser next to us was dried off after its wash, with sumptuous bath towels, on which I cast a covetous eye.

Nothing much happened on Saturday morning. A significant number of Californians still toil at the salt mines on Saturday mornings. By mid-afternoon folk began to trickle down the green carpeted dockways, trundling drink-laden trolleys. By Happy Hour every cockpit and afterdeck was abuzz. Sunday was a repeat performance, except that Happy Hour began at noon.

A few boats went out for a Sunday sail, but as it was 'winter' the serious racing programme had just finished for the season.

'The Ultimate Marina Experience,' I said to David as we splashed around in the club's pool. 'All the fun of boat owning with none of the hassle. You're not even expected to go out to sea.'

'The only effort that's required is to keep the payments up,' replied David. 'No one's got time to go sailing.'

However, we knew from our previous contact with L.A. that, for all its surface froth, its vitality was fuelled by expertise and accomplishment in a rich diversity of fields. The relentless drive for excellence spilled over from commerce into every facet of living and the sailing scene contained scores of skilled and dedicated yachtfolk.

We hadn't just come to M.D.R. as voyeurs. We had also come to see Howard and Roeanne, the perfect antidote to glitzville. We had met them in Panama, sailing an old, classic pilot cutter out from England. Now they lived in a charmingly rambling old wooden house, which had belonged to Howard's parents and had survived the rapacious re-development of recent years. It was tucked away among the peeling stucco and silted canals of Little Venice, a forlorn enclave of bohemia, just across the freeway from the marina.

They came to see us and left a spare car. 'You'll need it,' they said, 'even to get to our house.' They were right. Only a five-minute crow-flight, it took us over half an hour to negotiate the marina perimeter of shopping malls, car parks, forecourts, underpasses, overpasses, and walkways. These pedestrian ways were busy, but no-one was engaged in anything so mundane as walking, and we found ourselves being sucked along in a slipstream of cyclists, joggers and rollerskaters.

Because we had been lent a car we spent yet more precious time and money. We whirred (it was a V.W. beetle) along the five-lane freeways to shops with names like Gemco and Fedmart, each the size of several aircraft hangers. Day or night the freeways were full, not solid, but steadily flowing. It was as if some great heart was pumping millions of cars through a vast arterial system. It grid-locked the city and snaked around the perimeter hills. It ran alongside the ocean and off into the deserts to the east. Somewhere in the centre there were still, incredibly, the remains of the *pueblo* which, in the 1830s sent its hides by ox cart to the ships lying off San Pedro. It was the Pueblo de Nuestra Senora la Reina de Los Angeles, 'the largest town in California,' according to Dana, ecompassing 'several of the wealthiest missions.'

We loaded yet more stores aboard. *Moongazer* sank further in the water.

'How can we still be buying things,' I wondered aloud.

'Because we're on the doorstep of the world's biggest superstore – and who knows?.... the rest of the world out there might just be one great desert.'

'I feel a neurosis coming on.'

'A sure sign of impending assimilation. It's time to go.'

'But so soon?'' asked the kind folk at the Del Rey Yacht Club.

'We have to go to Newport Beach to re-rig the boat,' we told them. 'We have a friend in the rigging shop who's expecting us.'

Moongazer's masts were held by stays and shrouds of galvanised wire, still quite serviceable, but showing rusty signs of age. The rigging firm was one of the best in the country, and it was having a 'clearance' sale of odds and ends of wire and terminals.

We were quite unprepared for Newport Beach. The only thing it had in common with M.D.R. was MONEY, but Newport Beach had lots more of it, and for a lot longer. As a sheltered, sandy estuary it was once a beach resort for L.A. with holiday cabins by the shore, each with its wooden jetty built out into the water. Now we could see as we motored, awestruck, along the waterways, that the cabins had become opulent five-million-dollar homes, packed wall to wall with hardly a blade of grass in between. The rustic jetties were now smart regiments of private docks, each running out to deep water to accommodate at least two huge yachts or cruisers. Lined up behind the mansions, and massed in deep ranks were the merely-million-dollar-homes. Everything, even the 'Private' notices, reeked of Impeccable Good Taste.

At the Balboa Yacht Club the dockmaster, an Englishman from Plymouth, alloted us a berth where we could work on the rigging away from the public gaze. We were aware that it was 'not done' in smart marinas to work seriously on one's own boat.

We were just one day into the job when Brian arrived, in time to relieve me from my precarious position up the mast. I had not been happy hanging like a trapeze artist from the bosun's chair while I struggled, under orders from below, to dismantle one of the shrouds. In spite of David's continual reassurances of 'You're fine', I felt I might as well be up a tree, sawing off the branch which supported me.

Brian, because of our Alaskan detour, had long run out of the six months he'd told his girl friend it would take to go to the South Pacific. The vagaries of our mail-forwarding system had created a lapse in communications and he was having a few anxious thoughts about whether he should continue. A long, excited phone call to Australia, and an exceedingly patient girl-friend, reassured him and he was once more, to our delight, on-line for the South Seas.

At the club we became a magnet for those who cherished the dream of sailing off into the blue. 'Oh, but you must have had some wonderful adventures!' they would say, eager for some vicarious living. It seemed too ponderous for the dinner table to explain that the journey itself was the adventure. Our hosts were waiting to share some death-defying moments. But much as our days were fraught with incidents, I could never recall any that could be elevated, even in the re-telling, to the status of 'an adventure'. Maybe we'd had some and didn't know it. As Joseph Conrad wrote of his own seafaring experience: 'Adventures come like unbidden guests and at inconvenient times....and we often let them go unrecognised.'

Southern Californians are not so easily deflected from their goal. 'Well then,' they'd persist. 'Memorable experiences? Surely?'

It would have been true, but absurdly feeble to reply: 'the bacon sandwich in Hawaii; the first hot bath in Victoria.' Instead, I said, 'Ah! But there were so many!' which sometimes was all they wanted to hear.

We dined in the homes of folk who told us they were, 'going to do the same as you guys....when the kids finish school....or when the business can look after itself.... or when we can afford a bigger boat', but they probably knew they were only rattling the bars of the gilded cage. One frustrated sailor protested quite passionately, from the upholstered depths of his Mercedes, that 'This materialistic life has gone too far.'

Not for everybody in the eighty different municipalities that make up Los Angeles – as we found out when we tried to travel by public transport. We were bound from Newport Beach to Santa Monica, a half-hour car ride. Our journey took three hours and four buses. 'Nobody travels by public transport,' we were told. Our buses were packed with the nobodies, short, dark, mostly Latin-looking, who keep the wheels of Southern California turning; the gardeners, maids, cleaners, factory workers.....

We did meet one young couple who were taking active steps to flee the gilded ghetto. Pete and Lynne had been nurtured by its affluence all their twenty-odd years, but were now selling off their possessions to retreat to an island in the Gulf of Georgia and build a boat. Until then, they were living in a little flat above the garages at Lynne's parents house. 'They have a private dock, with a spare place,' Lynne told us. 'We'd love to have you come and tie up there.'

So we did, a few days later when *Moongazer* glittered with new stainless rigging and fancy turnbuckles. (All for less cost than our original galvanised stuff.)

Lynne's parents lived on Balboa Island, a rabbit warren of chic dwellings, with energetic inhabitants who pranced around the supermarket in tennis dresses and jogging shorts. Lynne's grandfather had bought one of the beach plots in the 1920s and now it was a hugely valuable complex around a little courtyard, shaded by a mature tree. On Balboa Island mature trees are rare and highly prestigous. Not that Lynne's parents needed to display prestige. They had it; they were Old Money.

Lynne's mother was interested to hear that *Moongazer* was made of ferrocement.

'My Daddy used to build ferrocement boats,' she told me, 'way back in 1917.'

'Really?' I was genuinely interested.

'I'll show you some pictures.'

She did. They were Liberty Ships, built when her daddy was president of the U.S. Board of Shipping.

She and her husband were self-effacing, charming folk. He, a retired engineer, spent his days absorbed in his workshop building an aeroplane.

Pete and Lynne already owned a wooden ketch, *Skylark,* given to them as a wedding present. They had sailed her up to British Colunbia and back ('It changed our lives, that trip') and had now decided to build a bigger and more modern one. *Skylark* was for sale. 'Had any offers?' David asked.

They both groaned. 'Have we ever!' said Pete. 'Last year, soon after we advertised it, a young couple came down with a little baby. They seemed very keen on the boat and asked if they could take photos of the interior. Then they said they'd buy it and paid a deposit. We settled on a date for the rest of the payment, and off they went. Then one day a friend of ours came across this brochure. We couldn't believe our eyes.'

The brochure was quite professional with a splendid picture on the front, of *Skylark* under full sail. It was entitled: 'God's Chosen Boat, The Vision, And The Plan.' Inside, it gave the details. God wanted them to go to the Pacific to save lost souls and He had even specified the boat – which matched *Skylark* exactly. The Plan ended:

> We believe that the Lord will pay for the boat by October 15th. This includes a half-payment on September 15th. We urge you to take on this plan in prayer – and to pray in faith, believing. God is faithful to answer and meet the need! Praise the Lord! The Bible guarantees it.(Phil. 4:19)

'And?' we asked, intrigued.

'They'd been travelling around to prayer meetings and such, trying to raise money.' said Lynne. 'They didn't know we knew, but we gave them an extension. We were so curious to know what would happen. In the end I'm afraid God defaulted on the payments.'

Skylark lay quietly beside us, looking most demure for one who was 'God's Chosen Boat'.

We spent the few days of our stay doing more

last-stop-in-civilization chores. I revelled in the use of unlimited fresh water and washed everything I could lay hands on. In the warm sunshine I dried our woollies on the dock, conscious that it must be the only 'naturally dried' washing for miles around. In our host's kitchen we bottled several dozen jars of turkey and beef. We made more shopping expeditions, accompanied by Pete and Lynne. They said they they found the trips, 'very instructive.'

David, ever firm about departure dates, smoothly disengaged us from Balboa Island's social grip and on the appointed day, at the appointed hour, we posed for photographs, exchanged goodbye hugs with our hosts and set off for San Diego.

We motored down the coast in the same hot and windless conditions that plagued Richard Dana's ship, 150 years before. It was bound for the hide depot at the San Diego mission, and spent two days drifting around Point Loma before it could make the harbour. We cleared the point under engine in a few hours. For the sailing ships, this great natural harbour was the most secure on the whole coast, but the entrance was difficult and only wide enough for one vessel at a time.

We hardly noticed the entrance. Our eyes were on the two warships, the aircraft carrier, and the submarine that seemed intent on running us down. All around, like distracting flies, buzzed high speed landing craft. Above whirred giant helicopters. On the north shore passenger jets roared in and out of the airport, and on the south shore navy planes screamed into the sky.

Our stay in San Diego was as brief as we could make it: five days to get our visas for Mexico, and our U.S.A. clearance. Five days of hassle, always on the move, like vagrants looking for a place to spend the night.

The pressure on waterspace in San Diego harbour made everywhere else we'd been look half empty. Acres of marsh and sand dunes had, by the clever use of dredging spoil become palm-shaded marinas already full with local boats. For most of cruising folk leaving the West Coast San Diego is the 'last fill-up before the motorway.' Some find the umbilical cord just too strong to break. Some would never admit it and live from season to season on excuses for not leaving. The harbour authorities cope with the pressure on waterspace by enforcing strict regulations and high berthage charges. Visitors' moorings are provided in various areas with a 72 hour limit of stay.

One old yacht basin had been left as a reminder of the laissez-faire days. We went to its entrance to have a look. We wouldn't have had room to go further, even if we'd wanted. 'Junk City,' commented David. 'I don't know how half of that stuff is even floating. Must be their dock lines that are keeping them up.'

Unaware of the situation when we first arrived, we swanned straight in to the San Diego Yacht Club. They had just had their fill of the type of cruising yachties who wash the laundry in the showers and hang it round the swimming pool, and for once we were not given the dazzling smile treatment. We were told to push off, immediately.

We spent the night at great expense at a municipal dock beside a cumbersome 20-metre steel ketch from Vancouver. The owners were Donald, a charming middle-aged Englishman and his tiny, vivacious wife, Lotte. They too had been unceremoniously ejected from the Yacht Club in spite of the fact that Donald, a flag officer of the Royal Vancouver Yacht Club, had written to book a berth in advance. This was one of several setbacks they had encountered en route and I could see that Lotte, despite her good humour, was having misgivings about the whole enterprise.

It had actually started eight years before when they had commissioned their dream boat to be built in England. They sold up, 'our beautiful home. oh, it was so lovely,' and went to England to collect the boat. They found it only half built and the yard in the hands of the receiver. After a year of legal tussle they returned to Vancouver, and had to wait four years before the boat was finally released.

Donald and his son then sailed it in its incomplete state to Canada, where it was fitted out. Sea trials revealed major deck leaks and it was taken to Seattle for modifications while Donald and his wife prepared to sell up again. In Seattle the yard welders accidently set fire to it and the interior was totally gutted. After more legal tussles it was partially rebuilt and the boat taken back to Vancouver to be finished. There, at the dockside the engine inlet hose broke, and the boat was partially sunk. It was raised and once more refurbished. Finally, the following season, they set off.

In order to make sailing bearable for his wife, Donald had stacked the boat with electrical gadgets as if it were a house – right down to the electric organ. To make a cup of tea they had to switch on the generator. Every time we met Donald we saw his back-end first. His head was always down a hole buried in a mass of wires. Problem followed problem. We were often on board; David to help sort out the problems, and Brian and I to be entertained by Lotte, who was a wonderful hostess, used to entertaining on a grand scale. We last saw them in Mexico. The refrigeration had broken down, but Donald's heroic enthusiasm was still undimmed. We often wonder what became of them.

After five days of moving *Moongazer* all over the harbour (the San Diego Shuffle) and of riding buses downtown to collect our Mexican visas, we were more than ready to go. We surprised the customs officers into allowing us some duty-free spirits. 'No one bothers these days,' they told us, 'You can get it almost the same price at the discount stores.' 'Almost the same price' was four dollars a bottle more; worth the effort to us, if to no-one else.

We wove our way out among the windsurfers and the warships, and every craft in between. After a few hours of steady motoring we suddenly sensed that California had ended – abruptly. In front of us, the sea and the air, were empty. The land, a few miles off, was scrubby desert, 'naked and level in appearance,' just as Dana had seen it. But, most of all, we were aware that the air had changed. For the first time in two months we noticed its smell – fresh and sweet.

23

The Fleet Prepares

'Cabo for Christmas,' was the word, 'everybody's going there.' Except us; we didn't seem to be going anywhere.

From San Diego we had sailed two hundred miles out of our way to look at sea elephants. We found them, on the strange volcanic island of Guadalupe, in their colony below black cliffs which towered upwards for hundreds of metres. The cows and cubs looked like large seals, but the bulls were huge, with grotesque snouts, which stuck out like a squashed-up trunk. It gave them a square-headed look, and when one swam out to have a look at us I mistook it for a half-submerged oil drum.

At one time these mammals thrived in abundance from Antartica to California, but in the nineteenth century it was discovered that their blubber yielded oil, and they were hunted to near extinction. Several times it seemed that the species was doomed, but each time a tenacious group just managed to survive. In recent years the breeding grounds have become Protected Reservations and their numbers are slowly building.

We drifted away from the black rocks of Guadalupe on the lightest of breezes, until we were barely moving. We had three hundred miles still to go.

'It looks like Christmas on the high seas,' said David.

'Right now,' said Brian, 'that seems more of a

blessing.'

Flat seas, sunny days and cool nights were too good to pass up. The clutter of twentieth century living dropped away. We only had to feed ourselves and plot our position. There was nowhere to have to go, no one to have to see, nothing that *had* to be done. For a brief moment it was Life Without Struggle.

'Before I took up sailing,' said Brian, 'I thought this is how it would be most of the time.'

'Just as well it's not,' said David. 'Or everyone would be doing it. We'd soon get fed up if it went on for any time.'

'Dying of scurvy would take the gloss off things.' I said, thinking of the Manila galleons, drifting around in these waters, eight or nine months out from the Philippines. The annual treasure ship would have left in August and lumbered eastwards along the thirtieth parallel, hoping for westerly winds. These were more reliable further to the north than the galleon, with its fragile cargo, usually dared to go. There was no accurate way of measuring longtitude, and it struggled on eastwards for months until the floating porra plant was sighted. This was the sign for the pilot to steer south and the ship's company to break into a *Te Deum*. Around the latitude of Cabo San Lucas the pilot would head toward land until he picked up the distinctive rocks at the Cape, which Thomas Cavendish's chronicler described in 1587 as being, '...very like the Needles at the Isle of Wight.' From there the galleon would have a free run to Acapulco, unless a pirate ship was on the prowl.

For the two hundred or so years of the Manila-Acapulco run, ambitious pirates and privateers dreamed of the galleon as the ultimate prize. Those few pirates who made it into the Pacific and up to Mexico, hung off the coast hoping to pounce on the galleon either on its way in to Acapulco, or on its way out, laden with silver from the mines of Nueva Espana.

Thomas Cavendish's early success in 1587 inspired sucessive generations. He took the *Santa Anna*, '700 tons in burthen', just off the Cape, set the crew and passengers on the inhospitable shore, and loaded up with a hundred and twenty two pesos of gold and '... silkes, satens, damasks, with muske and divers other marchandise.' Then after putting the *Santa Anna* to the torch, he '...set sayle joyfully homewardes towardes England with a fayre wind.' The abandoned Spaniards rescued the *Santa Anna* before she sank and sailed the remains on to Acapulco.

When England was at war with Spain, capturing the galleon became a Noble Deed, as well as making the victorious captains millionaires. The merchant adventurer, Woodes Rogers, captured one galleon and was beaten off by another in 1709, during the War of the Spanish Succession. In the following war, thirty years later, George Anson was dispatched to these waters with a squadron from the Royal Navy. The Jesuits had by then established an efficient intelligence network and Cabo San Lucas had become a lookout and provisioning post. Anson hung off for several months hoping to surprise the ship as it left Acapulco. But it had been alerted by the network and sat tight. Anson then sailed off to China, and eventually captured the elusive galleon the following season, on its way into Manila.

Our days of bliss were cut short by neither scurvy nor privateers, but by the wind which came literally from out of the blue and whipped up the sea into small slabs of concrete. Cabo For Christmas suddenly became a good idea.

We sighted the coast of Baja California on the morning of Christmas Eve. It looked just as Rogers described it in 1709, '...mountainous, barren and sandy.' The rocks at the Cape were still reminiscent of the Needles and we could have followed Rogers' directions for entering: ' Leave the outermost rock on the larboard side, and steer into the deepest part of the bay, being all bold you may anchor from 10 to 20 fathoms.'

That is, if the bay hadn't been filled with yachts and motor cruisers (later I counted over eighty). Our friends in 'Canada Row' had kept us a space beside them, near the beach. 'A bit too near, don't you think?' I asked deaf ears. I was watching the swell burst in a roll of surf, a mere few metres it seemed, from our stern. Like everyone else we ran out a stern anchor to keep our bows facing the swell.

'Customs office closes at four-thirty,' shouted our friends on the neighbouring boat. They added directions on where to find it. Plenty of time. We launched the dinghy and rowed smartly over the swell on to the beach without being dumped unceremoniously in the surf. (That came later.)

After twenty sweaty minutes along a hot, dusty road, we came as directed, to the Customs and Immigration Office. It was an ordinary house, like its neighbours with the owner snoozing in the porch. He regarded us through half closed eyes for a few minutes while we flashed passports and ingratiating smiles. With a great sigh he rose and motioned us to follow him into the darkened house. We crowded into a tiny office where a stereo was blasting rock music off the concrete walls. Our official worked slowly and in silence through the lengthy paperwork. Then, with a flourish, he stamped our papers and looked up, smiling broadly. 'Me, teacher,' he shouted above the din, 'Eengleesh.'

'Very good,' we shouted back. He held out an open palm.

'Feeftin dollars. Eet ees after ze hora, pliz.' We looked at our watches. It was only twenty minutes past four. There was some mistake?

'California time.' He grinned and pointed to the clock on the wall. 'Here we have Mexico time.' An hour ahead. We had forgotten the time change. We paid the fifteen dollars through gritted teeth.

The village was still disarmingly scruffy, heedless of the flashy pockets of tourist development creeping along the cliffs. The high-rise resort development of tropical Mexico hadn't yet taken hold on the rugged arid landscape of Baja but there were signs that it was earmarked for overspill. Every other day, we walked the two kilometres into the village to buy bread and vegetables and the occasional cold beer, but otherwise the local community impinged little on our life in the bay. Here was our own floating village.

All the motor cruisers and most of the yachts were spending the season on the coasts of Mexico and Costa Rica. They were already in holiday mood, geared up to the competitive business of Enjoying Life.

The daily grind started about seven a.m. with activity on the VHF radio.

'*Sunburst*, *Sunburst*, this is *Footloose*. Y'a hear me Betty?'

'Yeah, I gotcha. Howya doin' Marge?'

'Kinda hung over... But I gotta get goin'. Craig wants ashore by eight, I have to pick up Stevie at nine-thirty, be at the bank at eleven, and then there's a little party at Cliff and Jackie's at twelve....'

The eight a.m. slot on the VHF was given over to the anchorage 'phone-in'. We were much too British to join in, but we listened, fascinated at how much eloquent mileage could be squeezed out of such trivia. No thought was too humble, or secret too sacred, that it couldn't be shared with the anchorage – or even the whole village, via the fishermen listening on their boat radios. Regular topics of local interest included rip-off restaurants and lightfingered laundrywomen. We finally switched off for good when we found ourselves listening to a succession of lengthy and tendentious dissertations on a cure for the 'trots'.

Much more controlled, and used, in these parts, only by licensed operators, was 'mobile maritime' amateur radio. The 'hams' checked in regularly to networks around the Pacific and could, through a 'ham' back home, make telephone calls anywhere in North America. Tom, on the boat next to us, spent a great deal of time and frustration trying to get through to Vancouver to arrange this, or check out that. He was an ex-manager of a construction company and evidently only felt comfortable with a telephone in his hand. His favourite seat was in front of a large chart table. I expected any day to find his wife learning shorthand.

For the thirty or so yachts bound for the South Pacific the 'ham' radio was a fountainhead of rumour and gossip. 'Did you hear that the bond for French Polynesia has gone up 500 bucks?....Susie on *Vagabond* says someone she knows got kicked out of Nuka Hiva after 48 hours... Chuck and Marlene on *Windsong* have just had a baby in Bora Bora.' Every scrap of information, even the scare stories, helped to lessen the leap into the Great Unknown.

Tom's wife, Ann was having bouts of indecision about continuing. Her worry was how to help with the sailing and cope with an indefatigable three-year-old. When it finally dawned on Tom that they could use another hand, the word went out to the travellers camping on the beach. A number of hopefuls swam out to be interviewed, but the bond requirement for French Polynesia put most of them off. Finally they chose a personable girl from San Diego, just out of graduate school. She flew back, posted her bond, collected her toothbrush and re-appeared several days later, ready to go.

No one else was much ready to go. They were working on their boats, some making the jobs spin out. The dry sunny weather was ideal for painting and varnishing and I made the most of it, with Brian's help. David spent hours pouring over the circuit boards of our errant radar and autopilot, assisted by an electronics whizzo whose engine he'd fixed. It proved to be time well invested. Not only did our electronic gear behave itself from then on, but David was able to earn a few dollars along the way, fixing other people's.

When we felt like it we played. We swam and learned to windsurf. We went for walks and had barbecues, book swaps and beach parties. It all beat going to the office. It also beat going out into the ocean.

Brian's idyll came to an end one day when his mail finally caught up with him. His girl friend's patience was now understandably thinning. I knew he had set his heart on seeing the South Seas, but it would be another five months at least before we reached Tahiti.

'The Marquesas will always be there,' I reminded him. 'But Jenny might not.'

'I was thinking that,' he replied. 'How do I get to Australia from here?'

Next day a huge motor cruiser bound for L.A. came in to the fishing harbour to re-fuel. 'Sure, we could use a crew,' said the skipper. In record time Brian packed his bags, hugged us good-bye, gave *Moongazer* an affectionate pat and took off at full throttle, out of our lives – for the time being.

With Brian gone, David received the full force of my fussing. 'I'm just not happy about being so close to the beach,' I whined, more forcibly this time.

'O.K.' he said, knowing that now, back on a one to one basis, he was beaten. 'Choose your spot.' We picked up both anchors and re-set them in a space a couple of boat lengths ahead. We had new neighbours; it was like moving into a different street.

Back in 1709, Woodes Rogers had described the bay as being sheltered from the north through east, to south, but he warned that '...it is but an ordinary road if the wind should come strong out of the sea.' Several seasons after we left, the wind one night, did just that, and over twenty yachts were wrecked on the beach, including Bernard Moitessier's beloved *Joshua.* He wrote afterwards: 'I was careless. Much too close to the shore. When the swell broke under me, I was on the beach – just like that.'

Other yachts, near where we now were, suddenly found themselves that night in the surf line. Some tried to motor out and fouled their propellers in the tangle of stern lines. Others found their engine inlets blocked by the flotsam of cushions, awnings, towels and all-sorts. It was a nightmare of chaos in which, amazingly, no one was drowned. Some people lost everything they had worked for for years.

The day came when I noticed that David, instead of hauling stuff out of tool lockers, was now stowing it away. 'One more coat of varnish on the coachroof and then I'm ready,' I told him. Tom had already left, though no-one else showed much inclination to follow. 'They will,' said David. 'It just needs a few to go, and then suddenly no-one wants to get left behind.'

I knew how some of them would be feeling. That first ocean passage is a leap into the personal unknown. Here, in climes where one day is much like another, it's important to have a departure day, stick to it, and say, 'here we go, for better or for worse.' You head the bows out towards 3,000 miles of open ocean and hope that someone in The Big Control Tower Up There is watching your blip on the screen. After that you merely respond to whatever gets thrown at you. There aren't many choices. Life becomes quite simple.

The passage to Polynesia was known as the milk run, and unless the trade winds were acting up it would present no difficulties. But it wasn't the winds that worried some people – it was themselves, and whether they could hack the way of life. This was the moment of truth, the final departure from the mother continent.

All our friends in that row by the beach made it out to French Polynesia. Some went on, after a few weeks, to Hawaii and home. Like the Jones family who were doing it on a shoestring and had run out of money; or Dick who'd spent years preparing for the trip, and sailed off in a huff after a row with the *gendarme*.

Tom and Ann got as far as Bora Bora. Tom received a job offer, by radio, and they hotfooted it back to Vancouver.

The rest spent the next six months crossing the Pacific. One lost his boat on a reef in the Cook Islands. Another narrowly missed the same fate among the atolls of the Tuamotus, but went on to the Western Pacific, and more near-misses. One couple, ever unsure about where they going, left their boat in Fiji and flew home to Seattle to sort themselves out. They came back for a second try and sailed home via Japan. The Clark family carried on to New Zealand where they sold their exquisite, home-built boat and continued their travels by plane. Don and Carol sailed into Brisbane and found their computing skills were in high demand. They swallowed the hook, sold their boat and bought a house. Our good friends Kathy and Terry spent some time in New Zealand and Australia to let their bright little daughter get some schooling. Then they moved on to teaching jobs in Papua New Guinea, where we ran into them again.

When each of those folk left the mountains of Baja behind them, not one of them would have dared to make a firm prediction on how things would turn out. For some the outcome was a disappointment, for others, a relief. A few with heavy odds against them, amazed everyone, and themselves, by their achievments.

But much of the magic of the venture lay in the uncertainty of the outcome, and for some the pre-voyage excitement turned out to be a great deal more fun than the voyage itself.

'...yet the sea is a terrible place, stupefying to the mind and poisonous to the temper ... the motion, the lack of space, the villainous tinned foods,... I cannot say why I like the sea; I regard it as the highest form of gambling; and yet I love the sea as much as I hate gambling.'

Robert Louis Stevenson - letters to Sydney Colvin

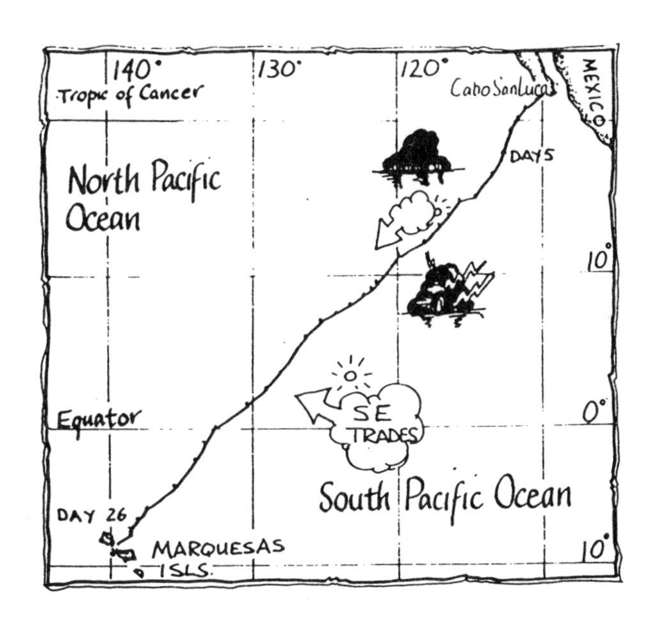

24

Back Before The Trade Winds - Mexico to Marquesas

A slow start, fifty miles yesterday, an average of just over two knots. I don't mind, it gives me time to adjust to passage living, to ease myself in. I'm not one of life's 'deep-enders'. We have a long passage ahead, most of it before the trade winds. Somewhere in the middle, the doldrums lie in wait. At present we keep our ears cocked for any hint of stray Tehuantepecers shooting out from the Gulf of Mexico. We listen most religiously to W.W.V. these days. 'There are naa-ow weather warnings for the traa-pical Paa-cific'. We hope it stays that way.

The log notes read:

FEB. 9th., DAY 5: Even the jellyfish overtake us. 250 miles of progress so far. Moving on occasional light puffs of wind. Sea flat.

2 a.m: Brilliant moonlight reveals a rock pinnacle, yards away. Rochas Partidas, nasty surprise. Have been swept west 30 miles in the night. A current of 4 knots?

DAY 7: Gloomy and squally. W.W.V. forecasts a Tehuantepecer to the south, and Kona storm (75 knots) in Hawaii, north of us.

DAY 11: Could this be the trade wind? Blue sky, fluffy clouds and a steady breeze from the N.E.

6p.m: Wind strengthening, sea building, twin headsails up – in the groove now!

DAY 12: Ugh! Suddenly into squalls, rain, gloom and fickle wind. Doldrums? For how long? Lightning on the horizon. Some progress in the squalls. Hot and sticky. We languish.

DAY 18: Picking up the south-east Trades now. Spray flying, have to close hatches – cabin like an oven.

Paid devotions to Albert (Most Important Gear). Works without complaint, 24 hours a day. Doesn't screw-up or argue.

DAY 19: Crossed the equator (for the third time) Pleasant day, sea down. Baked bread, washed, put on brand new knickers (present from the U.K., big treat)

The days and nights pass, some good, some bad. Wedged against the motion, we read, cook, bake, sew, navigate and mend things. Little petrels are the sole signs of life.

Nights are long – 12 hours of darkness. Watches are uneventful, 3hrs. on and 3hrs. off. David listens to B.B.C. World Service. I mostly ruminate and reflect. David calls it 'dozing'.

DAY 25: Getting close. Squalls push us on, then hold us up. Sails up, sails down. Patience!

Sunset flushes pink and orange across the sky and throws up shadows on the horizon – land! Unmistakably. We drop the sails and drift slowly. Behind us the moon is rising, showering the sea with cold, pale light. Another passage draws to a close. The doldrums lasted for only a few days. The jibs have flown, poled out for almost all of the twenty-six days. The trailing log has spun out 2,680 miles on its dial. We are rested, washed, well-fed (except for a lack of vegetables) and well-read. But I am ready to look at something other than the cabin, cockpit, sea and sky and to hear real voices other than our own.

A slow drift under a brilliant moon. This time the Marquesas enfold us in a gentle welcome.

25

Changes

We had made a promise to ourselves and we had kept it. We were back beneath R. L. Stevenson's 'austere and feathered mountains'. The moist spiced smell of greenery wafted out to greet us and awakened memories of that first impact two years before. It was a landfall still unmarked by man, still as Stevenson saw it: 'There was no beacon, no smoke of towns to be expected, no plying pilot.'

But we knew that up on the high plateau, bulldozers had been at work, making an airstrip for passenger jets. Nuka Hiva was now connected to the outside world of instant travel.

As we came round into the great amphitheatre of Taiohae Bay I scanned ahead, bracing myself for some discordant sign of the island's new status. The bay looked much as we had left it. About a dozen yachts lay at anchor; the French flag fluttered from the residency garden, and behind the palm trees and hibiscus, the village dozed.

David took a closer look through binoculars. 'Uh-uh, a new building, near the market,'

'A bank, I'll bet. Thoughtfully provided so that we can lend the administration 3,500 dollars for a few months.'

That was the sum, equivalent to two air fares home, that we had to lodge in the French Bank, until we left French Polynesia. On our previous visit, yachtsmen from E.E.C.

countries were exempt, but now, even the French had to pay up.

The bond was a source of great indignation to the yachting community. 'They can't do this to us,' was a familiar refrain. When I was feeling energetic I'd counter this with a little lecture:

'There are actually less restrictions now than there were twenty years ago. In the early sixties the Smeetons were grateful to be allowed ten days in Niku Hiva. In the thirties, visitors of any sort got twenty-four hours. Thor Heyerdahl had to get special permission for his stay. The Keep Paradise Clean campaign has been running a long time. Lots of countries all over the world don't admit tourists without an onward or return ticket.'

I'd go on to tell whoever was left listening that even Australia and New Zealand required visas and proof of means of support. And as for the U.S.A. – there we had to pay for a cruising permit and notify customs of our every move. Yachtsmen from countries not on the U.S. cruising agreement list have to check in and out, and pay, at every single harbour as if they were entering and leaving the States each time.

This last bit usually came as news to my American listeners but they could never quite see what it had to do with the iniquitous French in Polynesia.

'This is an infringement of our rights. I'm gonna write to Washington.'

Indignant outrage over visitors' restrictions was not confined to Americans or to French Polynesia. We found it among yachtfolk all over the world. Maybe they had got too used to being too free. It saddened me, particularly in the newly independent countries of the Western Pacific, to see how insensitive some yachties could be to cultures and economies which are fragile and vulnerable.

I was right about the new building. The little box of

glass and plywood bore the grand banner, 'Banque d'Indo-Chine Suez'. The manager, who seemed to be the sole employee, greeted us pleasantly. Podgy and pasty-faced, with a thin moustache which caught the sweat as it trickled down his nose, he told us, above the whirr of his desk fan, that his name was Bernard. He was from France of course, but for many years living in Tahiti. He had just moved with his wife and family into the new house beside the bank. We exercised our rusty French. Yes, he liked living here, except, perhaps, it was a little lonely.

'But often in the evenings I dine at the restaurant of Frank and Rose.'

Restaurant? Frank and Rose? 'Yes. They are Americans. They came on a yacht and now they have bought the house of old Monsieur Duval, up there, above the bay. Soon they are building cabins for an hotel. Now that we have an airport there will be tourists.'

'But what about the locals, don't they want to be in on the hotel business?' I asked. Bernard rolled his eyes heavenward.

'Pouff! Only if it involves no work. Why do you think all the shop-keepers are Chinese?' He mopped his face and waved the sodden handkerchief at the window.

'There is so much that could be done here. I tell you, it is a struggle for a banker to be busy in Paradise.'

Curiosity took us on for a beer at Frank and Rose's place. They were toiling away, or rather Rose was. Frank was acting amiable host to a group of Americans from a large yacht, who had made themselves at home around the table. Rose was in the kitchen rustling up surprise lunch for twelve. 'That's how it goes,' she told me later. 'Some days we see no-one, other days we're run off our feet. And we never know what supplies we'll have in hand.' Frank was a former airline pilot, and this was their 'retirement' project. Planning permission had been granted for the bungalows and the ground was being cleared. 'But so slowly,' groaned Frank. 'The locals work as the mood takes them. They wander off in the middle of a job and come back a few days later. Big smiles, no explanation, no apologies.'

He took us round the fine old colonial house, pointing out the modifications he was making. 'It takes forever to get building materials. "On the next boat" is the most well-worn lie around here.'

It was salutary to remember that they'd once been yachties too. They'd lost that weathered glow that their customers exuded. I made a mental note; paradise is only for playing in.

For the next two weeks we made the most of it. We swam, lazed, hiked, nosed around, socialized. We even managed to entice Maurice, the funny old Scots Marquesan, from his musty shop to have dinner with us on *Moongazer*.

Several of our friends from Cabo arrived, elated and amazed with themselves at having completed their first ocean passage – as we had been, when we crossed the Atlantic.

The joy of arrival apart, not everybody was captivated by their first South Sea Island. 'A bit oppressive, these mountains. And the water, I didn't expect it to be so murky. You can't see what's swimming around beside you,' Tom told us. He continued 'Ann's being driven nuts by these noe-noe bugs. She finds this dinghying ashore a bit of a hassle with the little one, so we're off to Papeete. We can tie up to the quay there.' Through his ham radio, Tom had fixed himself up with a job back in Canada, so their sights were already on home.

For others, the islands weren't primitive enough. There were no bamboo huts and grass skirts. Mopeds, fridges and rock music took the edge off the romance.

But for us there was romance enough, although we had to seek it out. We sailed back up to the north coast, to the bay of Anaho where R.L.S. had first dropped anchor:

> It was a small sound, a great event; my soul went down with these moorings whence no windlass may extract nor any diver fish it up; and I, and some part of my ships company were from that hour the bondslaves of the isles of Vivien.

His yacht was immediately surrounded by canoes, full of 'stalwart six foot men in every stage of undress' trying to trade or 'offering us island curios at prices palpably absurd'.

We ran under the jib into the majestic bay, turned sharply into a little bight and dropped anchor, less significantly perhaps than the *Casco* but still moved by the power of our surroundings. *Moongazer* lay in oddly quiet water, a solitary, insignificant speck beneath the shattered mountains. In vain I looked to the shore for stalwart six-foot men, dressed or otherwise, but the village and all its inhabitants were long gone. Only the wind stirred in the coconut grove, or so we thought. .

We had fixed the awning over the deck and were assembling the cockpit table when we noticed a two-man canoe coming our way. 'You might be in luck,' said David, 'One of them looks well over six feet. Hardly stalwart, though.'

They introduced themselves; Jacques, pale and languid, fresh from Paris and Henri, more seasoned, from Tahiti. They were building bungalows among the trees. 'We have only just started, the permission took so long to come. But one day there will be an hotel,' Jacques told us, with a wave of his well-manicured hand. He had been an advertising executive working in New York and Paris, and had been married five times. Wife number five was Chilean, a former international fashion model. She was at present over the hill in the next village nursing their new baby.

We asked who the guests were going to be in this inaccessible spot. Jacques seemed optimistic. 'The French who work in Taiohae, they like to get away for a change. And maybe even those in Papeete.'

They stayed chatting late into the night, eager for company and in no hurry to return to their little tent and the waiting squadrons of mosquitoes. Next morning when we went ashore they showed us around their domain. The coconut grove was cleared of underbrush, an impressive achievement. But somehow we felt they were in the early stages of a Robinson Crusoe fantasy. During the next few days they would be in Taiohae ordering materials. We wished them luck for what lay ahead, with more show of confidence, I hope, than we felt.

After some days of exploration around the wild and tangled shores of the bay we extended our horizons to Hatiheu, over the hill. A stony path wound tortuously up to the knife-edge ridge between the bays. While we rested at the top, feasting our senses on the stunning views, a couple appeared over the brow of the hill, the man astride a horse and the woman struggling on behind. We exchanged *bonjour*'s, and they disappeared, slithering down the path to Anaho. We followed the path they had come by, plunging steeply down into a cool green forest of breadfruit, orange, mango and banana.

Stevenson thought the village of Hatiheu, 'a place of some pretensions,' even while disease was daily plucking off the inhabitants. It was then the 'university' of the northern islands, where those that were left of the male population between the ages of six and sixteen were compulsorily sent to school. The school, and its priests had been moved from Taiohae since the memorable occasion when the pupils of both the girls' and the boys' schools had broken bounds and made off into the forest for a few days of extra-curricular activities..

Now the village nestled sleepily among the foliage, in a breathtaking setting of green spikey mountains and surf-rimmed sea. We picked our way down the pathways, lined by walls of black stone. Everywhere we saw the old, stone, house-platforms, half swallowed by the jungle. The Marquesans didn't always have an antipathy to hard work. Religion, customs and warfare were powerful spurs to activity.

One of the little plywood bungalows among the blossoms sported a sign advertising Hinano beer, and we made for it like moths to a light. Within minutes we were pouring the deliciously chilled stuff down our throats as if it had just saved our lives. The owner, a plump, middle-aged lady, with two front teeth missing, watched happily. She was eager to chat and spoke good simple French – the kind we could converse in.

Five years ago, she had been to New Zealand, for three months. Her husband, who was the mayor of the village, needed open heart surgery and the French Government flew them to Dunedin. The New Zealand doctors were 'Magnifique!' she said, her eyes shining at the memory. 'In Papeete they are...ppfff!' The people of New Zealand were also 'Magnifique!' But oh, the cold! It was strange to have to wear boots and stockings, and things to cover the hands and the head. And snow! she had seen pictures before of snow on mountains but she didn't realise how it came. Like bits of torn-up paper floating down. Her husband was now fully recovered, but he was away just now to Taiohae, 'on business'. The ills of the Western World are all-pervasive.

One ill in particular was dogging our tracks. The pressure of Time had chased both of us all our lives and to my great disappointment there was no sign of a let-up. Deadlines governed our every move; admittedly we measured them now in weeks and months, instead of hours and minutes, but it made the weeks flash past even faster.

We had to be in Tahiti before our cruising permit ran

out in June. Before then we planned to be in the Tuamotus for a month, and to arrive there during full moon. This gave us a date for leaving the Marquesas. 'We can't hang about,' reminded the Cruise Director. 'There are three islands we haven't seen yet. And it might take some time finding the *tikis* on Hiva Oa. We should be on the move every three or four days.'

Anchorage hopping in a cruising yacht is like moving from hotel to hotel with no chance to unpack your suitcases. Living comfortably at anchor involves using an amazing amount of junk, like awnings, snorkelling gear, water carriers, wash tubs, windsurfer, barbecue etc. The thought of stowing it all, only to have to reverse the operation hours later, paralyses many folk into remaining where they first arrive, and cancelling the side trips to paradise. My natural inclinations toward inertia were always checked by David's goading and by an insatiable curiosity to see 'over the next hill'.

From the wild northern shore of Nuka Hiva the next 'hill' was the easternmost island of Ua Huka. Upwind of the other islands, it gets less attention from yachts, so on our approach we were surprised to see another mast rolling in the main bay. We were also pleased, because we were ready for some company.

Bill and Lavonne turned out to be very good company and to this day, many travels later for all of us, we still keep in touch. From San Francisco they had been cruising Central America for two years in their home-built sloop *Matreya*. They were true sea gypsies, committed to the way of life and prepared to live on slender means to keep on travelling.

In Ua Huka we were treated to our first truly Polynesian feast. It was a thank-you from Moe the woodcarver, to David and Bill for fixing his outboard motor. Under the gaze of some of their twelve children we sat down with Moe and his serenely smiling wife, to a table of roast pig, baked chicken, marinated tuna, rice, breadfruit, banana and papaya. The next day he took us lobster hunting and we had all the lobster we could eat for two days. Feast was having a field day. Famine, we knew was just around the corner.

Faithful to our deadlines, we extricated ourselves (literally) from the hospitable embraces of Moe's family, waved *Matreya* au revoir, and headed south, into a stygian night of flashing thunder squalls. Daybreak came, grey and comfortless, and with it, a strong north-easterly which carried us on toward the cliffs of Hiva Oa, and what I silently suspected would be disappointment.

We had long been looking forward to our return to Ozanne's place, the past scene of our brief Polynesian idyll. Now, with the swell bursting on the northern shores of the islands we knew, even before we saw it, that the anchorage would be untenable. Between the gaunt red cliffs, the choppy bay looked lonely and unfriendly.

But even if we'd been able to anchor we would have found the valley deserted. We learned later that Ozanne's responsibilities had caught up with him and he was back in Atuona, with his wife and family, working in his uncle's shop.

'We should know by now,' remarked David, as we ghosted down the lee of the island, 'to leave a good memory alone.'

The main anchorage looked little changed except for a few more yachts, rolling to a gentler swell – thanks to the wind being in the north-east. One of the yachts, a large yellow trimaran flying the Dutch flag, looked familiar. After we anchored, I remembered. 'Madiera,' I told David. 'They were in front of us – with two little toddlers.' I looked over and saw that there were now two little boys and a dog.

The long hot road into the village was now surfaced and a number of mopeds buzzed past us, each looking dangerously overloaded by its occupant. Two new 'supermarkets' had opened in the village. Chinese stores by another name, but with self-service shelves for the tinned pilchards and Camp coffee. At the check-out desk was a large stool where even larger customers could take the weight off their feet while they chatted over the check-out.

We saw no sign of any hotel but there was a new restaurant, run inevitably by a European. As we approached the small open bar we heard a shrill, tense voice.

'I tell you – I'm having a breakdown in Paradise.' A pale, blonde young woman was sounding off before a group of yachties who'd come in for a cool quiet beer. 'They won't pay their bills, they won't work – but oh, they like to eat and drink!' She paused briefly to acknowledge our presence and draw breath. 'I have to let them run up credit or I wouldn't have any business at all. They run up huge bills and then I find they haven't got a penny. The *Gendarme* says there's nothing he can do. And I can't get anyone to stick at any work. They slope off when they feel like it and come back smiling as if nothing had happened. As for suppliers! You wouldn't believe the stories they invent. I thought I understood these folk – my husband's Tahitian – but they've got me beat. They're driving me crazy!'

She sounded like she might be right, and David nudged me into moving off. He shook his head and sighed. 'She comes here because it's strange and exotic and then gets all uptight because the locals won't jump through the same hoops as we do in the West.'

This was a favourite topic of Stevenson's: 'All the world must respect our tabus, or we gnash our teeth'.

I thought of him, as we trudged along the roadside. A true romantic, ever-struggling against his middle class upbringing in Victorian Edinburgh, he was fascinated to find a race whose cultural roots had no contact with Greece or Rome:

'I was now to see what men might be whose fathers had never studied Virgil, had never been conquered by Caesar, and had never been ruled by the wisdom of Gaius or Papinian.'

Stevenson met many native islanders on his anchorage hops, and studied them, more as a reporting journalist than a novelist (much to the disappointment of his public). With a skipper and five crewmen to tend the chartered *Casco*, he and his family entourage of four could relax ashore. He was free from the nagging worry of dragging anchor which, in these squall-ridden islands, dogged all our extended jungle hikes.

The arrival of a 30-metre schooner, one of only four yachts known to be travelling in Polynesia at that time, was a great event, worthy of a village turnout. Whether Stevenson wanted it or not, the presence of his yacht was an act of involvement with the community, from which there was no escape, bar going to sea. (We were to experience this ourselves, in remoter parts of the Solomon Islands and Papua New Guinea)

Now, it seemed to me that yacht travel in Polynesia was more like a private travelling circus, a moving community with its own built-in entertainment. Each anchorage, or even each country, was only a change of backdrop for the ongoing soap opera of daily life, played out in our own self-contained culture capsules.

The anchorage at Atuona was a good example.

YOUNG BANANA PALM

26

Memorable Yachts

The dowager of the anchorage was a gnarled, but still noble, three-masted Baltic trader, the *Sophia.* Over 30 metres long, she lay across half the inlet and formed a breakwater for the rest of us. She had plied the Baltic as a cargo vessel for over forty years and, except for her American flag, still looked much as when she was built in 1921. Her decks were clear above the caprail with no deckhouse additions which clutter most renovated sailing craft. The masts and rigging were free of interloping scanners and aerials.

'Unusual for a boat that big,' said David, when we first arrived. 'It's got to be carrying passengers, either fare-paying or sponsored. That usually requires some electronic gadgets for safety. I wonder if it's even got an engine?'

'Ho! Ho! I know what it does have.' It was my turn for the binoculars. 'There's a little cubicle on the stern rail. Presumably a concession to privacy. So much for mod. cons.. Authentic Adventures – for 1,000 dollars a week you can experience all the privations of the old days of sail!' I handed David the binoculars.

He scanned the ship slowly. 'The folk on the deck look a bit young for 1,000 bucks a week. Blonde tousled heads and bare torsos.'

'No women?'

'Oh, yes! Better than any French boat!'

It wasn't long before we were invited on board and David got to meet the real object of his curiosity, 'Junie Babie'. Old and cantankerous, she was lovingly looked after by Norman, no youngster himself. His little pigtail was greying and his lean frame was wrinkled at the corners. He patted the huge flywheel. 'It takes four crew to start her up. One on the compressed air bottles, one on the flares, someone on the fuel pump and one on the controls. Not what you'd call an instant start.' A two cylinder, 125 h.p. Swedish-built antique, she was the *Sophia*'s original engine.

'But mostly we use sail power,' said Norman. 'This baby's too noisy, dirty, hard on the nerves – and expensive. We run a tight ship here.'

'We noticed. What's the scene?' I asked.

'It started with a co-operative venture in 1969 and it's still going. A bunch of students from Oregon got together and bought *Sophia* in Sweden. She'd just been retired so there was a huge lot of work to be done on her. Some of us bought in at the beginning – I paid 2,000 bucks.'

'So, who owns her now?'

'About fifty folks. Most of them started as crew members, paying their way. Right now it's ten bucks a day. After a year or 3,000 bucks, you become an owner. Then you stay virtually for free. You can leave and re-join any time you like – for life. The majority of crew come for a few months and then move on, but there's a hard core of veterans.'

'They run the ship, then?'

'Everybody, no matter how new, has a say. We've never had to compromise our original ideals of power sharing. Even the captain gets elected.'

Our minds boggled. Power sharing on *Moongazer* was fraught with impasse. What it was like with eighteen multi-national wayfarers we couldn't imagine. Norman provided some insight.

'It does take up time, I guess. Right now we've spent three weeks trying to resolve the problem of where to go next.'

We were to see more of the *Sophia* across the Pacific, to lounge under the awnings on her wide working deck, and to sit in the pine-clad saloon, round the twelve-foot table which had formerly been a hatch cover.

Once, in Auckland harbour we slept aboard. It was a memorable night. I lay awake in a spartan, mildewed bunk listening to the rustle of cockroaches. I saw a huge one scuttle across the floor and under my bunk. The occupants of the other bunks, long inured to nocturnal scufflings, snored contentedly.

Then I heard a soft footfall heading in my direction. I knew what it was and sat up instantly. I'd been warned that the ship's pet had taken a fancy to my berth. 'You might get evicted,' someone had joked. 'The Varmitt doesn't go along with the sharing thing.' That was a relief, as The Varmitt struck me as a most malicious mascot.

He looked like a long-snouted racoon, but was a coatimundi from Costa Rica. He had been with the *Sophia* for seven years, the longest serving member, and he ruled O.K. His bite was vicious and random, but there were those that loved him, and apparently had their love returned. Under New Zealand quarantine regulations he was supposed to stay in his large cage, but he made such a din in it that he was allowed free run of the ship.

I hissed at The Varmitt and he scurried off in surprise to another bunk. There, in a fit of pique he rummaged and raged, and woke everyone up. Finally, with a loud curse, a naked male leapt from the bunk above, grabbed the creature and carried it, struggling and squealing to the saloon. There he threw it in its cage, which was evidently next to the bulkhead beside me. From then on, sleep was a lost cause. For three full hours The Varmitt rattled and shook his cage in impotent fury.

Shortly after, the *Sophia* sailed to Nelson, on South Island, for a major refit. The boatyard at Nelson was second home to *Sophia*, as during her previous circumnavigation she had spent nearly a year there. This time she carried hardwood timbers bought in Central America to replace some planking and it was reckoned that she would be laid up for the same length of time again.

On arrival at Nelson, the temporary crew members dispersed and we met some of them during that winter, wandering around New Zealand. They told us the work was progressing well, and, if finished in time, there was a film role waiting for the *Sophia* in Auckland.

Months later, when we were back in the U.K. on a flying visit, the newspaper on a friend's breakfast table caught my eye. A small column was headed, SIXTEEN SAVED AFTER FIVE DAYS IN LIFERAFTS. The *Sophia*, on her way to Auckland and film fame, had gone down in heavy weather off the North Cape of New Zealand. One crew member was lost, a girl who'd joined just after they'd left Nelson. He didn't get a mention in the newspaper but The Varmitt also went to a watery grave. 'I'll bet the cockroaches didn't,' David said. 'They probably swam ashore, the bastards.'

Later, back in the scene, we pieced together snippets of the story. During the re-fit in Nelson there had been dissensions among the crew and most of the hard core had left, including the vital engineer. It seems that before the ship was overwhelmed she was already labouring, half full of water with both pumps out of action.

This sequence of cause and effect had a familiar ring. We knew of other sinkings and shipwrecks where the seeds of disaster were sown months and even years before the final ending. And always, the fault lay not so much in the weakness of the boat, but in the frailty of human organization.

In Taahuku Bay, nestled beside the *Sophia* was the smallest boat in the anchorage. Measuring less than seven metres, it was made of plywood painted bright yellow and had no engine. Phillipe, a skinny French lad, had sailed it from France. His last passage, from the Galapagos had taken seventy-two days.

He had been earning some money in Atuona by teaching, or trying to, in the girls' school. 'They just sat and giggled and ate jars of peanut butter. No-one paid any attention except to laugh at me.' So he had given it up and was moving on. His mother sent regular food parcels and entreaties to come home.

At his next stop, in the southernmost island, Fatu Hiva, he fell in love with a local beauty, and in the best traditions of the wandering sailor moved ashore. We heard later that, along with the food parcels, his brother had been dispatched to Tahiti to find him and bring him back to France.

In any anchorage it takes only a couple of days to become an established resident. Then with the other residents you can appraise the entrance of all subsequent arrivals as if they were 'strangers riding into town'.

We did this more than usual one day when an immaculate 20-metre ketch made its entrance. Two young lads and a man were on the bow and a woman was at the wheel. They all looked squeaky clean in yachting clothes, as if they'd just been out for a day's sail from Rhode Island. The boat was in marina-mint condition. Not a trace of weed, barnacles, oil, rust and all the usual marks of a 4,000-mile passage.

We found out later that they had stopped in an outlying bay to scrub and polish the yacht for its entrance. Harvey, the owner, was the only person I knew who consistently wore socks and deck shoes in the tropics. 'Shoes and socks!' everyone would remark in amazed disapproval, just as they would have said 'barefeet!' back home. Harvey stuck to his long shorts and button-down shirts all across the Pacific. This seemed so remarkable to us all, that at a fancy-dress party in Fiji, someone came dressed as 'Harvey.'

The scruffiest boat of the fleet, and anchored perilously close to the surf-line, was a small, heavily built double-ender, with two short stubby masts. We invited the owners, Al and Helen, on board for a drink and they came, each clutching a half bottle of something.

'You didn't have to,' I said. 'We're well stocked.'

'Well, we were on Don and Betty's boat last night, and hell, no-one told us they were Seventh Day Adventists. By six-thirty I had severe withdrawal symptoms,' Al told us. 'So this time we're taking no risks.'

'Still it's nice to have company,' said Helen. 'First time we came here we were the only yacht. There was another one up in Nuka Hiva.'

'You've been before?'

'Yeah, this is visit number four.'

'What! This is your fourth time around the Pacific?'

'This is our fourth time around the world.'

Stunned silence for a second. 'Wow!' (That was the nearest we could get to an American reaction.) We were amazed. They looked just like any ordinary couple. But no ordinary couple circumnavigates twice, let alone four times. For nearly twenty-five years they'd been travelling in their faithful ketch, *Myonie*.

'We're from Florida,' said Helen, by way of explanation. 'And each time we returned we liked it less and less. In fact, we began to hate Fort Lauderdale with a passion.'

It struck me that there must be easier ways to avoid Fort Lauderdale.

Myonie was stout and seaworthy but spartan and devoid of gadgets, even of a self-steering gear. 'With the tiller on a bungie cord,' Al told us. 'She steers herself. We only ever take the helm going in and out of harbour.'

Our paths crossed a number of times over the next few years and we were always pleased to see them. Al was a complex and contrary character who viewed most of his fellow men with cynicism. His rock was Helen, a warm and loving lady, whose lot in life was to be hitched to such a man, for all the joys and agonies it must have brought.

They nearly lost *Myonie* in the Cook Islands. Her anchor chain snapped during a sudden and vicious onshore storm and she dragged onto a reef. By good seamanship and the stark spur of knowing she was all they posessed they managed to get her refloated with minimal damage.

They lived on slender means and I remember Helen telling me that she hoped they would stop in American Samoa to work and get some money together. 'I could do with treating myself to a little bit of luxury.' She closed her eyes for a second in a dream of indulgence. '...Like a new dinghy.'

They stopped in Samoa, but there Helen took seriously ill and had to undergo major surgery. When she recovered they continued on, round the Cape of Good Hope ('We always go via the Cape') and back to Florida. That was where we last saw them, tucked away in a little backwater canal. They were fitting out a van to go camping and *Myonie* was up for sale. Sitting quietly in the still water under the overhanging trees, she looked like a faithful workhorse put out to grass. But, unlike their owners, boats are allowed several lives, and one day someone with a dream will find *Myonie* and she will lead them back to the South Seas.

We had a reason for returning to Hiva Oa other than to socialise with our neighbours, or to go on forays with Phillipe into the forest for wild bananas, or to dive with Frans, from the yellow trimaran, for lobster and clams. We wanted to see the great stone *tikis*, the statues in the jungle that so stirred the young Thor Heyerdahl.

They were near the village of Paumau on the northern coast. As the anchorage in the bay of Paumau would be untenable, we would have to go by road. A new one had been cut across the plateau, and along the tortuous north coast terrain. I met a French woman who had travelled on it, but, seeing how she shuddered at the memory, I wished I hadn't.

We enquired around but no-one, it seemed, was desperate enough to take us to Paumau. Just as we were on the point of giving up, we met a jaunty, stringy-haired Tahitian who was prepared to take us in his jeep, – at a price, and it had to be the next day, a 5.a.m. start. If it looked like rain he wouldn't do it. 'Trop dangereux'.

To share the cost, we rounded up others who had expressed an interest; Frans and his family and a young German couple, Anne and Rolf, who had just arrived from the Galapagos. (We had no clue then, but several years later we were to share many jungle hikes with Anne and Rolf in the Western Pacific.)

We dug out our sun hats, filled our water bottles and went to bed early. I was too restless to sleep. I lay with Thor Heyerdahl's book, *Fatu Hiva*, before me and read:

> There are incidents in everyone's life which may be casual and yet prove to have vital consequences in future development, even to the extent of sidetracking an entire life. My introduction to the Paumau stone giants during an attempt to return to nature later resulted in switching me onto a new track that was to guide my destiny for many eventful years to come. It set me asail on rafts, led me into continental jungles, and made me excavate Easter Island monuments as high as buildings of several stories.

No one could tell him who had carved the strange figures or why. The locals had told previous explorers that the statues were already there when their ancestors arrived and drove an earlier people into the mountains. Heyerdahl reckoned they looked similar to the statues that lay scattered in the Andes, from San Augustin to Lake Titicaca. The seeds of his curiosity grew and took root, and gave the world the *Kon Tiki* expedition, as well as starting a fashion for adventurous theory-testing.

Until recently there was only a track to Paumau, and Heyerdahl went on horseback:

> It was like riding on a Pegasus without visible foothold. There was a mountain peak in front of us and another behind. Between them passed a ridge so sharp that the trail filled it completely.... On either side, our feet dangled above slopes that ran into nothing except the bands of surf far below.... all we could hear was a general hiss carried up from the depths below.

I put the book down and switched off the light. I prayed the new road would be an improvement.

27

To The Tikis – Notes From The Log

6 a.m: We race the sun up to the high plateau. No rain clouds in sight. The road winds ahead – a red slash of hard baked mud. So far, bumpy but O.K.

Our driver, Aroma. French father, Tahitan mother. Was a mechanic in the army; now the engineer at the T.V. video station.

Keeps turning round to talk while driving. At the first stop we change the front passenger for Anne (who speaks fluent French). Maybe this will focus his attention more ahead.

10.a.m: We reach the northern coast road, wider now than Heyerdahl's horse track, but just as terrifying.

Noon: Relieved and rewarded by the sweeping sight of Paumau Bay.

1 p.m: We drive through the village and smiling children hitch a ride. They know what we've come for. 'The tikis – we will show you the way.'

Suddenly, through a banana grove, we see them staring at us.

Two – three metres high, each carved from a single block of volcanic stone. After the Easter Island giants, they are the largest stone carvings in Polynesia. Carbon dating puts their erection on the stone platforms around 1500 A.D., but who by, and for what reason, still remains the tikis' secret.

We feel the presence of the past all around us. I think of the Haida Indian village in the Queen Charlotte Islands, and Emily Carr's words...' a place more poignantly desolate for having once known man.'

2.30 p.m: We slip away quietly and leave them to their secrets and their solitude.

28

Heyerdahl's Virgin Island

We had 'done the *tikis*'. Now we were ready for the Marquesas' Grande Finale – the island that Heyerdahl chose, above all others in the world, to fulfil a childhood obsession. In 1936, while studying zoology at Oslo University, he resolved his determination to see if he could, as he put it: '... resume the life abandoned by our first ancestors...Be independent of everything except nature.'

His fiancee was to share in the experiment, and together they pored over maps of the world. At first they looked for something that didn't exist – a tropical, fertile, uninhabited island. Next best was Fatu Hiva, 'Mountainous and lonely. Rich in sunshine, fruit and drinking water. Few natives and no white men.'

There was no doubt about our next stop. No one would be able to say this time 'My God! They missed Fatu Hiva.'

We sailed first to the nearby island of Tahuata and motored south under the lee of a wall of mountains. We anchored in the bay where Mendana had raised the Spanish flag and where, 200 years later, the second European visitor, James Cook, came in the *Resolution.* He and his men were sorely in need of fresh provisions after three months of epoch-making explorations in Antarctic waters. They traded with handsome, heavily-tatooed men for breadfruit, pigs, and coconuts. At first the natives were pleased to accept nails in return, but several young officers, acting without permission, offered a large quantity of red feathers. The trading was immediately spoiled as the feathers were seen to be much more desirable than nails and from then on the natives refused to part with their goods unless more feathers were forthcoming. Cook and his men also had to contend with vicious squalls which buffeted them 'with prodigious violence.' One such squall, roaring down off the mountain ridge, caught Cook and his botanists in the longboat and only the 'extraordinary address of our oarsmen' saved them from being smashed on the rocks. We, too, suffered the 'prodigious violence' of the squalls and after a sleepless night at anchor we left for Fatu Hiva.

Fatu Hiva, a mountain barrier astride the trade winds, lay a night's sail to the south-east. It was a weary night of struggle with truculent winds and troubled seas, but daylight brought its reward of our first view of the island. It seemed a composite of the wildest features of the other islands – and then exaggerated some.

Half-way along the coast, four yachts, just tiny white specks, dwarfed by towering cliffs and mountains, gave a clue to the anchorage. We knew from previous accounts and photos that Hanavave Bay was possibily the most scenically stunning anchorage in the South Pacific. Even Eric Hiscock, a practitioner of understatement, was moved to write: 'As a spectacle we had seen nothing quite the equal of this for a very long time.'

However, when its splendour opened up before us, our eyes were cast downward, not in humility but in concern. The yachts were lying in different directions leaving little room to anchor. Frans shouted over from his Trimaran. 'We've had strong gusts off the mountain. They send us round in circles, and the holding ground is bad.'

We sniffed around for a suitable spot, dropped the anchor and pulled back, and back, and back.

'Not holding,' yelled David from the bows. 'What's the depth?'

'Sixty feet, nearly seventy now,' I replied.

He shook his head. 'I've put out most of the chain. Better try again.'

He pulled on the winch lever but nothing happened. The chain, running straight down into the dark water didn't budge a fraction. It seemed caught.

'What's up?' I shouted.

By way of reply, David strode down the deck, looked at the depth-sounder and turned a knob. 'Christ! We're in sixty bloody *fathoms*, that's what's up! A hundred foot of chain and a forty-five pound anchor, dangling straight down. No wonder the winch won't lift it. God knows how *I'm* going to!'

Eventually, inch by inch we got it up, with toil, mud, sweat, and for me, nearly tears – mostly of mortification.

On the second attempt, the anchor bit into the floor of the ledge, but we ended up close to another boat. With our last remaining strength we ran out a stern anchor to keep us off, and this held well for a few days. Then a three a.m. blast roared down from the crags and had us all re-anchoring.

Mighty blasts from a dark mountain, were in keeping with the scene, which could have been a stage set for *Gotterdamerung*. Above all, it was a triumph of artistry for the Director of Lighting. There was no overhead light, only a deep indigo canopy of brooding clouds. Shafts of sunlight pierced the gloom from seaward, where we could see blue skies and shining water. The sun went down like a giant footlight bathing us, and our fantastic backdrop, in a brilliant golden glow.

One day the threatening clouds fulfilled their promise and dumped a torrential load on us – for twelve hours. The cliffs foamed white with waterfalls, and the bay choked up with jungle flotsam and hundreds of coconuts. But most days the clouds just hung on the ridge tops, glowering and oppressive.

When the Heyerdahls sailed along the coast in the copra schooner looking for a place to be set down, the captain warned them against Hanavave. 'An unhealthy climate,' he told them. 'The valley is very moist and the air is filled with water vapour. The natives here suffer from all kinds of diseases that may infect you too. Elephantiasis is terrible here in Hanavave.' Now, forty years on, modern medicine and education had made themselves felt, though we occasionally saw old folk with the grotesquely swollen limbs that signify elephantiasis.

Some of the younger villagers were much more forward than their fellows in the other islands. There they had treated strangers with a dignified reserve. Going ashore in Hanavave we were accosted by folk asking for T-shirts, tapes, jewelry and cosmetics. For the first time in the islands I saw a young woman wearing lipstick and sparkly drop-earrings. It was a shock to my Western sensitivities to see natural beauty so mocked.

'That's the last time I give out candies,' said Jackie, our aggrieved neighbour. 'Yesterday I gave some to the kids playing on the beach. To-day I get angry mothers telling me I missed out their kids!'

Why the behaviour of the locals here was different from those of the other islands, was a matter of some discussion. Perhaps it was because they were more isolated and yachts were their major contact with the outside world. During the past few years the villagers had come into contact with an increasing number of yachtfolk for whom this was the first stop since leaving California, and for some, their first experience of a foreign land. Eager to make contact and be welcomed by 'the natives', and often mistaking the villagers' simple lifestyle for poverty, some yachtfolk had lavishly dispensed hospitality and gifts to all and sundry. It seemed to me that such misplaced generosity must inevitably cause jealousies and resentments and disturb the delicate balance of village life. It also created a 'red feathers' situation where some locals would only trade for ridiculous offers, like a tape player for a few grapefruit. I saw all this as a kind of 'social pollution', a view which I noted with sad surprise, often evoked blank looks from among my fellow travellers.

I took some comfort from learning that in the 1950s a certain Father Albert was bemoaning an even worse state of affairs. Bengt Danielsson, a member of the *Kon Tiki* voyage, was passing by on his way to settle at Hiva Oa, when he met the priest. He mentions their conversation in his book, *Forgotten Islands Of The South Seas*:

> Tourists came to Fatu Hiva very seldom, and Father Albert was very angry with the few who had come, for he considered that it was they who had corrupted the inhabitants. According to him the only visitors were circumnavigators and other people on long voyages in small boats. They stayed as a rule only a day or two, as there was no safe anchorage, so they almost always wanted to make the most of their time. They were really interested in only two things; roystering and amusing themselves with women, and collecting Marquesan antiquities. Both men and women from the valley used to ask for spirits or cash in return for their gifts and their hospitality and the parties inevitably ended in orgies.

Unless we were missing something, things had changed. Opportunities too. The modern yachtsman was usually accompanied by his yachtswoman. Nor were we so gullible about 'antiquities'. Some of us were interested in the present-day handcrafts, carvings and tapa (decorated material made from pulped bark) but finding and buying good specimens was akin to treasure hunting.

We mustered the energy one day for a hike up the dark

humid valley to a rock pool in the mountains. It was fed by a waterfall cascading down a cliff-face hundreds of metres high, and was said to have been where young girls of high rank prepared themselves, often for several months, with the help of their handmaidens for bodily perfection on their wedding-day. Some must have spent a pleasant number of years in this pursuit of perfection as it was the Marquesan custom for women to take a number of husbands.

All along the track we passed overgrown stone platforms and walls (all built without the help of wheels, carts or animals) and now the only traces of the three mighty tribes who once lived in the valley. Possibly we passed the Taboo Place where Heyerdahl found the pile of bones and skulls. We marvelled that he and his wife managed to live more or less off the forest and with few western utensils for over a year.

It was a heroic struggle which was almost cut short when they developed large ulcers on their legs. To get to Hiva Oa and medical aid, they had to patch up an old rowing boat and brave the ocean – and the surf-pounded beach at Atuona. It was while convalescing there that he came across the stone *tikis* of Paumau.

When their ulcers healed, they went back to Fatu Hiva for another try. In the end they were defeated, not by nature, but by humanity. To survive, they needed contact with the locals for their knowledge of jungle living, but the contact became an intrusion which the Norwegians couldn't handle. Their last days on Fatu Hiva were spent hiding in a cave, hoping that a ship would come and take them off. They had gone through hell to discover that 'Paradise' lay within themselves, and, as Heyerdahl said at the end of his book: 'One can't get there by buying a ticket.'

The moon grew fatter and set later, sending a ripple of activity around the anchorage. Everyone was preparing to escape from under the glowering clouds. Some, unable to repress that craving for steak and salad which assailed us all, were heading straight for Tahiti. Others like us, were going to have a go at finding those classic Isles of Paradise – the coral atolls of the Tuamotu.

Awaiting us would be smiling natives and languid lagoons, but the catch (and there's always a catch) was that they were hidden in a current-swept labyrinth of seventy-eight atolls, each barely higher than the crest of a wave. Named on the old charts as the Dangerous Archipelago, it was given a wide berth by sailing ships coming up from the Horn. Insurance companies excluded it from their field. Stevenson admitted 'It was not without misgiving that my captain risked the *Casco* in such waters.'

But it was his description of the lagoons: '..rippling like an inland mere' which appealed to me. I was fed-up with rolly anchorages and with beaching dinghies through the surf. To escape the unremitting pulse of the ocean, I was prepared to brave the fangs of hell itself. I noticed, when I said those words after a few drinks, how easily they rolled off the tongue.

Loaded down with grapefruit and bananas and with four days in hand before full moon, we sailed out from under Fatu Hiva towards Stevenson's 'causeways in the sea'.

Everything depended, as it always does at sea, on the weather.

29

Village On A Coral Strand

The atolls are beautiful...Not even the wild hurricanes...or the bitterness of a life slipped past can subtract one portion of the crystal beauty of these miraculous circles in the sea.
James Michener

Tues, 3 a.m.

Twinkle, Twinkle, little star.. Antares, Deneb, Peacock, our signposts in the sky. This evening we trapped their altitude in time, in the moments before darkness swallowed the horizon. Daybreak will bring it back again, but it will also steal the stars, so we have to catch them quickly.

In all our previous wanderings we've never felt the need to take star sights. Now we want to know precisely, not roughly, where we are. A running fix leaves too much to the caprices of the current. So far we haven't noticed much, but from now on it could play all sorts of tricks. David's calculations put us fifty miles off Takaroa. We've dropped the sails and jog along gently, on the windage of our rigging. I'm on watch, looking, listening, comforted by the brilliance of the moonlight. The heaving ocean glitters – like crumpled foil.

It was the sort of night that the lookout on the crow's nest would have prayed for. Magellan sailed this way in blissful ignorance, sighting only a few outlying atolls. How many of his followers were snared on unseen reefs we shall never know.

In 1616, the Dutch merchants Schouten and Le Maire, after opening up the route round Cape Horn, came upon Takaroa and found natives who knew about iron. They tried to draw bolts and nails from the ship which suggested some previous contact with Europeans or their wreckage.

It was over a hundred years before the next visitor, Rogeveen, nosed in among the atolls. His search for the Southern Continent almost came to an end on Takaroa's neighbouring atoll, Takapoto. Of his three ships, he lost one and only extricated the other two with difficulty. His countryman Schouten had named Takapoto, 'Bottomless Island'. Rogeveen left it with the name 'Disastrous'.

From the mid-1700s, the rush was on to find Terra Australis and a succession of expeditions poured into the Pacific. Those who came across the Tuamotus, Byron, Wallis, Carteret, Bougainville and Cook, stayed only long enough to gather coconuts if they could, and note the lack of anchorages and the hostility of the locals. Even Cook, the most skilled and sensitive in his dealings with natives, found the Takaroans, 'resentful of our presence.'

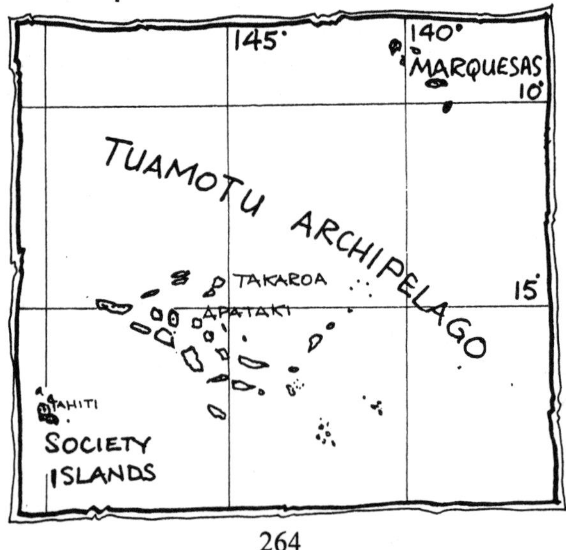

Such a reputation spared the atolls the attentions of the white man, and left them to war against each other. In the early 1800s the warriors from one of the more fertile atolls, Anaa, overran the eastern group, Takaroa included. The vanquished were eaten and their women and children taken as slaves. But even then, the growing European influence around Tahiti was spreading eastwards, mostly on the zeal of the missionaries, and by the 1830s the Paumotus ('Conquered Ones'), as they were then called, became safe enough to support a flourishing trade in pearl shell. There were the occasional grisly relapses, which did nothing to deter the pearl trader. By 1880 the lagoons were almost empty of pearl shell. Trade switched to copra, employing the new German method of sun drying the coconut kernels. French citizenship brought legislation and land registration, which in turn stimulated the planting of coconut palms. The uninhabited atolls that the sailor aloft strained so hard to see, were mere clumps of brush and pandanus a few feet high. The waving coconut palm, which has become the trade mark of coral islands and paradise packages, is, as Stevenson noted, 'a mark...of man's intervention.'

We made a text book landfall. Right on time a grey tuft appeared ahead on the wave tops. It was so barely there we had to look hard to believe it was land, about six miles off. The Mighty Navigator took a modest bow, and received that most acceptable gift so rarely given by wives – praise.

Then a thought struck me. 'How do we know it's Takaroa?'

David sighed. 'Remember why we chose Takaroa as a landfall?'

'Ah,.. because the *County Of Roxburgh* sits up on the reef.' Driven ashore in the hurricane of 1906, the rusty iron hull was likely to be the most distinguished feature on the earth's surface for hundreds of miles.

We bowled along and the grey fringe began to grow into a clump of parsley hung with the mist of the exploding surf. We closed the northern end of the fifteen-mile long atoll and ran down the lee. Now, from a mile or so off, we could make out the surf line, the reef, the beach strand and palm tree topping. At random intervals there were gaps in the topping, where the ocean washed over the strand into the lagoon beyond. We could see through the gaps and right across the lagoon to the thin grey fringe of palms on the far shore.

We sailed alongside the reef at a respectful distance and after an hour or so I caught sight of a rusty hull high up on the beach. 'O.K. All doubts dispelled. We're at Takoroa. Proceed to the pass.'

It was as well for my peace of mind and shipboard harmony that I didn't know I had missed the *County of Roxburgh* and was looking at the wreck of a Korean fishing boat.

Our concerns were now with the pass, the only thing that stood between us and the promised land of the languid lagoon. When the Hiscocks first came this way in 1953 in little *Wanderer III*, they found a current boiling out of the narrow cut from the lagoon into a rip of white water: '...to enter was impossible.'

Nor did The Pacific Islands Pilot, Vol. III offer reassurance: 'The currents in this channel are very strong, local knowledge is essential and it should be entered only in case of necessity.'

However, it did suggest there might be a moment of respite: 'There appears to be slack water at the moon's lower meridian passage.'

'The moon's lower what?' I asked the Master Astronomer.

'We'll use the time-honoured technique,' said David, 'and have a go if it looks O.K.'

The lay-out of the pass at Takaroa was etched in my mind. It had been, ever since I'd read Bernard Moitessier's riveting account of how he and his wife sailed *Joshua* through the long coral-flanked channel, tacking in the teeth of a south-westerly. For Moitessier it was the sublime experience: '...this light shining round the boat....these tremendous electrical discharges which surge through your vitals and guide you on.....It was the finest experience in the whole of my sailing career.'

For we lesser mortals who sail on a different, less incandescent sea, I knew that just chugging in under engine would activate my vitals quite sufficiently.

A white church spire, poking up from the palms, gave notice of the village, and beside it the pass. A deep cut of blue between two islets, it looked smooth and quiet. Slack water? We looked at each other and nodded.

Instantly we switched from ocean mode to inshore mode and ran around unlashing the anchors and dinghy. We fired up the engine, blew it a kiss of encouragement and headed for the channel between the reefs. Coral-bottomed waters rushed up to meet us. I stood on the bow watching ahead. The wind was strong but the channel looked strangely smooth. We slid past the village quay, now crowded with children and a number of adults. I waved, but the response was muted. The adults stared sullenly. I remembered Cook's description of natives: 'resentful of our presence'. Well, we would anchor well away from the village and keep a low profile.

'What does the bend at the end look like?' shouted David against the wind. 'There's a lot of pull on the helm already.' Shades of blue and green flashed under us. Pale jade loomed up ahead.

'A bit on the shallow side,' I shouted back, 'with some ripples. The current's gathering strength.'

We were past the point of no return. My eyes were fixed on the right-angled bend and on the keel-ripping coral that waited if we failed to make the bend. For a second *Moongazer* faltered at the turn. Then she answered to the helm and we shot over the shallows into the lagoon.

And then for the first time I looked up at the lagoon – my first much longed-for real lagoon. I stared in disbelief. Angry white water tore towards us, whipped up by the trade wind across fifteen miles of uninterrupted lagoon. We were safe enough from the ocean. We could hear it thundering on the reef outside.

But where to anchor? 'Slow down,' I yelled, 'I can't see the coral properly. The water's too rough.' The lagoon was studded with pillars and clumps of coral reaching to just below the surface. With every yard I expected to come to a keel-crunching halt.

'I can't slow down much more,' David yelled back. 'We'll lose steerage way in the wind. Hey! Look, a yacht! *Matreya*!' My sliding spirits rebounded upwards. We threaded our way towards it and found they were in a little bight near the shore, protected from the worst of the chop by some submerged reefs. We anchored, with difficulty, and Bill and Lavonne swam over – having decided it was too rough to row their rubber dinghy. We put out the boarding ladder and greeted them like long lost family. They answered above the wind, 'Welcome to Paradise.'

So this was it? The longed-for haven of my imaginings? Where was Stevenson's 'inland rippling mere'? Or Michener's 'haven that captivates the mind and rests the human spirit'? Or Charles Darwin's 'shallow, clear, and still water'? Or Jack London's 'huge and glassy lagoon'.

Moongazer was plunging up and down to the nerve-grinding rasp of anchor chain sawing through coral. I had been lured to the atolls by literary licence.

A few whiskies and a good snooze did much to improve my outlook. I began to take a second look and to see that we had entered a stunning world of light and sparkle. With every footstep we made new discoveries. We trudged over the coral clinker that apparently nourished thickets of mangrove and pandanus palm and even plantations of slender coconut palms. On the ocean beach we picked our way across the lunar landscape of old dead reef. There the surf tore at its edges and sent spindrift high into the air. It was disquieting to be reminded of the power of the ocean and see the wrecks up on the reef. It was, as Stevenson described, '...a place accursed and deserted, the fit scene only for wizardry and shipwreck.'

We prefered the palm-hung shores of the lagoon. We snorkelled, and dived for shells among the coral clumps and brilliant fish. Then I saw my first shark.

'Only a reef shark,' scoffed David. 'They're harmless. Just bark at them and they'll scuttle away.' I tried this, but I never knew if it worked, because as soon as I barked I scuttled away too.

Of the village and its inhabitants, we saw no sign. 'Odd,' remarked Bill, 'I'd have thought curiosity would have brought someone out.'

On our third morning we heard an engine. We thought it might be the other yachts we were expecting, until we recognised the hum of an outboard. A long open boat shot past and several wild looking men smiled and waved. 'I'm glad they smiled,' I said to David, 'because they were waving machetes.'

'Copra workers,' said David. 'Sun-dried atoll kernels give the best oil. They don't get rained on like in the Marquesas.'

We looked at the sky which wrapped around us. Puffy white clouds in serried ranks ran off, Magritte-like, into infinity. 'No rain in this lot,' said David, 'We should go carefully with the water.'

Just before dusk we heard the engine of the copra workers' boat and as it passed there was a thud and scrabbling in the cockpit. We looked out and found dinner, a large blue land crab with finger-crushing pincers, bound with string.

The four of us made short work of it, for we were all beginning to weary of beans and rice. We were even running out of flour.

'We're going to have to make a sortie to the village,' I told the others. 'I take it from the present of the crab that the locals are not unfriendly.'

'The peace offering to lure you ashore,' joked David. He was nearer the truth than he thought.

The village had looked quite important when we saw it from the pass. The red-roofed spire of a church peeped above the tallest palms, and official-looking buildings were grouped around the quay. Now we approached it by the back door, splashing through the shallows, disturbing little sand sharks in our path. We followed a walkway of coral hard-pack so dazzlingly white it hurt our eyes. On either side were familiar signs of the past – abandoned houses and overgrown pathways. But there was none of the mournfulness of the Marquesas. The sun and wind met with no barriers and everything was bathed in brilliance and sparkle.

'Woof! woof!' Our arrival had been noticed. With every further step another dog woke up, and made the most of a rare chance to bark at strangers.

The lived-in part of the village was neat and tidy. Little plywood bungalows and the occasional grand one with glass louvred windows lined the roadway. Women smiled and waved and children laughed and ran before us. They showed us to *Le magasin*, a large empty hall, whose owner lay curled up asleep in the doorway beside her dog. We stepped over her and she struggled to her feet. I looked at the dusty display cabinets and yellowing pictures from Mormon folklore and, without much hope, asked if she sold flour. 'No, but perhaps Monsieur Herman did...' There was another shop.

Like his name, Monsieur Herman's house, garden and shop bore an unmistakable Teutonic imprint. He was a wiry little Austrian, recently retired from the French Foreign Legion. Now he lived with his Tahitian wife and three children, running his shop and tending his mound of imported topsoil (the nearest you can get to a garden on an atoll)

The spick and span shelves of his shop gleamed with the wearingly familiar cans of pilchards and mackerel and processed cheese. No, he had no flour.

'Everyone orders it by the sackful from Papetee. It comes on the ship, with the rice and sugar, at a reduced rate for the islanders.'

We wandered, followed by the giggling children, to the quay, where, we had been told, there was a weather station, *le meteo*. Almost as if he had been expecting us, a short burly man burst out of a building and greeted us warmly. He introduced himself as Tehina, and, although he wore only sport shorts, the size of his watch and girth denoted he was a man of importance. '*Le Directeur*,' he told us, ushering us inside. We were introduced to his assistant, Gerard, a small, lean French-Tahitian. Gerard could speak English, a relic of the days when he was restaurant manager at one of Papeete's top hotels.

There followed an intensive tour of all two rooms of *le meteo*, and a detailed explanation of all that went on, like launching weather balloons and reporting measurements to Papeete. Tehina said nothing about reporting yachts, but I saw by the radio a notepad with the names *Moongazer* and *Matreya* scrawled across it.

The conducted tour continued on, across the road and into Tehina's house where we were introduced to his wife, his mother, her mother, and a string of other female relatives. They plied us with lemonade, made from lemons from Papeete – a special treat. I asked where I could buy flour. Tehina's wife led me to the food cupboard and pointed to a sack. 'Take as much as you want.' she said, and as I murmurred weak protests she began filling up a large bag. She also added bread and cakes and a slab of rice pudding. Probably to her eyes, we looked like famine victims.

Dusk was falling before we could decently disengage ourselves from their hospitality. Tehina shook our hands in turn with a bone-crushing grip and thanked us for coming. 'We are so glad you have visited us. When you anchored away from the village we could only think that you wished to be left alone.'

'Not at all, you must come and see our boats.'

'Thank-you, that will be a pleasure,' Tehina replied. He opened his mouth to say something further, thought about it, and said instead, '*Au revoir*, my friends.'

From then on the pace of life quickened. Our friends on *Spellbinder* and *Contagious* arrived, much to our relief as we were beginning to worry a little. The next day two more yachts arrived, an American and a Canadian, and squeezed themselves into the anchoring spot. The wind slackened to a brisk breeze and I began to relax.

The copra workers (the only youngish men we had seen) dropped by on their way home from work, with presents of crabs and coconuts. They appeared again on Sunday afternoon along with Gerard and some toothless old characters, ukuleles, and a case of beer.

Tehina came the following morning, not to stay, he said, but to invite us to his daughter's birthday party. 'Everyone from the yachts, tonight at six o'clock.'

At five-thirty we assembled on the beach, clad in our mildewed best and bearing fresh-baked offerings. In single file we trooped along by the edge of the lagoon, paddling through the shallows where the vegetation overhung the water. The beach was alive with hundreds of shells of every variety, scurrying from our path on the pincered legs of their occupants, the hermit crabs. The undergrowth rustled with rats and land crabs, and from the water beside us came the odd sinister splash. It was a welcome sight to see the lights of the village hall and even to hear the hum of its generator.

We found forty entrancing little children, washed, scrubbed and bedecked, jumping up and down with excitement. The birthday girl was four and she sat in the seat of honour, clad in a bright new *pareu* and crowned with an exquisite corona of frangipani blossom. Each child came forward with a *lei*, a long necklace of cowrie shells, and hung it round her neck. By the thirtieth *lei* she was wilting under the weight, but she stuck it to the end, buried shoulders to nose in shells.

We took our places at the long trestle tables, surrounded by the children, while mothers waddled around with dishes of food and jugs of orangeade. Tehina sat at a top table with the village dignitaries (the only other men present): the chief, the policeman, the teacher and the generator engineer.

It was much like a birthday party anywhere, except that from the children we heard only laughter. There were no squabbles, shovings, showings-off or tears. Over half the children were siblings or cousins, and the rest would be related in some way. By virtue of being from the same village they would all consider themselves one extended family. There are no Polynesian words for 'Uncle' and 'Aunt'. All adults are 'mother' or 'father.' These children grew up, confined within a five hundred yard strip of coral clinker, and with few material possessions. But they were Fortune's Favourites. From the minute they were born, they were kissed and cuddled by every human they encountered and they all grew up together like puppies in a litter.

After the meal we were entertained by the star dancers. For seven year-olds, they gave a remarkably sophisticated performance of the *tamure*, the notorious hip-waggling dance that so affronted the missionaries they had it banned throughout Polynesia.

To our surprise, at the party's end, Tehina made a special address to 'Our guests from the yachts.' As the children hung *leis* round our necks, Gerard translated: 'The people of the village are very disappointed that none of the yachts have come to the dock. They would like to meet you but you are too far away.' He went on to tell us how welcome we were in the village, and to use the water from the *meteo*'s storage cistern – a generous offer.

We proffered our thanks, bade our farewells and, taking off our best shoes and sandals, filed off into the darkness .

As we padded along, guided by the leader's torchlight, I reflected on how Tehina hoped we would come to the quay, but was too polite to ask us. That was what had been on his mind when we first met. I thought of how we arrived and motored past the quay. The sullen faces were not, as I'd assumed in my Western way, a sign of disapproval. I just wasn't used to seeing adults display disappointment so openly.

There was no way we could now escape being at the quay. One by one, next morning, the yachts made their way up the channel, at what we had calculated (wrongly) was slack water, to an enthusiastic welcoming commitee. From then on we had to get used to living in a goldfish bowl.

The children were the least inhibited, and even in the cabin our every move was followed by a row of large brown eyes peering in the windows. We gave coffee parties, each yacht in turn, for the mothers. They would gaze round the interiors, pat the upholstery and happily settle themselves down for the day.

Tehina planned our days with the verve of a tour guide. He swept us off in his motor boat to see the new pearl shell farms. We saw, dangling in the water, rows of lines festooned with the plate-like shell of the pearl mussel.

'The Japanese come and insert into each shell, a fragment which we hope will grow into a pearl,' Tehina told us. 'It will be several years before we know how successful we are. It is run as a village co-operative, and I am the President.'

'Maybe one day you'll be rich,' said someone, and Tehina laughed.

'Then I will make the authorities build a high school in Takaroa and everyone with older children can come back to the atoll. And all the men who are away working in Tahiti, I would pay them to come back and stay with their families.'

He was being optimistic. It wasn't just money that took the men off. It was the need to have something to do. Warfare and its rituals had long been stamped out but nothing had taken its place. The men were, in a way, redundant warriors. The women continued on as they had done for centuries, now more securely and comfortably, bringing up the children.

Tehina took us to the fish traps when the mackerel were running in from the sea. We ladled basketfuls into his boat – enough for several meals for everyone in the village, and us. One old woman, who was helping to string the fish together into bundles, said to me, in English, 'Here, God looks after us. In Papeete, you no work, you no eat. Here you no work, but still you eat.'

Darkness brought no respite from village activities. Each evening a group wandered down with ukuleles, followed by families trailing bedrolls, children and dogs. As the singing got under way they bedded down the children and crawled in beside them . By ten-thirty the quay was like a refugee station, covered with bundles of bodies and sleeping dogs.

In keeping with his role of chief organiser, Tehina laid

on some 'special entertainment' one night. 'American movies', to be shown in the Mormon hall. It was a vast building, built in more optimistic days, and now in dire need of repair. Apart from the projectionist, his family and attendant relatives, we from the yachts were the only audience. We sat on the eight wooden seats that had been set out, while the projectionist's entourage snugged themselves down among bedding on the floor. I had the feeling even then that they knew something we didn't.

The film was M.G.M's version of the *Battle of Thermopylae* dubbed in French, an epic four-hour yawn. For the final hour the scratchy soundtrack competed unsuccessfully with loud blissful snores from the projectionist's family.

When it ground to its interminable end we we rose stiffly, and as we turned, saw to our horror, the projectionist loading another film. 'Yes,' he beamed, 'There is another.'

Fortunately it woke us up with a laugh, not Elstree Studio's original intention when it was made in 1933. The so-English expedition to darkest Africa to find the man-eating giant albino gorilla had our attention immediately, particularly as the first ten minutes of film had been spliced on upside down.

One morning shortly after we arrived we looked from our bunks to see a handful of people loitering on the quay. 'Odd,' I said, nudging David. 'They're all carrying radios or cassette players.'

David groaned. 'The word must be out. I managed to fix Gerard's yesterday.' He looked through the window at the hopefuls who had now formed a definite queue to Moongazer. 'Lost causes,' he sighed. 'I can tell from here. They've all been opened up before and mangled with scissors and sticking plaster.'

He won rapid promotion the following morning when

the line was elbowed aside by none other than the generator engineer. Both dynamos, only three months old, had broken down. Next on the list were the huge outboard motors of the copra boats. 'Most of the trouble,' David told us, 'stems from misuse and lack of maintenance. Spare parts are no problem. There's a graveyard of outboards behind the boatshed. When the engine packs up, they order a new outboard, and bang goes all the copra money.'

For over a week David went off to work with his lunch box and his tool bag. He returned at the end of each day, bearing the fruits of his labours – literally (usually a large green paw-paw) and garlanded like a hero with *leis* round his neck.

Two weeks flashed past and the renewal date for our cruising permit loomed nearer. We thought of the other atolls on our route, and of the idea of a few days to ourselves. We all decided that the yachts should leave together, which would give Tehina an occasion for organising a grand farewell.

He pulled out all the stops – a party on the quay, open to all. We barbecued fish, sang to ukuleles, danced 'rock and roll' to Tehina's loudspeakers, and submitted to more 'movies'. This time Tehina operated the projector using the wall of the shed as a screen. The films were French, in black and white with incomprehensible plots, made more so in that we saw only the first half of one, about fighting in Malaya in 1870, spliced straight into the second half of the other, about a loony mass murderer in 1930s Paris. The audience sat among their bedding, attentive throughout. I wondered at the notions they must have of life in the West.

Tehina rounded off the evening with a long speech of farewell, translated by Gerard. He hoped we would come back again some day, but most of all he hoped we would never forget the people of Takaroa. We would go back to our countries and our friends and we should tell them about our stay here. The people of Takaroa wanted the rest of the world to know about them.

We smiled and nodded and said yes, with a feeling that these days of honest welcome were numbered for the Takaroans. I knew that a little box of electronics was about to bring press-button navigation to the many. In the past ten years the average number of yachts stopping each year at Takaroa had risen from eight to around twenty-five. The development of satellite navigation would almost certainly bring more yachts to Takaroa. I hoped it wouldn't also bring disenchantment.

The yachts left next morning, one by one, waved off by a solemn little crowd of early risers. We sailed out into a heavy, running sea and went our separate ways, soon lost to each other in the troughs of the swells. Three of us were heading for Apataki, one of a group of atolls to the south west. If all went well, it would show up on the horizon next morning.

30

Raw Edges Of Paradise

The dawn had come with pearl-grey clouds, veiling our stars. It was now mid-morning and David had been three times up the mast, standing on the spreaders to look for our atoll. 'Nothing but grey sea,' he reported. 'No sign even of the other yachts.' We had lost sight of their lights during the night. We rolled along before a moderate wind, holding the course which should have taken us by now within sight of Apataki, or even the other atolls in the group.

'Either we have less current with us than we estimated, or we've been swept sideways,' I said to David as he measured out our logged distance once more on the chart. 'And what do we do if nothing shows up by nightfall,' I continued, honing my instinct for worry. 'Do we turn north or south?'

I looked at the chart. Each of the atolls had long stretches of totally submerged reef. The pilot book referred to them as being: 'in calm weather, even dangerous by day, as then there are no breakers and the current is always strong.' The impassive measured prose had a chilling ring to it. My imagination buzzed with disaster scenarios and the memory of all the wreck tales I had read. The noise of the impact always seemed the most horrifying part; rending, tearing, crashing. I wondered how *Moongazer*'s concrete hull would sound. David broke in on my imaginings.

'The sun's bound to come out soon,' he said brightly, looking at the leaden sky. 'Then we'll have at least a position line.' I envied his optimism, and wished it were more infectious.

We sat in the cockpit eating bread, canned butter and sardines. I would have given a great deal for a tomato, a slice of cucumber, a lettuce leaf even. I gazed into the distance in a vegetable reverie. After a few seconds I realised I was looking at a long grey ribbon of palms not more than two miles off. Surprise! Relief! Joy! Immediately tempered by thoughts of the pass into the lagoon and where to anchor. The village was at the southern end of the atoll, conveniently at the mouth of a pass, as at Takaroa. 'We should make it before darkness,' said David. 'Assuming this *is* Apataki.' I made a strong and silent prayer.

All through the afternoon we ran alongside a broken and uneven fringe of green. Sometimes the palms gave way to little tufts of bushes; sometimes even the tufts disappeared. But always there was a continuous line of surf where the ocean spilled up onto the reef.

Night follows sunset swiftly in the tropics. The eastern sky was already darkening and still there seemed no break in the unremitting line of foam. Then in the last moments of daylight a gap suddenly opened up and we could see the pass and the quay, empty beside flat water. We tied up, unnoticed, except for a few curious but silent dogs. The village had obviously retired for the night, to our relief. All that we required of life at that moment was a quiet drink, supper and bed.

After the intensity of community living at Takaroa, we were ready for a few days to ourselves. We stole away early in the morning into the lagoon, through one of several small channels in the inner reef, marked by rusting, drunken-looking posts. For twelve miles we motored carefully into a light wind and a rising sun. The lagoon was iridescent with the changing colours of the sky. According to the chart, the coral in this part of the lagoon was well below the two metres we needed to clear the keel. With each hour the climbing sun shone more directly down through the crystal water. By the time we reached the the coral and white sand shallows of the eastern shore we could pick the exact coral-free spot to drop the anchor. The water, sheltered by the tall palms on the *motu* was like glass. *Moongazer* looked ethereally suspended, more like a balloon in the air than a boat in water. On the other side of the motu we could hear the dull roar of the ocean. We were snug in an oasis of crystal beauty.

Here at last was my dream picture of travel brochure Paradise, but much more searing to the senses than any photograph. No ink can reproduce the radiance of cobalt in the distance, the nearer glow of burnished jade and emerald; the white hot slash of sand on the *motu* or the velvet-rich shadows and glossy brilliance of its greenery. There is that same quality of colour that glows from the great windows of the Gothic cathedrals and with the same breathtaking power.

For several days we played, snorkelling and swimming – nature's naked children. The land, sea and air for miles around belonged only to ourselves. Or so we thought.

The first signs of an interloper in paradise came from the garbage bin.

'Been shredding up silver foil for something?' I accused.

'Me? No?' said David sounding genuine for once.

'Then we've got company – with sharp teeth!'

'What! A mouse? A rat?'

'Or a giant cockroach,' I added unhelpfully.

We looked at each other. We had heard some nasty rodent stories. Shipboard rats were difficult to catch, had teeth like lasers and were even more desperate for a tasty meal than we were.

'We can't poison it and have it crawl into a corner and die,' said David. 'So without a trap, we have a problem.'

I fell asleep that night, reflecting that our toes presented the only fresh, uncanned protein on the boat.

Next day we found more evidence that ratty, for the moment, was seeking other sources – with astounding determination. David, delving in the deepest bowels of a distant locker for some nuts and bolts, brought out a plastic carton full of washers. The edge of the lid had been gnawed through. 'That carton, if you remember,' he said, 'used to hold egg powder – three years ago.'

I began to worry about our other plastic containers – cooking oil, shampoo, lubricating and fuel oils. They would make an interesting cocktail in the bilge. We were under a determined attack from an enemy within, and we seemed to be weaponless.

We sat in the cockpit, gloomily considering our plight. 'Maybe you should wait for it tonight and zap it when it pokes its head out,' I suggested.

David was considering his reply when a sail hove into view on the lagoon horizon to the north – followed by another. They were *Spellbinder* and *Contagious*. We learned later they had been only miles from us the previous day and had gone into the lagoon through the northern pass. As they moved nearer it became evident they weren't stopping. Kathy on *Spellbinder* shouted, 'We're going on to the village, while the sun's still high. We're both out of flour and sugar. See you there.'

'You don't have a rat trap, by any chance?' I shouted back. *Spellbinder* stopped, circled, and came back. Kathy tossed over a package. 'You're in luck. We were given it as a joke leaving present.'

That evening David set the trap near the rubbish bin and

we retired to the cockpit to eat our supper of 'crusty garbanzo casserole'. I was making coffee about ten minutes later when I noticed the trap. 'For God's sake, David,' I said. 'The idea of a trap is that you bait it with something.'

He shot into the cabin. 'I did! The cunning bastard! He's picked off the cheese!'

We had heard tales of smart rats who'd sussed out traps. Until now we'd thought them apocryphal. 'We'll try again, maybe he'll get careless,' said David. 'He's certainly desperate if he eats this stuff.'

'Well we eat it.'

'That's what I mean.'

The cheese came out of a tin, looking and tasting like high density polythene, but the crews of the galleons would have mutinied for it.

Several hours later I was in bed, slowly succumbing to sleep, when a whip-like crack brought me bolt upright. It was followed immediately by heart-tearing screams. David shook off my stricken grip and leapt out of bed to deliver the *coup de grace*. When finally I opened my eyes and took my fingers out of my ears, I heard him say: 'bopped it over the head with a winch handle. A big fellow, bright looking. Extra titbit for the sharks.'

'Ugh! Poor old ratty. I suppose he'd had enough of coconuts,' I said in a wave of remorse. 'What a pity he couldn't have come for his food like a cat. We could've kept him as a pet.' As a child I'd had a white rat called Wuffles. David threw me one of his looks.

We weren't natural hunters or fishermen, but lately we seemed to be doing a lot of killing. Every day we speared fish and lobsters for dinner, poisoned shellfish and hermit crabs for their shells, and swatted hundreds of flies and mosquitoes for being a nuisance.

'The raw edges of paradise,' I said, still a little

unnerved by ratty's screams. 'Maybe it's time to join the others back at the village.'

'O.K.,' said David settling down to sleep again. 'But this time we let another yacht have the pleasure of being next to the quay – and adventurous rats.'

When we arrived at the quay we found several yachts already tied up, so we happily berthed on the outside, next to *Spellbinder*.

Life was quiet at Apataki. Most of the younger adults were away, cutting copra on a neighbouring atoll. There was no Tehina to take charge of the rest and only the more curious adults hung shyly around the quay. The children, never shy, laughed and giggled and showed off their diving aerobatics by leaping off the roof of the copra shed into the pass.

The pass was fringed with the most prolific and colourful coral heads we had yet seen and we spent our first afternoons on snorkelling expeditions. We were the privileged viewers of an exquisite underwater garden and wildlife park, a stunning contrast to the sterilty of the surface land. They both shared the same foundation – a limey build-up of millions of years' worth of coral skeletons around the crown of an ancient and slowly subsiding volcano. When the delicate balancing act between the rate of subsidence and the growth of build-up keeps the living coral within reach of warmth and light (up to about fifty metres below the surface) the reef lives. It provides a home for thousands of colonies of corals, plants, marine animals, insects and fish, all existing in a fragile symbiotic interdependence.

We would swim slowly along the surface, gazing down through our masks into grottoes and forests of corals of every configuration and texture, with pertly descriptive names: staghorn, brain, lettuce, pipe, mushroom, star, vase... Schools of rainbow-coloured fish paraded across their territories, ignoring us. They, too, looked like creations of an artist's fancy with appropriate names like: Sergeant-major fish, angelfish, butterfly fish, triggerfish, parrotfish, trumpetfish.... We took deep breaths and dived down to peer among the bejewelled coral crannies. There lived the masters of disguise, the clam shells and cowries, and lurking solitary fish, like the big grumpy groupers which eyed us suspiciously from the shadows.

Then, on the third day we saw some unusual, mean-looking sharks, fat and silvery with pointed snouts. They had come in from the ocean and they circled around, unafraid of us. That was the signal to exit, 'calmly', as it says in the books. I was sure the tell-tale thudding of my heart would be travelling underwater like a sonar sounding. Four of us arrived simultaneously at the dinghy and heaved ourselves in at the first go. Normally it took me several hauls to get myself over the gunwhales. I often just rested with my legs dangling in the water. Not this time. The sharks stayed around the pass and effectively put an end to our snorkelling, even in the lagoon.

SHARK AND REMORA

From the little huddle of poker-playing ladies who gathered daily in the shade of the copra shed we learned that the copra boat was expected soon and it would be bringing supplies for the islanders.

'And for the shop?' I asked

'Oh yes, of course.'

'Onions?'

'Well, perhaps, if you are lucky.'

So we decided to wait for the copra boat.

We were all working on our boats one morning when we noticed a yacht approaching from the sea.

'Coming in from an odd direction,' I said. 'Must have overshot. Heavens! It's Ned. Remember Ned, in Cabo San Lucas.'

No one there would have forgotten him, especially his arrival from California. He had only just reached the anchorage at Cabo San Lucas and was unhooking the anchor when to everyone's entertainment, his female crew was seen to launch the dinghy, throw a couple of bags into it, follow them and row purposefully towards the shore.

We had first met him, or rather heard him, on a bus in San Diego, where he was complaining, even then, about the difficulty of keeping crew. He looked cheerful and pleasant, but pebble-lens glasses and a booming voice always made me feel he was addressing a huge crowd behind me. He found it difficult to establish the one thing he wanted most – intimacy.

When we left Cabo he was still searching for female crew, and we never expected to see him again. So when he sailed into our lives again we all looked up attentively and noted the blonde young lady on the bow. She threw us lines as they came alongside, and as they were tying up I waved to Ned.

'Where've you come from?' I asked.

'Ahe' (An atoll about ninety miles north of Takaroa.)

'How was it?'

'Well we didn't stop. Funny thing, I couldn't find the pass. Went all the way round – twice. Sure beat me. It was getting dark so I just laid course for Rangiroa instead.'

As he stopped to draw breath, I cut in lightheartedly, assuming he'd changed his mind. 'Ha! Ha! You *do* know this isn't Rangiroa?'

Ned and his crew stopped in their tracks and stared at me. 'What d'you mean, ''This isn't Rangiroa''?' he asked slowly.

'Well... it's Apataki.'

'APATAKI!' they shrieked in unison.

'My God! Where's Apataki?' The girl looked at me in stark disbelief. 'Oh come on,' she pleaded, 'You're kidding us!'

I shook my head. A stricken look spread across her face.

Ned gave a shrug and a thin, forced laugh. 'Well, what the hell, it's good to be tied up somewhere,' he said and carried on tying up the lines.

There followed a stunned silence among the yachties, as the implications of his mistake sank in. Whispers and muffled giggles came from the locals on the quay. Everyone had been listening. Ned and his crew had come through the most providential deliverance and they didn't even know it.

The girl, who introduced herself as Candice, brought out the chart and we pointed to Apataki. 'Good God!' she breathed, and, clutching a satchel, began climbing over the yachts to the quay. She plonked down on the first bollard, lit up a cigarette and stared blankly across the lagoon.

'Still having crew problems,' observed David.

We went over Ned's navigation with him and worked out what happened. His initial landfall was ninety miles too far south. What he expected to be Manihi and Ahe, were actually the atolls of Takaroa and Takapoto. His navigation had been sloppy rather than wrong, too thick a pencil, adjusting his dead reckoning to where he would like to be each day, and making too many assumptions.

The course he set for Rangiroa that night miraculously took him between reefs of Apataki and its neighbour Aruatua. He sailed unwittingly down the slot, headed for the hidden fangs of the huge submerged reef of Kaukura. They were saved only by the fortuitous timing of daybreak. Ned, from the mast top spotted the thin line of palms that marked the southern end of Apataki. Rangiroa, he assumed, and headed for it, ignoring the fact that the compass bearing didn't agree with the chart. 'I just thought it wasn't working right,' he told us.

The story of Ned's arrival in Apataki spread and entered the cruising folklore of that year. He became known as Ned the Navigator. Several years later we heard of him in the Western Pacific. By then he'd bounced over a few reefs and was known to the cruising folk there as Ned, the Reef Hopper. His boat was a handsome sturdy double-ender, built by himself, possibly with a view to bouncing over a few reefs. But it was with the name that he showed uncharacteristic foresight. He had called it *Tangaroa*, after a venerated Polynesian God.

The arrival of the copra boat was heralded by much bustle on the quay. Families sat, surrounded by their dogs, excited and expectant. Around noon the little boat hove into sight, listing heavily to port and bursting with humanity. Immediately it docked a stream of villagers jammed the gangplank, making, it turned out, for the shop on board. We saw them return ashore, happily clutching such treats as packaged frozen chicken, or wrinkled-looking apples, at prices we knew would be far above our budget. Throughout the afternoon burly crewmen, glistening with sweat, unloaded supplies – building materials, drums of paraffin, boxes and sacks of provisions. The quay became, to our eyes, a chaotic jumble of sacks and boxes, but everyone seemed to know what belonged to whom and one by one each family claimed their basic staples of flour, sugar, and rice and trundled off, some with laden wheelbarrows. Only the shopkeeper was left to sort out the remaining boxes and roll away the fuel drums. I hailed him.

'Onions?'

'Not this time – but maybe on the next boat.'

At the onset of darkness the quay was suddenly flooded with light from the boat's searchlights. The business of loading copra was enacted before us like a play, accompanied by an odour that would have driven most audiences away. The sour, sickly smell of rancid coconut meat is for me the most evocative smell of the tropics. It hangs permanently in the air around docks, sheds and ships long after the copra sacks have gone. At close quarters to even one sack the odour swells to a powerful stench.

About sixty sacks were lugged across the quay to the ship and stuffed into every corner of the deck, including the stern which was also the passenger 'accommodation'. During the loading the passengers sat around the quay, chatting, laughing, eating, some even singing. I watched as an enormous Polynesian mother washed her six small children at the cistern tap and changed their clothes while their spindly little Chinese father cooked supper over a camping stove. A sharp toot from the boat's horn sent everyone piling back on board to the stern deck. There they clambered among the smelly, crawling sacks and settled themselves down for the night. With another few toots the scene was plunged into darkness, leaving only the feeble glow from the the navigation lights. To shouts of farewell and the slow thunk of marine diesel, the boat pulled away from the quay, turned sharply in the pass and, still listing heavily, chugged off into the night. The thick smell of copra floated back on the air, and with it, above the engine throb, the strains of singing.

Not being able to get onions hastened the departure of the yachts for Tahiti. Apart from coconuts (which we were all heartily sick of by now) onions had been our last remaining item of fresh food. They had been crisp and sweet, New Zealand ones, bought at Maurice's in Taiohae Bay. For most of us, our last normal shopping had been in Mexico, six months previously. Signs of ill-nourishment were beginning to show. Cuts and scratches infected easily and were slow to heal. Some yachtfolk complained of headaches and tiredness, split nails and dull hair. All of us had lost weight, to the extent of becoming skinny. Some of this was no doubt due to the stress of living precariously, through months of uneasy days and nights on the tenuous links of an anchor chain. It seemed ironical to think that here, in the ultimate antidote to high-tech living, we were all suffering from the effects of stress and poor diet.

We had ample quantities of nourishing, processed food and drinks, but it was fresh stuff that we craved. The obsession intruded into every conversation. 'My first meal in Papeete' became a favourite game. Paradise was being forsaken for the supermarket.

As we bustled around our yachts next morning, preparing them for sea, we heard through the 'ham' radio on *Spellbinder* that a yacht from San Francisco had gone up on the reef at Ahe, the atoll that Ned had missed. It had happened around seven a.m., and both crew had been asleep below. Ahe had already claimed two other yachts that season.

The news sent a chill through the yachtfolk. We re-checked our charts and calculations and carefully timed our departures. Late enough for the sun to have climbed in the sky but early enough to clear the neighbouring atolls before darkness. After that it was a clear two-day run to Tahiti.

But *Moongazer* was not quite through with paradise. We wanted a last look in on our way to the supermarket. Among a group of atolls to the south-east was 'a special place.' Someone had told us, marking our chart with an X on the north-west corner of Tepuka. 'It doesn't look it, but Baie Otaho is a break in the reef between two motus and forms the perfect anchorage. A family lives there and loves having yachts. The rest of the atoll is uninhabited. It's the nearest you'll get to heaven.'

It would have seemed churlish to pass it by.

31

One Atoll, One Family

Tepuka hid its secret well. We had taken the sails down and were motoring in for a closer look. Not too close, I thought, the reef could be just ahead. I eased the controls into neutral and we began to lose way, wallowing in the swell.

'For God's sake!' came a bellow from above. I'd forgotten David was aloft. Clinging to the cross trees, he was rolling with the mast like a bob on the end of a pendulum. 'Get going – the reef's miles off!'

Inured to exaggerated claims, I crept on cautiously until the details of the *motus* started to make sense. 'O.K. I can see it all now,' came the word from above. 'The entrance is clear. Just keep going, it'll get shallow in a minute.'

Quite suddenly, the deep ultamarine of the ocean changed to mottled green. We went through the gap in the reef and the mottled green washed out into white sunlit sand, seen through five metres of clear water.

It was, as we'd been promised, a perfect anchorage, a pool of jade between two islets, sheltered from the atoll's lagoon by a coral shoal. What I didn't expect was the rusting little coaster that lay moored in the middle. Her crew seemed to be ashore. On the beach we could see a ship's boat drawn up beside two local boats, and from the shacks in the palm grove we could hear voices and laughter.

'It'll soon be dark,' said David. 'They'll be eating. Maybe we should leave going ashore till to-morrow.' So, forgetting already the lesson of Takaroa, we stayed on board and dined on a spiced-up concoction of canned vegetables. If I had foreseen our dinner menu for the next few weeks I'd have gone gourmet and tipped in a can of corned beef.

Next morning I awoke to sunlight streaming through the window. '*Bonjour*,' I heard David say in the cockpit. 'Come aboard.'

'*Merci*,' replied a husky female voice. It continued in Polynesian French: 'I've brought some coconuts, green ones for drinking.'

I rolled out of my bunk, stopped long enough to rummage for a respectable sun top, and got to the cockpit at about the same time as a lusty Polynesian lass, clad in bra and shorts. She held out her hand. 'My name is Laiza, you must come and meet my family. Why did you not come last night?'

'We thought you had company,' replied David. 'We didn't want to intrude.' Laiza looked puzzled. He added quickly 'We were very tired.' She nodded in acknowledgement. That was something she could understand.

Ashore, everyone was busy stringing fish into bundles, ready for the coaster to take back to Tahiti. Laiza led us over and they all looked up and smiled expectantly.

'Maman.' said Laiza, introducing a short stocky lady with dark wavy hair drawn into two long plaits. She smiled shyly, showing a row of pearl-white teeth, normally only seen in younger folk. Behind her, beaming from beneath a tousled shock of sun-bleached hair, stood a powerfully built young man. This was Taupiri, her son, her pride and joy.

A small, thin girl beside him gave us a brief, but guarded smile. Laiza ignored her and led us on, past two of the ship's crewmen, to a figure sitting comfortably in the shadows on the only chair I could see. He was a genial-looking Chinese gentleman in a tailored shirt and shorts. 'This is Albert, the captain. He has been very kind to us,' said Laiza. Albert smiled modestly and bowed politely. 'His family have a fish stall in the market at Papeete and he buys all the fish we can catch,' Laiza continued. 'He has helped us with outboard motors and materials for the fish traps. This time he brought a generator from Papeete. And delicious peaches. I must give you some.'

She moved us on to one of the huts. Like the others, it was a decrepit affair of warped and peeling hardboard with gaps where panels had given up the unequal struggle to cling to the framing. It was roofed with rusty corrugated iron and at the corners stood two even rustier steel drums to catch the rainwater.

'Poppa is in here,' Laiza explained as she pushed open the rickety door. 'He has been sick for a long time but today he goes with the ship to Arutua, where his brothers live and where there is a doctor.'

On an iron-framed bed lay a very large man reading a magazine. He mustered a weak wave and a smile. A buxom girl and a lean young man were packing a box on the other bed. They smiled and waved too. When we were outside Laiza told us, 'That's my sister Valentina, she's seventeen – a year older than me, and Ramon, her fiancee. They have terrible fights. I'm glad she's going with Poppa to Arutua. We'll get some peace'.

It was almost dark before the fish were loaded and Albert nosed the rust-streaked *Raroa Nui* through the pass. We all stood at the water's edge waving to Poppa and Valentina until they were swallowed by the distance and the darkness.

There was a subdued quiet for a while as preparations for the evening meal got under way. By the light of a pressure lantern, Maman fried fish after fish over a propane burner. The fish were from the lagoon, about hand-size, some filleted, some split flat, and some whole with bulging eyes. Ramon tended the bread oven, a fifty gallon steel drum on a fire of coconut husks. As we gathered around the long rough trestle table conversation resumed its normal noisy level – a mixture of Tuamotan grunts and lilting French. It was school French, like ours, so we understood each other perfectly.

Before us were dishes heaped with fish, rice and coconut bread, the basic and, we were to discover, the never-varying components of this and every meal. Taupiri, at a signal from Maman, shut his eyes tightly and uttered a brief grace. That over, everyone attacked the plates with gusto as if fish and coconuts were a rare treat. Laiza had set down knives and forks, but only for our benefit. After some self-conscious usage we fell into line and abandoned them for fingers and scoops of bread. Around our feet was a scrabble of dogs, cats, chickens and piglets, fighting it out for survival. The smartest dogs could catch fish skeletons in mid-air and swallow them, heads, tails, the lot, in one gulp. The flies were one jump ahead of the game and took their mouthfuls from the plates, even before we did.

We rounded off the meal with the remaining mainstays of the food chest – Nescafe and condensed milk. Laiza brought out her guitar, and Ramon turned the pressure lantern to a lower, softer light. Maman whispered in my ear, 'Laiza went to school in Papeete, and she learned many Tahitian songs. And...' Maman paused and said with pride, 'She was the champion for boxing and karate.' I didn't doubt it for a minute.

The others joined in as Laiza picked chords and strummed happily. Taupiri looked especially relaxed, his arm round his *vahine*. I had been told her name was Frieda, but nothing more. She had a frightened furtive air and said very little. Around her, everyone sang and cracked jokes, late into the night. The departure of Poppa and Valentina was already a distant memory.

Our days began to fall into a pattern. Ramon, the 'engineer' of the family, had the job of setting up the generator and he and David spent many hours trying to breathe life into it. They worked also with Taupiri on the fish traps in the shallow pass into the lagoon. The traps were a maze of submerged coral walls built by Taupiri's grandfather. Now they were repaired or extended with wire netting and bamboo stakes and every day they needed tending. This was where the fish for Albert were caught; mackerel-type fish which swam in from the ocean and became trapped in the man-made pools.

Sometimes I helped with the fish traps; other times I worked with the women, baking bread and preparing the meals. What I had really hoped to do was to draw and paint, but such a solitary pursuit would have been misunderstood and I lacked the singlemindedness for that not to bother me.

Every day we swam in the lagoon with Taupiri while he speared reef fish for the evening meal. Up until now we had been wary of eating reef fish because of the danger of ciguatera poisoning. This is a poison which, apparently harmless to the fish, builds up in its flesh as the result of eating toxic algae. It is passed on up the food chain to the larger carnivores, and eventually to humans where it attacks the nervous system with distressing symptoms. There is no known antidote to the poison and we had heard tales of horrible deaths. It is known in all coral waters around the world but appears and disappears indiscriminately. Sometimes the fish on one side of a reef are poisonous while those on the other are safe to eat, and there is no way of knowing until they are eaten. The books advise: 'seek local knowledge.'

Safe in the hands of Taupiri's 'local knowledge,' we tucked into our platefuls of fish each night. 'How is it you know which fish are safe?' I asked him, to my immediate regret.

He shrugged. 'I don't. Not until we have eaten them. Then if they have the poison we get sick and have headaches. But it soon passes.' He burst into a hearty laugh at the look on my face. After that we surreptitiously picked out only the tiniest fish from the serving plates.

When Taupiri went hunting he didn't swim after the fish, but sat on the bottom until something swam past his gun. His activities usually attracted a few black-finned sharks which he totally ignored. Strangely, I felt safer swimming beside him. I could imagine him taking on a shark with his bare hands.

I wasn't far wrong. One day we saw him in action in the fish trap. Two reef sharks, about five feet long, had broken in and were working their way through the fish. With a mask in one hand and a steel rod sharpened to a point in the other, Taupiri jumped into the chest-high water. He bent down and looked through the mask for a few minutes at the sharks. They sensed immediately that an enemy had arrived. They left the fish alone and began to swim nervously round the trap perimeter, thrashing their tails. Taupiri singled one out and slowly began to stalk him with the spear. The other shark, to my surprise, cowered motionless in a corner. I saw Taupiri lunge. There was a great scuffle and thrashing and then he surfaced, grinning broadly, with a writhing shark on the end of his spear. He had aimed right between the eyes. 'The only way to kill a shark,' he said. Then he slid back into the water and finished off the other.

He took home the heads and after careful cutting and much scraping he presented me with two razor-toothed jawbones. It was a generous gesture. Albert would have been only too willing to buy them for the tourist stalls in Papeete. We added them to our growing cargo of little treasures that friends had given us, all worth a modest rip-off in the market but priceless to us.

Soon it was time for Albert to return. 'I would like to have some lobsters for him to take to Papeete,' Taupiri told us one evening. He looked up at the sky. 'No moon tonight, light wind, this is a good night to hunt them. You are coming?'

After the evening meal we helped slide the long wooden skiff into the water and loaded it with two heavy batteries, long cables and two sealed-beam spotlights. David chucked in our snorkelling gear. 'What about sharks?' I voiced. 'I thought you said we should never swim at night.'

'I meant in the ocean. The lagoon is different. You saw how easily the reef sharks are frightened.'

'Maman's coming to handle the boat,' I said. 'I think I'll stay with her and keep her company.'

Taupiri started up the outboard and headed not for the lagoon but for the pass in the reef. I looked at David. 'You know where he's going?'

'To the drop-off, it would seem,' he replied, a twinkle of excitement in his eyes.

The drop-off is where the outer rim of the atoll rises from the deep and where the fish and coral are at their most exotic. On the weather side of the atoll the breaking swell makes swimming impossible, but here in the lee, the swell was much less. We could see, as we sped through the darkness, the thin white line a few hundred yards beside us, where the ocean met the outer reef with only a gentle sigh.

Taupiri cut the throttle. 'Here!' he said, pointing to blackness. Maman took a small paddle and sat on the bow, paddling first on one side and then the other, keeping the boat in position as it rose and fell with the swell. When the men were ready she laid down the paddle and said, 'First, a prayer.' So, under a star-studded sky, we knelt and bowed our heads. Maman incanted a lengthy piece in Tuamotan. I'd never seen them take anything so seriously before. Silently I slipped in a prayer of my own.

The men slid into the black water, each with a speargun in one hand and spotlight in the other. The reef lit up like a giant aquarium, glowing pinks and purples. I saw a vertical wall of grottos and canyons, faced with fronds and fans of waving corals. A glorious pageant of coloured fish swam to and fro, ignoring David and Taupiri. They worked along the reef face, diving among the huge fans of gorgonian coral and peering into the teeming holes and crevices.

Maman sat on the bow, cross-legged, working her little paddle, one side and then the other. With skill she kept the boat nose-to the reef and moving with the divers without tugging on the the light cables. Outside the perimeter of the searchlights' beam, was inky blackness – the lurking place of large predators. I curbed my imagination and turned my attention to Maman.

She was telling me of her early days on the atoll, when the children were small and they had no outboards and generators. Every day she used to work the fish traps with Poppa, paddling to and fro in their little canoe. The acquisition of a small outboard motor enabled them to take their fish to Aratua, thirty miles away. They would bed the children down in the open boat and set off at night to avoid the heat of the sun. I thought about the big seas and the likely state of the outboard motor. Whoever she said those prayers to, they were definitely on her side.

Every so often, while she was speaking, there was a thunk as a lobster landed in the boat. They were of a kind I hadn't seen before. Not the usual pincer-less Pacific spiny variety but one with a flat rectangular carapace: 'bug-eyed' lobster, I heard it called later.

Maman, still cross-legged on the bow, paddling and sensing every movement of the boat, continued with her tale. In the early days Poppa used to work so hard but now he did nothing but lie in bed. The doctor in Aratua could find nothing physically wrong. She said it without rancour and just a touch of sadness. Then she looked at me and brightened. '*Moi, j'aime le travail.*'

Just as well, I thought. These women dwellers in the wilderness seemed all to have a taste for unremitting toil. The ones I had met were not adventurous, romantic figures, but solid down-to-earth types who get through mounds of work wherever they are.

The bottom of the boat was becoming alive with crawling lobsters. Spiny legs were striking out in our direction. Maman gazed steadily ahead at the thin white line of surf. Albert, she told me, had brought a big improvement into their lives. They had a ready market for the fish, and he brought things which made life much easier. He took the fish as credit and everyone was happy with the arrangement. But the best of all, she confided in me, her eyes brimming with pleasure, was that Albert was Laiza's fiancee. They were to be married in August.

'Marriage' is a word used loosely by the Polynesians, but not, I knew, by the Chinese. It sounded as if Albert came from a prosperous and established family who might take a less enthusiastic view of the union than Maman. However, I gave her my good wishes.

By now the spiny legs were searching out my toes, and I was squatting uncomfortably on the thwarts. I wished the men would come back. They had been in the water over an hour, more than enough time I thought, to give a tiger shark ideas for dinner.

Eventually Taupiri appeared at the side of the boat and heaved himself in, followed by David. They surveyed the catch. 'It's O.K.,' said Taupiri, obviously having hoped for more.

'A bit small, aren't they?' I ventured.

'But those are the best eating,' replied Taupiri.

I tried another tack. 'Why do you come so far from your bay to find them?' I asked.

Taupiri laughed. 'Because they know they are being hunted and they move farther away from me.' Then he added with a shrug, because he knew what I was too polite to say: 'Besides, there is plenty of reef left and only me to hunt on it.'

I didn't ask how long it had taken to 'fish out' the reef within a mile around his house.

The return of the *Raroa Nui* was greeted with excitement, but Albert had come only for a few hours before he went up to Arutua. 'I'll be back the next day. You can come with me if you like,' he said to us, in passable English. 'We leave at three in the morning.'

We just made it. The *Raroa Nui* was already slipping her mooring when we entered the wheelhouse. Albert greeted us and so, to our surprise, did Laiza, tucked up in his bunk, reading comics.

Once clear of the reef, he glanced at the radar, measured across the chart with a cigarette packet, and set the autopilot. Then he relaxed and leaned back on the bunk beside Laiza. Two powerful brown arms crept round his middle and joined in a handclasp. Albert offered no encouragement, neither did he desist. He merely smiled happily and picked up a magazine.

Out from the shelter of the atoll the *Raroa Nui* began to roll. Laiza clung on more tightly and I began to fear for Albert's ribs. I had seen those arms wield a machete and split a coconut husk at the first swoop. Just one of them could reach over the stern of the skiff and tilt up a 50h.p. outboard.

I wedged myself across the chart table and dozed. A few hours after daybreak we closed with Aratua and headed for the pass on the weather side. A heavy swell was breaking just off the entrance but Albert carried on, hand steering his ship as it surfed down the breakers. A school of porpoises streaked alongside, leaping and spinning into the air. In a boat that wasn't ours, we could share their exhilaration. Albert enjoyed it too, even though he had done it many times. Laiza looked terrified.

Arutua was a bustling lively place. Because it had a secondary school, the population was more balanced. Laiza's uncles were important persons – with large wristwatches and large middles, and they lived in European-type houses with glass louvred windows. In their yard, dozens of women surrounded by dogs and children, were stringing and packing fish. For several hours, boats ferried the bundles out to the ship to be packed in the melting ice in the hold. There was no pause in the operation because in the tropics mackerel-type fish develop a poison in their tissues after death if left in the warm air for any time. This scombrotoxin is different from the toxins resulting from spoilage. It develops earlier and displays no outward signs.

The lagoon was a network of fish traps, and I wondered how long it could sustain such large catches every couple of weeks. Albert made no secret of why he came to the Tuamotus. As he so disarmingly said, 'because around Tahiti the fish are now so few and so small.' This only seemed to make the Tuamotuans feel one-up on the Tahitians.

By noon the loading was over and we were on our way to the next fish stop, an atoll which had no deep water pass through its reef. We lay off, rolling heavily while a flotilla of little boats dangerously laden with fish came labouring out to us. The swell made loading difficult, but the genial Albert had a quip for everyone. Then one man came with no fish, but with something serious on his mind. When he'd gone Albert told us 'An empty boat has been found. It should have held a father and his two sons. They have asked us to keep a lookout.' He gave a shrug of hopelessness.

We headed off, into a beam sea, lurching and rolling.

Below the wheelhouse was the galley, now exuding tantalising smells. After half an hour of torment Albert said 'We eat!' and we followed him into the dark, dripping cell that was both galley and mess room. On the filthy table a crewman laid a roasting tin with two legs of sizzling, garlic-spiked lamb. We almost dissolved in an orgy of salivation. Laiza turned and bolted through the door. Albert gave her a passing glance and started to hack slices off the lamb with the only knife. The accompaniment was slices of stale white bread, and salt (which I noted came from Stoke-on-Trent).

I nibbled on the crispy bits of skin, savoured the full flavour of the fat, and chewed and sucked on the juicy pink wedges which Albert offered on the point of his knife. I ground to a halt only when I was painfully full. David wiped the last of his bread round the inside of the roasting tin. 'So much for thinking that we could easily be non-meat eaters,' he said.

'Anyone can make virtue out of necessity,' I replied pertly. 'But you're right, we just failed the test very convincingly.' Albert had been amused by our gluttony and a little concerned. As we lurched out into the cooling wind, he said 'When you come to Papeete you must come and eat with my family. On Sundays we gather at our beach house and have a big party. We always roast a calf or a pig on the spit, and there are many dishes of our own fruit and vegetables.'

To me, it seemed like Satan whispering in the wilderness.

'MOD CONS', TEPUKA

32

Paradise – Lost Or Found?

There was no doubt that soon we would have to leave for Papeete. Not to keep a Faustian pact for steak and salad, but because our permit renewal date had already passed. Also, our mail would be piling up in Papeete and folks back home would be getting anxious about our silence.

The question was, whether to move on westwards, across the Pacific, or to return to Tepuka. 'There is so much here you could help me with,' Taupiri had said. As the acting head of the family he was brimming with the enthusiasm and impatience of the recently promoted.

He was right. David had the skills and the tools and he enjoyed being useful. I could be happy anywhere with books, pen, paper and paints and the time to use them.

Ahead of us lay 4,500 miles of ocean, strewn with island groups like The Societies, The Cooks, Tonga and Fiji. To be safe in New Zealand before the cyclone season we had less than four months to see them all.

Or we could return to Tepuka. With a replenished food locker we could relax and enjoy a few months rest. It was a rare spot which combined all the right ingredients for 'Paradise': safe anchorage, good friends, not too isolated, and an outlet for our different pursuits.

'But what about cyclones?' I reminded David.

'Taupiri says they don't get them this far east.'

I was thinking of Jack London's classic tale, where the natives of Hikueru were sent flying through the sky, still tied to the palm trees – their last refuge from the engulfing ocean. David picked up my thoughts. (Perhaps it was this living-close-to-nature, but his antennae were more finely tuned these days.)

'...Well only every fifty years or so. We'd have to wait here till the cyclone season around Fiji was over – which would mean that we couldn't be in New Zealand until the end of next year.'

While we were chewing over the implications of this another diversion was sending a buzz through the camp.

'The *Astrolabe* is coming!' Laiza told us excitedly, pointing to the radio, which was blasting out rock music.

'Oh, yes?' said David, looking up at the sky.

'It's a ship,' I told him. 'The government boat; I'd guess it's named after La Perouse's flagship.' La Perouse was the distinguished French navigator who came after Captain Cook, and vanished while searching for the Solomon Islands.

Laiza explained that the ship toured the islands, bringing the doctor, dentist, policeman, magistrate, and whoever else was needed. There was a message on the radio for Taupiri. The policeman wanted to see him to discuss maintenance payments for his wife and child in Papeete.

It was the first we had heard of Taupiri being previously married. Later, as I helped Maman gut fish at the water's edge, she told me:

'He was eighteen when he went to Papeete. She was twenty-two and had been married three times before. A good-time girl – they're all like that there. They look for a man who will go out and earn money while they spend it. Taupiri got a job loading bags of cement while she went out dancing. He wanted to be here, where we needed him, so he brought her back. I knew she would never stay. Three months after their son was born she left, taking him with her.'

Maman paused and looked across to the cookhouse where Frieda was helping to grate coconut. Laiza and Ramon were there, chatting and joking, but Frieda, as usual, was silent. Maman's frank and trusting look disappeared. Her eyes hardened.

'He went back last month, to look for a wife, but we could only spare him for two weeks – we must catch the fish to pay Albert, or he will stop coming, and take back the engines. Two weeks is not enough time to find a good girl. And Taupiri deserves one. *Il est un homme **tres** gentille*'

'So, ...you don't think Frieda will make a good wife?' I probed.

'She has already caused unhappiness among us. She has opened our private chests and taken things. Now we have to keep them locked. But she is Taupiri's *Vahine,* so no-one can say anything.'

I was saddened too. They had few material possessions but each of them had a tin trunk in which they kept their personal 'treasures', out of reach of rats and cockroaches. Human predators in Tepuka were unimagined.

Maman stood up and stabbed the distant Frieda with her eyes. Then she turned to me and hissed with startling venom, '*Elle est une femme sauvage*!'

The Baie Otaho could accommodate the little *Raroa Nui* but it was too small for the *Astrolabe*. There was an anchorage and a deep water pass on the southern side of the lagoon, twenty miles away, where we would rendevous with it. Quite when this would be, no one was sure, except that it would be soon. It went without saying that we would be coming too.

Next morning we came ashore early. Maman and Ramon were already baking coconut bread. Taupiri took our water carriers and we helped to fill them from a rusty oil drum under the cookhouse roof.

'You don't have a big cistern?' I asked thinking of the concrete water tanks at Takaroa.

'Come, I'll show you,' said Taupiri, and we followed him through the bushes to the centre of the islet. There stood a large square concrete cistern – roofless, and with greenery sprouting from the cracks. Taupiri laughed. 'Built by my grandfather, when he worked the copra here. Now it is useless.' He was to be proved very wrong about that one day.

We packed supplies into the longest of the wooden skiffs; water, bread, rice, coffee and green drinking coconuts. From our own stores we added more coffee and some cans of corned beef, sardines and sweet corn. We had never advertised the contents of our food locker, because we would have been expected to share it until it was empty. As David remarked, 'That's what they would have done – which is why Polynesians make such hopeless shopkeepers.'

The dogs followed us to the waters' edge, whining pitifully when they realised they were being left behind. We helped to pushed the skiff into deeper water and climbed aboard. The big Johnson outboard purred into life, and we slid slowly through the false pass, past the fish traps and into the copper sulphate-blue lagoon. Taupiri opened up the throttle and headed for a mottled patch of shallows. Weaving and twisting, we zipped past pillars of coral, reaching almost to the surface, close enough to rip the boat apart if Taupiri muffed it. Laiza whooped encouragement and egged her brother on. This was his sports car and he could handle it superbly – or so I told myself.

Half-way down we pulled in at a *motu* of fine coconut stands. Maman explained: 'A family from Fakarava is living here for a month to work on their plantation.'

Fakarava was a nearby atoll and Robert Louis Stevenson's first taste of a coral island: 'I was never weary of calling up the image of that narrow causeway ...lying coiled like a serpent, tail to mouth, in the outrageous ocean.'

The schooner *Casco*, having failed to sight Takaroa, made its landfall there in September 1889. The Stevensons rented a house in the village, long enough for him to pen a sensitive, but unsentimental, portrait of atoll life, still recognisable today.

The village on Fakarava was the administrative capital of the Tuamotus but when Stevenson visited it, it was half empty. Many of the villagers were away, tending what he referred to as 'their cocoa-patches' on other atolls.

This 'cocoa-patch' that we were now visiting was well-tended – a sylvan glade of curving palms, cleared of undergrowth. The homestead was tidy and well-organised. The chickens were penned, two banana palms grew from tubs of soil and the roofs of the huts were linked by gutters to an enormous concrete cistern.

But in spite of the order, the flies were almost unbearable. 'It's the copra,' explained Ramon. For the moment the attractions of copra had evidently palled in favour of my eyes, nose and lips, and no amount of swiping and brushing seemed to have any effect. The singing of a huge black kettle on a fire of coconut husks signalled lunch. We sat in a large circle with the other family which included three strapping teenagers and, amid babbles of French and grunts of Tuamotuan, passed round assorted cans of food. I didn't talk much. I was afraid I might get a mouthful of flies. No one else seemed to mind, and occasionally someone did spit out a fly or two. It took intense concentration to get each chunk of bread-borne corned beef up to my mouth, rid it of its passengers, and clamp my teeth over it before the next sitting landed.

The conversation centred around an outbreak of 'the poisoning' on Fakarava. It seemed that badly affected people developed an intolerance to fish. The toxin could lie dormant, like malaria, and a mouthful of fish, or even alchohol, could aparently trigger off symptoms. It struck me that 'the poisoning' possibly carried the blame for a number of ills.

Much later I began to read of more sinister speculations on the source of 'the poisoning'. About a hundred miles to the east lay Muraroa Atoll, the centre of the French nuclear testing project. The tests were conducted in the atmosphere until 1975 when worldwide opposition forced them to continue underground. 'Underground' in an atoll is the old mountain top underneath the coral and there is much controversy about the stability of the explosion chamber. Facts are difficult to come by and the area is out of bounds to private observers. Many of the world's conservationists are worried that the local waters are possibly being contaminated by radiation seepage. I had never heard any of the Tuamotuans mention the testing, and when I asked they talked enthusiastically of relatives who worked on the project and earned 'much money'. Only Maman shuddered a little when we spoke of bombs. Radiation was a more difficult concept. Taupiri and Ramon shrugged and laughed, in the way that they laughed at all life's perils.

When the shadows began to lengthen it was time to pack up and move on. The other family, it seemed, was coming too. We helped to slide their boat down the beach. It was a typical, long, narrow skiff and they used it to travel on the open ocean, back and forth to Fakarava.

As we came to the southern corner of the lagoon, the clouds in the west were aflame with sunset. There was no sign of the *Astrolabe*. We put in at another fine plantation, this one silent and deserted. Little huts of woven bamboo stood in the clearing, dominated by the ubiquitous cistern.

'Tonight's Beachcomber Inn,' I said to David, reminding him: 'this will be the first night for over a year that we haven't slept on *Moongazer*.'

At the mention of the name we each involuntarily scanned the sky. In the east night was darkening the clouds, but there was nothing ominous.

'Looks O.K.,' said David. 'Anyway, she won't go far. The anchor chain's wrapped well around the coral.'

We hauled the boats high up on the steeply sloping beach with the help of palm-trunk rollers, kept in a pile for that purpose. Then we gathered coconut husks and made small fires beside the up-wind wall of each hut. Laiza and Maman dampened them off with green palm leaves and watched in satisfaction as each hut filled with smoke. No mosquitoes survived to make it to the door.

We sat round a campfire, which contrived to smoke us out as well, and drank sugary coffee. I wasn't sure whether I preferred mosquito bites to streaming eyes, but I was almost too sleepy to care.

Just when it looked as if everyone might be heading for bed, Taupiri jumped up. 'Come on!' he said, 'The tide is out and the moon has yet to rise. The lobsters will be out on the reef.'

I sat up with a start. This *motu* was on the weather side of the atoll. I could hear the dull thunder of the surf. Surely they weren't going diving? 'We're going on foot,' said David reading my face. 'There's nothing to worry about.'

I would always find something to worry about, but I didn't want to miss anything. I followed through the thickets out into the surf-lashed wild of the ocean beach. The tide was out, exposing the broad shelf of dead reef, fissured and pot-holed and teeming with intertidal life. Taupiri led the way with the pressure lantern and we slithered behind him, trying to keep up with the light. I stumbled in and out of rock pools, my flip-flops floating from my feet.

'Careful you don't stand on a sea urchin,' shouted David, above the roar of the surf. 'And watch out for moray eels.' Sea urchins and other nasties were already on my mind, but I'd forgotten about moray eels. I thought immediately of a girl who had shown me a horribly deep scar on her leg, the result of accidently treading on one.

Taupiri strode steadily ahead, out near the edge of the reef. Every now and then an extra large breaker hit, sending water swirling round our thighs, threatening to suck us with it in the backwash. Taupiri and a couple of lads were well ahead, still stabbing vigorously at the rock pools, and whooping when they made a kill. The rest, left in the darkness, were beginning to tire, and I, already exhausted, lay down on the coral shingle and waited.

Hunting for fish, I reflected, had been the atoll dwellers life force. It was in Taupiri's genes. But a century ago a night fishing party wouldn't be for fun. The dark harboured all sorts of terrors, far worse than moray eels. Conversion to Christianity had done nothing to allay their dread of returning spirits. 'A cannibal race may have cannibal phantoms,' was how Stevenson put it. The spirits of the dead came ashore from the ocean. That 'accursed' ocean beach, the scene of 'wizardry and shipwreck' was also, Stevenson added, '..in the native belief, a haunting ground for murderous spectres.'

Now, three generations later, the young hunters laughed and sang snatches of pop tunes as they returned along the reef, dragging a full and squirming sack.

We ate most of the contents of the sack that night, boiled in a pot over the campfire. David and I were the only ones to wince when we saw the size of the lobsters. As Taupiri had said, young lobster makes very tasty eating.

He lay outstretched before the fire with his arm round the silent Frieda, laughing and joking with his mates. Among them he was the undisputed King of Tepuka. Someone strummed on a ukulele and the company began to sing, in the hauntingly melodious way of Polynesians. Taupiri had said often of his atoll, '*Il est un paradise*,' and at moments like these it was. The logistics of living were beautifully simple. But, I thought, as I watched Taupiri and Frieda, the personal life was lived as deeply as anywhere else and, because of the absence of distractions, probably more keenly felt.

In bringing his family to eke out a living on this uninhabited atoll, Taupiri's father had committed an un-Polynesian act of individualism. To his fellows on Aratua he had taken a step backwards on the Great Western road to 'civilization'. Like the other wilderness dwellers we had met, he marched to the beat of a different drummer.

I used to think that people who chose a life of physical toil sought their pleasure from self-denial (I even thought it of sailors who crossed oceans in small boats). But I was discovering how toil and hardship change meaning when they are met through choice. Then they become the forces of fulfilment.

For centuries the idea of 'civilised man' re-embracing nature has excited the European imagination. It has inspired many practioners, most of them, like the young Heyerdahl, searching impractically to recapture that balance and harmony enjoyed (before the white man's impact) by those favoured children of nature – the Polynesians and the American Indians.

I thought of the families who had made a success of wilderness living – the Witmers and others in the Galapagos, Gunnar and Lassie in Alaska and the family here on Tepuka. They hadn't denied the 20th century and they used its gadgets with circumspection and common sense. They lived simple lives rich in humanity, a stark contrast to our urban Californian friends, mired in the clutter of high-consumption living, and keeping pace in the lonely crowd.

I thought of the millions on the Santa Monica Freeway, driving to Dreamsville, insulated from nature as if it might contaminate them (which there, it just might). Odd to think that living as we were, tuned to the vagaries of wind and water, sun and clouds, night and day, the size of the waves, the movement of the fish... is described by distant observers as 'escaping reality.'

I wouldn't care to define 'reality ' – but I could certainly recognize what it was not.

That night, for what was left of it, I slept surprisingly well – in a bamboo hut shared with Taupiri, Frieda, Maman and Laiza, who all slept on the shingle floor. David and I had the guest bed – a plywood shelf, four foot long.

Breakfast, of stale bread and cold fish, was well under way when I joined the others round the still smouldering camp fire.

Quite when the *Astrolabe* was due, no one knew. 'Today?' I asked, expecting anything. Laiza shrugged and answered 'I think so...perhaps?' No one else seemed very concerned. We tidied up and settled down to wait. After an hour or two of desultory chatter I began to wish I'd brought a book. My mask of repose was cracking. David had found something to tinker with, but the others were blissfully free of our hang-up on Productive Use of Time.

At last, the *Astrolabe*, white and gleaming, came steaming round the corner. She dropped anchor well out in the lagoon, and immediately lowered a boat. As it came towards us, I scanned the passengers. 'No sign of any officials,' I said to David. 'Looks like locals.'

But when they jumped from the boat and waded ashore, I saw that they were sunburnt Europeans in T-shirts and shorts, carrying briefcases. One T-shirt read '*Gendarme National*.' Our party moved forward and exchanged handshakes and kisses.

I tried to imagine a similar scene in a British colony. I stretched it to include shirtless officials – but the policeman greeting the natives with a kiss...!

Under the shade of the coconut palms the assembly sifted into little groups. Laiza accompanied the gendarme and Taupiri, to act as her brother's reader and adviser. As a child he had slipped from under the net of compulsory schooling and had never learned to read or write.

When, after an hour or so, all the business of the day was done, there was a reverse re-enactment of handshakes and kisses before we dispersed our separate ways.

But our outing wasn't quite over. Taupiri couldn't resist the food stops on the way. The first was for coconut crabs which he winkled out of their holes and immobilised by tying up their huge pincers. The rest of us filled up the boat with old coconuts which had started to sprout. 'For the pigs,' Maman said 'They like them.' Just as well, I thought, as the alternative was fish bones.

We stopped next at a small bushy *motu*, bereft of palm trees. Frigate birds soared above us. We looked inquiringly at Taupiri. He grinned and said only, 'Wait!' and disappeared up the beach into the bushes. We heard much squawking and crackling, and after a bit Taupiri emerged, triumphant, red weals across his face and holding four squirming frigate bird chicks by the feet. He dumped the large down-covered chicks in the boat and we finally made for home. The chicks struggled to their feet, but even with a wing span of four feet they were not yet old enough to fly. They made up for it in aggression. Throughout the homeward journey I fought to ward off attacks from long pointed beaks, perched unsteadily as I was on a pile of coconuts and crabs.

We returned to a welcome of yelping of dogs and the sight of *Moongazer* serenely at anchor. The frigate bird chicks enjoyed the briefest of lives in their new surroundings. Within twenty minutes they were headless, plucked, disjointed and in the pot. Several hours later they were the only the memory of a tasty stew with not even a bone left by the dogs to remind us.

The dogs were less keen on crab, so the fly-borne mound of crab litter which piled up on the table was eventually tossed to the fish.

Afterwards, when we sat with our coffee, David said quietly to the company. 'Soon we will have to go to Papeete. The day after tomorrow.' He said it in such a way that they knew we weren't coming back. There was a hush of disappointment round the table. No one tried to persuade us to stay – that would have seemed rude and selfish. David and I had hardly even discussed it ourselves. (Over trivial matters we could fight tooth and nail, but important decisions were more often mutely arrived at through some instinctive conjugal feeling.)

Taupiri broke the silence with a brave smile and an announcement; 'Tomorrow, we have the best feast of all – we will make it special.' Maman's face lit up in anticipation of the work ahead.

We rowed back out to the boat, under a night sky heavy with rain clouds. The wind had dropped and it was strangely quiet without the rustle of the palms. We lay on our bunk, stretched out side by side on the sweat-hardened sheets. (This is the moment of twilight in David's day when his mind and body are in repose long enough to be receptive to discussion. I have to be quick because he gives up readily to sleep.)

I opened: 'D'you think they understand why we're not coming back?'

'I don't think they waste too much time on the 'why's', sighed David without opening his eyes.

'Maybe I've something to learn from them.'

'Maybe.'

'It would've been very pleasant to stay for a bit,' I said, watching for a reaction. Not a muscle moved, but there was still breath in the body. It mumbled back at me.

'Not a good enough reason. Anyway, it's a mistake to

go *looking* for pleasure.'

Pleasure was a funny thing. Like adventure, it popped up unbidden at unexpected times and in odd places. More often it seeped in slowly, on the backwash of achievement.

David continued, his eyes still closed. 'Think back. What have been the best parts? When we were stopped or on the move?'

Odd, the times we stopped specifically to enjoy ourselves were now blurred recollections. But the memory of every day of our slog up the Alaskan passages was vivid. We were propelled on, to see round the next corner, over the next wave, to discover the unfamiliar, to see those shores the 747 can't reach, to touch that 'virginity of sense'.

We sailed with the passionate curiosity of the Traveller. That our journeys were made across tracts of uncongenial emptiness only heightened our perceptions – as it did for those legendary travellers of the great deserts. Freya Starke, smitten by Arabia, knew why: 'I wanted space, distance, history, and danger, and I was interested in the living world.'

We, less specific in our wants, had nonetheless found a way of life which embraced them all. With our home on our back we need never stop.

'How long do you think we'll keep going?' I wondered out loud, only half-expecting an answer. The only sounds were the patter of rain on the cabin roof and the deep snores of a contented man.

Our farewell feast was to have been roast pork – or more specifically, roast Napoleon, the engaging little piglet who scurried round our feet at mealtimes, but I demurred and saved his bacon – for the time being. 'You should be thankful it wasn't one of the dogs,' David reminded me.

We brought the last of our beer and some watered-down whisky, something we'd previously kept quiet about. Maman hung beautiful shell *leis* around our necks, made in secret for the occasion. David presented Ramon and Taupiri with tools to fix the outboard. I gave the household a little painted plaque showing *Moongazer* at anchor in the bay. We took photos of the present-giving and Maman wept a little.

We had hoped to slip quietly away at dawn. At first light we woke to hear the skiff alongside. They had come with fish, coconuts and new-baked bread. The live chickens we had to refuse – regretfully. We hugged and kissed and took more photographs, and Maman wiped away more tears. They climbed back into the skiff and waited to escort us to the pass. *Moongazer* was even more reluctant to leave. We were firmly tethered to a clump of coral. The women climbed back on board for more tearful farewells while Ramon and Taupiri dived to unravel the chain. After half an hour we finally tugged ourselves free from Tepuka.

As we went through the pass, the skiff dropped back and Taupiri cut the engine. We hoisted the sails in salute and returned their waves. The warmth of their farewell was quite moving and, in a way, poignant. Though they were bound together by powerful bonds of love and friendship, they were a vulnerable little group, already at the mercy of the march of 'progress'. I saw difficult times ahead and felt anxious for them. (I couldn't have guessed how difficult, and been more wrong about the cause.)

Long after we could see them only through binoculars, they were still sitting in the skiff, watching and waving.

(Old Tuamotus hands will know the atoll I am writing of. Its real name is not, of course, Tepuka.)

33

Half A World Nearer

Three days later we were in Papeete Harbour, at the foot of Tahiti's green mountains. The dull roar behind us was not the sound of surf on the reef but of traffic on the boulevard. Office and appartment blocks rose flat-roofed above the flame trees. Buses, street lights, shops and restaurants almost persuaded us that we were in small-town France. Only the long snaking line of yachts, moored two-deep among a tangle of shore-tied stern lines, reminded us that we had reached that once-great crossroads of the Pacific, the last stop for the merchantmen before Valparaiso and Cape Horn.

We had motored through the pass on a sparkling morning, into a harbour alive with ferries, fishing boats, coasters, and a magnificent three-masted barque in full sail. Behind the docks lurked the grey presence of the French Navy. The line of yachts stretching westwards from the quay had looked dauntingly impregnable, but halfway along familiar voices had hailed us and the ranks opened to let us squeeze in. Kathy had rowed over with fresh pineapple. Someone else brought cold beer and another friend brought gossip. Everyone, it seemed, was here. Some had been in situ for months; some had even been here since last season. Out there, in the islands around Tahiti were some of the most beautiful spots on earth, but in the hierarchy of human needs beauty was well down the list, below companionship, security, shops and a fresh water tap. None of us would have made very good wilderness dwellers.

From the sternposts and mizzenmasts of the yachts, fluttered the flags of the world – the affluent Western world, with English, in all its variations, being the predominant language. A brief study of the harbour entry records confirmed our guess that just over half the two hundred and seventy-odd yachts passing through that year came from the U.S.A., mostly from the West Coast. Yacht traffic had been increasing steadily since the sixties, with a big jump-up in the early seventies and signs of levelling-off in the eighties. The numbers of Australian and New Zealand yachts venturing up from the western Pacific had increased, accounting for about ten per cent of the traffic. British and Canadian yachts each averaged out around eight per cent, followed by the French at seven per cent and West German at about three per cent. Yachts from Sweden, Switzerland, Holland and Belgium each represented about one percent. Norway, Denmark, Finland, Poland and South Africa came next on the list, each with a few yachts from year to year. Less frequent were those from Spain, Portugal and Italy. A rising newcomer to the cruising scene was Japan, and we began to meet more Japanese yachts in the western Pacific.

Even as we arrived in Papeete there were signs that the party was coming to an end. While French Polynesia seemed almost 'seasonless', in that it was rarely visited by cyclones, the seasons of gales or cyclones in more distant destinations loomed inexorably closer. Yachtfolk heading for Canada and California via Hawaii were already running late, and facing the reality that the best of times were probably over. The rest of us, bound for New Zealand or Australia, had about three months' grace to work our way westwards before the threat of cyclones would chase us from the tropics.

Our departure date from French Polynesia was 'after the Fete', the annual display of competitive dancing and canoe racing which marks France's day of national re-assurance every 14th July. For this we sailed up to Bora Bora, Polynesia's most glittering gem, much-mentioned as the 'most beautiful island in the world.'

The Fete passed, but the exodus of yachts was slow and reluctant. Day and night, the booming of the surf upon the reef reminded us that the swell, born in the wintery Southern Ocean, was running high. The trade wind, too, was in boisterous mood, ruffling the iridescent waters of the lagoon and frosting the wave-tops in the ocean. Each day the rumble and clank of anchor chain would signal a departure and we would watch as the yacht laboured out over the corrugations of swell in the pass, flanked on each side by plumes of exploding surf. It was a sight which inspired compelling reasons to stay for just one more day.

By the end of July the caravan of yachts was rolling westwards, fanning out to the atolls of the Cook Islands in the north and Rarotonga in the south. The camaraderie, born of sharing common trials, flourished and deepened as we encountered an increasingly truculent Pacific. Cross swells, squalls and strong trade winds harried us until, near the islands of Tonga, we ran into our first severe storm. *Moongazer* weathered the white screaming fury of it all in her slow and steady way. She brought us through with the loss of nothing more than five coats of varnish, rainblasted off the cockpit coamings, the anodising off the compass casing and the signwriter's paint off the stern.

From Tonga and Samoa the yachts trickled into Fiji, gathering by the yacht club in Suva or by the beachcomber hotels in sunnier Nandi Waters. It was a time of 'eat, drink and be merry for soon we will have to make passage for New Zealand.' By mid-October the airwaves of the 'ham' radio bands were sounding the 'all clear'. Winter had left New Zealand. It was time for the fleet to migrate a thousand miles south to temperate climes. For us it was a slow passage. Protracted calms and teasing headwinds tested our patience before we gained the green waters of the Bay Of Islands and were rewarded with the much-missed sight of greening buds and the smell of rising sap. We anchored among friends already arrived and waited for more to join us.

On the last Thursday of November the Americans invited everyone to Thanksgiving dinners of barbecued lamb and the crews of over eighty yachts joined in a heartfelt recognition of the occasion. There was an air of 'graduation' in the camp. Many trials and vicissitudes had been weathered; many joys had been shared. The class was now dispersing for the summer, some to find work, some to buy old cars and vans and tour around and a few to sail further down the coast.

The summer's end heralded the start of the reverse migration back to the tropics, this time without *Moongazer*. She was snugged down for the winter in South Island, swinging to a fishboat mooring in the natural harbour of Akaroa. Her hull glittered with newly sprayed coats of polyurethane. Some surgery to her insides during the summer had made her even more comfortable. Her owners were in the scenic wilds of Central Otago, on a high-country sheep farm, transformimg tractor parts into ski tows, old sheds into ticket offices and themselves into a credible Ski Patrol. This was the New Zealand version of how we had spent our Canadian winter. It brought as much fun, as much skiing and rather less money. As the spring sun nibbled at the snow we could hear warm, seductive voices urging us to stay. More powerful was the pull of *Moongazer*, tugging at her mooring. Just two days before we left New Zealand, Brian arrived from the U.K. to sail with us to his new country of residence, Australia.

Our Australian sojourn took us from the tropical waters of Queensland to the wilderness haunts of Tasmania. It was a route rich with familiar moments; renewing old friendships and forging new ones; sailing into a great harbour and under a famous bridge; dogging the tracks of Cook and his successors in lonely inlets and keeping company with the Albatross.

It was while we were in Sydney, preparing to leave for the islands of Melanesia that disturbing tales of extraordinary weather in the tropical Pacific began to reach us. We heard that yachts bound for the Marquesas from Panama had encountered westerly winds for the whole passage, a nightmare of beating and tacking which for some, lasted two and a half months. In the islands, the westerly winds had chased everyone from the normally sheltered anchorages. The trade winds had apparently vanished from the whole tropical Pacific. Cyclones had hit French Polynesia.

The rhythm of nature had missed a beat and not, we learned when we read about it later, for the first time. Every five or six years the temperature of the Equatorial Pacific rises and upsets that pressure gradient which normally causes the winds and current to flow from east to west. Low pressure moves into the eastern Pacific bringing westerly winds and a warm west-flowing current. The phenomenon is known as *El Nino* because South Americans feel the effects of the current around Christmas, the time of the Christ child. This was a particularly maverick *El Nino* and its effects reverberated throughout the Pacific rim; drought in Australia, Indonesia and Mexico; floods and storms in California and Ecuador; the disappearance of plankton from the coasts of Chile and Peru and with it, the fish and birds. The abnormally high water temperature had fuelled a succession of cyclones which rampaged across the eastern Pacific.

We heard that Tahiti had been hit by six cyclones in three months. Almost all the yachts sheltering in the islands were damaged and many were wrecked beyond repair. The last and most powerful cyclone passed through the Tuamotus. We wondered and worried about the family on Tepuka.

When we left Australia it was to keep one last lingering date with the South Pacific; to explore the chain of islands which run from Vanuatu (formerly the New Hebrides) through the Solomons to Papua New Guinea. En route, the Tasman Sea sprang a nasty surprise and swiped us with our second severe storm, a tropical depression moving down from Queensland. Again, *Moongazer* plodded through the chaos, unimpressed by a close encounter with the cruise ship *Oriana* which, we learned later, was having her own problems.

For the next nine enchanted months, we flitted from anchorage to anchorage working our way up through the islands. Years of anchorage-hopping could never fully cover this wild corner of the Pacific. We sailed among green mountainous islands whose steamy jungles seemed remarkably recovered from the ferocious war which raged across them forty years before. The people and their villages were even more unmarked by time. This was a rare part of the world where the intrusion of the white man was violently and successfully resisted right up until the end of the last century. Now the people welcome visitors with smiles and kindness, but still the white faces among the crowd belong mostly to the missionaries and development workers. Overshadowed by the dazzle of its Polynesian neighbours, this off-beat corner has so far escaped most of the more destructive attentions of the West.

I had to take my leave of the Pacific some months earlier than David. Back home, people and property needed attention. Within days I was back in the U.K., covering a distance that would take *Moongazer* two years. David continued on his own, sailing north to the Admiralty Islands and west through the Bismarck Archipelago to the northern coast of Papua New Guinea. He came south, down the east coast, round the Louisiades and into Port Moresby. Just a week before we met up again in Darwin, he finally left the Pacific by way of the Torres Straits. It was an impressive piece of singlehanding; over 2,500 miles of tricky navigation in unmarked, reef-strewn waters.

At Darwin we were once more on the threshold of a new ocean. Six thousand miles of Indian Ocean, with islands on the way, lay between us and South Africa but it held less of the promise which had so thrilled us at the edge of the Pacific. We saw it as the road home, an obstacle to be overcome. We were back among the mainstream of yachts preparing for the passage to the other side of the world, some via the Red Sea and the Suez Canal, others like us, via the Cape of Good Hope. Our nearest neighbours on the anchorage were Bob and Betty, from the east coast of the U.S.A., also heading home via the Cape. By chance it emerged that they, too, had known the magic of Tepuka. They had spent some weeks with the family, just before the cyclones. From what they told us, there had been changes since our visit.

Poppa had died, from a heart attack, of all things. Albert had vanished from the scene, and so had the Johnson outboards and the generator. Laiza was married to a middle-aged Tahitian and had two baby boys (presumably twins). Ramon was no longer 'engaged' to the absent Valentina, but was apparently playing suitor to Maman. The inscrutable Frieda had gone back to Tahiti and Taupiri was now 'married' to a beautiful and pregnant sixteen-year-old from Moorea. Times sounded harder. There were no pigs in the sty. Fish boats and supplies came seldom. The only outboard was (as it always is when all else fails) an ancient Seagull.

Bob and Betty had been in Tahiti when the last cyclone tore through the atolls. 'We heard on the news that some of the villages had been devastated,' Bob told us. 'The reporter said that the Rangivaru family on Tepuka were found alive and well, and had been taken to Fakarava. That was as much as we knew.'

Having been in two storms only half as strong as a full-blown cyclone we had some small inkling of the terrifying forces that would have been unleashed on the atoll. The very existence of an atoll looks so tenuous at the best of times, but atolls, like their inhabitants, are more resilient than they look. I couldn't imagine Tepuka devastated and stripped of its palms. It still sparkled in my mind. We had seen many islands since, but for us it remained our perfect 'desert island'. Now we were reminded that nothing in this world comes without its price. Had we stayed to enjoy Tepuka's bliss we would certainly have been caught up somewhere along the way in the havoc of El Nino.

I'd often wondered if boats, like cats, were allowed nine lives. I had a feeling that *Moongazer* had already used up a few. It was as well that her bows were pointing homeward.

It is a dark soft night. The sounds and smells of early evening drift out across the anchorage; barking dogs, woodsmoke, Caribbean cooking. There is laughter, a snatch of singing, and somewhere a radio is pounding out a reggae beat. From the other yachts, mostly bareboat charters, come the clink and chatter of happy hour. We have just arrived, tired and salty from an exhilarating thrash to windward from the Grenadines. We sit quietly in the cockpit, drink in hand, soaking in the scene. It is a very special moment. Here, in the Caribbean island of Bequia, we have finally crossed our outward tracks. Eight years before, we had anchored in this lovely bay, dazzled by the novelty of it all and excited by the thought of what lay ahead. Even then we had no specific intention of sailing round the world. That came as a by-product of our curiosity. Conveniently, the world happens to be round and we have ended up crossing our tracks. Still, it is a 'classified achievement' and I enjoy a quiet moment of satisfaction and almost, surprise.

Bequia looks less changed by the passage of eight years than we do. We have become rather lean and leathery on the outside; and on the inside? .... perhaps it's too early to tell. Certainly in the last few months there have been endless ocean nights with time unlimited to reflect and let thoughts drift.

We have travelled from Darwin in the last year without detours or much respite. The Indian Ocean treated us fairly well and provided islands to add interest to the four-month crossing. We rested in South Africa and travelled inland to see more of friends and that beautiful and troubled country.

From Cape Town it has been a long run up to the Caribbean. St. Helena and Ascension Island offered brief diversions but their open anchorages brought no respite from the ocean swell. Night after night we watched the Southern Cross sink lower over our wake, until it was finally swallowed by the brooding skies of the doldrums. For ten days we flopped around in the windless gloom before we were found by the north-east trades. They picked us up, slowly at first, under a night sky which glittered with old friends first met in childhood. We gathered steam as the trades swung into their stride and sped us on to Grenada, to the mercifully calm harbour of St. Georges. There, for the first time in two and a half months, *Moongazer* was still.

Some of our fellow travellers had already arrived from Cape Town. Among them were Bob and Betty, our first visitors. They came with more news of Tepuka. A letter had finally found its way to them, written in perfect French by Laiza and signed by each of the family.

Laiza told of the tragedy that had befallen them only two weeks before the cyclone. One of Laiza's babies had died and they had gone in the skiff to Fakarava for the funeral. Three days after they returned to Tepuka, the winds hit.

Laiza described their terror. They took refuge in the only solid structure around – the old roofless water cistern that Taupiri had shown us. They lost everything – the huts, the cooking utensils, their treasure chests, the animals – all washed and blown away.

They were determined to stay and rebuild. 'Already we have started,' wrote Laiza. 'We work by moonlight.'

She had ended: 'We are all well and we have each other. That is all that matters.'

It's two weeks now since I heard those words and they still echo in my brain.

We are all well and we have each other. That is all that matters.

She is a fortunate girl to find that out, at the age of seventeen. It had taken me half a lifetime, and several years of travelling with the wind, to learn the utter truth of it.

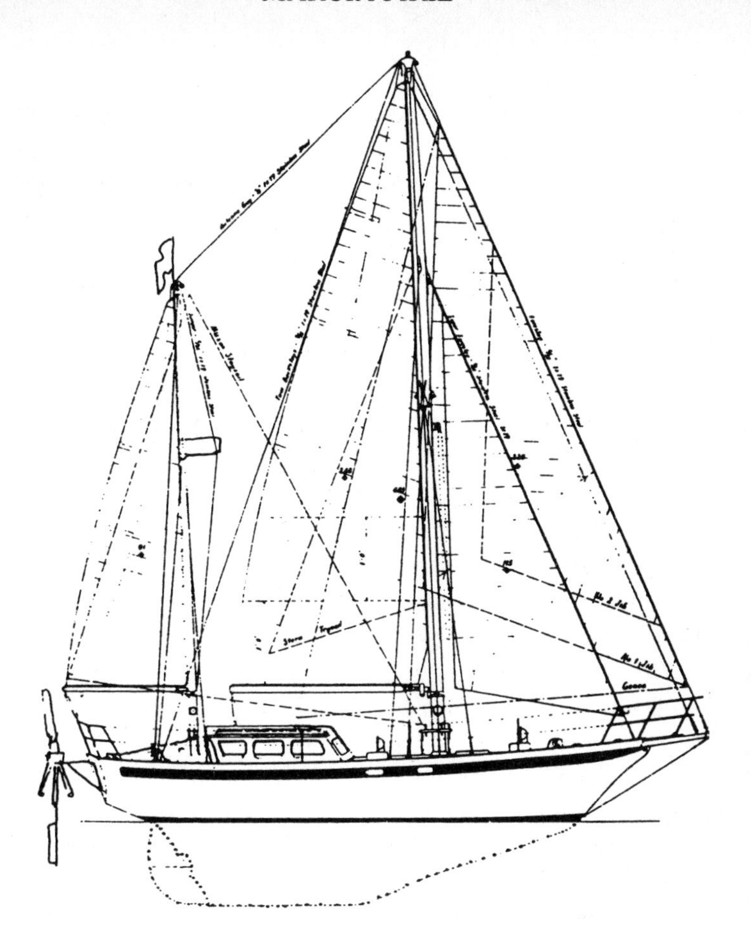

Dimensions:

L.O.A.	11.9m (39′)
Hull length	10,9m (35′4)
Waterline length	8.1m (26′8)
Beam	3.3m (11′)
Draft	1.6m (5′3)
Displacement	9,350kg (9.2 tons)

Appendix

Details Of *Moongazer* And Equipment

Moongazer is an Endurance 35 auxilliary sailing ketch, a design which won the top award in 1967 from the International Amateur Boatbuilders Society in the U.S.A. The brief called for a blue water cruising boat capable of being handled by two people, that was comfortable to live on, had ample stowage space and the provision for storing a dinghy on deck.

Moongazer did all of these admirably, especially the storage, as we carried a considerable amount of gear, provisions and paraphernalia. Most of all, she was sea kindly in heavy weather and rode two severe storms (65 knots plus – off the end of the wind-speed dial) well under control. We carried towing warps but never felt the need to use them. The down side of this was that she was sluggish in light airs.

MATERIALS AND CONSTRUCTION

Hull: This was built by Windboats Ltd., using their 'Seacrete' ferrocement process. Apart from initial cosmetic problems, ferrocement proved to be an ideal material for long term immersion in tropical waters. Although our hull seemed to attract barnacles more than most, we were free from the usual worries about corrosion, toredo worm or osmosis.

Deck: Construction from the bare hull up was done by ourselves following traditional methods of wooden boat building. The beam shelf was pitch pine, through-bolted to the hull. Beams of laminated oak supported the 18mm plywood deck which was overlaid with 10mm teak planks.

Coachroof and cockpit: This was built from 25mm marine ply, sheathed in G.R.P. The cockpit coamings and seats were 28mm teak.

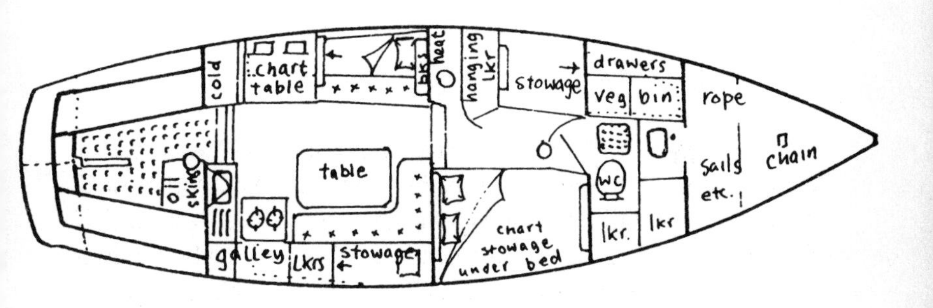

LAYOUT

This was to our own design, based on our previous cruising in the Irish Sea area. Anything which seemed snug and cosy there, like our high-sided cockpit, had its drawbacks in the hot sticky Tropics. After a few years the size of our double bunk began to irk and in New Zealand we made a major alteration to enlarge its width to a comfortable 1.5 metres. We did this by dismantling the heads compartment which was undeservedly taking up prime accommodation space in the middle of the boat, and rebuilding the double bunk in its place.

We made a new heads compartment in the focs'le under the forehatch, together with a workbench and storage bins and this was altogether a great improvement.

RIG

A cutter ketch with self-tacking staysail. The rigging was oversize -10mm s.s. wire on the main shrouds and forestays, and 8mm on the mizzen.

SAILS

We carried a mainsail, mizzen, mizzen staysail, genoa, heavy genoa, cruising spinnaker, two working jibs, two storm jibs, a staysail, a storm staysail and a storm trysail.

The sails had been used for four summers before we left the U.K., but they deteriorated much faster during the next four years. We took a large stock of roll-ends of sailcloth and with our domestic sewing machine and small generator, made numerous repairs and new panels. Eventually, in New Zealand, we ordered a new suit of sails from Hong Kong. They arrived on time and excactly as per order and proved very satisfactory.

For downwind sailing we found the most trouble-free arrangement was to have twin high-cut jibs poled out on each side, suspended from rotational fittings just below the cross-trees. The poles were stored hanging from their fittings and were raised and lowered, clipped to the clew of the sail, with no guys or downhauls to worry about.

In Australia David, undaunted by my scepticsm, replaced one of the forestays with a home-made roller-furling luff spar. After the Indian Ocean crossing I became a fervent convert when I saw how effortlessly, and safely, we could reduce sail. For running, we still poled it out opposite the working jib, and were then able to choose the sail area to match the conditions.

During the wet season of light airs in Papua New Guinea, David made a cruising chute from our roll-ends of spinnaker cloth. This was much more manageable than a spinnaker and we ended up using it for ocean sailing more than we'd anticipated.

HEAVY WEATHER HANDLING

In following winds above 25 knots we put up unpoled storm jibs, reducing to one jib and then to bare poles over 35 knots. *Moongazer* ambled along very comfortably under bare poles, so in some sea conditions we resorted to that for the sake of comfort in winds upward of 25 knots.

On other points of sailing we reduced sail in rough seas when the hull speed reached around five to six knots. The sequence was: one reef in the main; next stage, no main; then no jib, only staysail and mizzen. For gale force winds forward of the beam, we used only the staysail, tightly sheeted amidships. With the Aries steering, the boat forereached comfortably at about two to three knots, taking the seas on the bow quarter. In extreme weather (over 50 knots) the windage of the rigging alone provided enough 'sail' to keep us moving at about three to four knots with a drift to leeward of around one knot.

We've read a number of books on boat handling in

heavy weather and agree with the general conclusion that each design behaves uniquely and so does each storm. We handled *Moongazer* in severe weather more by instinct and feeling, based on long experience of her capabilities, than by any rules.

ENGINE

A Perkins 4.108 marine diesel. This was bought secondhand and rebuilt by David three years before we left. This intimate association and subsequent nurturing paid off, as the engine ran for the whole of our nine-year trip without a missed start or a falter (acknowledged by envious fellow yachtfolk as a remarkable record.) Regular maintenance and *use* kept the mechanical systems relatively trouble-free.

Diesel fuel was carried in two interconnected steel tanks with a total capacity of 250 litres. On ocean passages this was adequate for clearing land or making landfalls in light airs or headwinds, but not for motoring through mid-ocean calms. For those we had to use patience.

Separate batteries and charging systems ensured that should the ship's system become over-used, one battery was always in good condition for starting the engine.

GROUND TACKLE

For most situations we used a 20 kg C.Q.R. with 100 metres of 10mm chain. We dragged anchor on four occasions for no particular reason although we knew that the C.Q.R. often lay on its side, only half-dug in, and pulled out under a shift in wind direction. Later we acquired a 30 kg Bruce which we felt performed better. We also carried a 15 kg C.Q.R. but used it only rarely for a Bahamian moor or such, when swinging room was restricted.

On the stern we kept a 20 kg Danforth with chain and nylon warp. The Danforth was particularly good in soft mud where the C.Q.R. would plough straight through.

We carried 100 metres of spare chain and anchor warp which we fortunately never needed to use. We did know of others who snagged their anchor at 30 metres and had to cut the chain – and others who saw the lot disappear into the deep because the bitter end of the cable wasn't held fast!

SELF STEERING

Ninety per cent of our steering was done by the Aries. It could handle everything except a light following wind and we felt it to be our most important item of equipment. We experimented successfully with different areas of plywood wind vane, right down to a tiny one for storms.

For windless motoring in coastal regions we used an electric autopilot. Like a prima donna, it was marvellous when everything went right and terrible on 'off' days. Tracing faults took hours of work, but this applied to most of our electronics.

ELECTRONICS

Radar: We rarely used this in the tropics as the visibility was usually excellent. Also, rolling in large swells made it difficult to pick up a reliable signal. However on a few occasions of zero visibility in Spain, Tasmania and Alaska it proved very useful.

Log and windspeed/direction: these became temperamental after a couple of years' continuous use. Mostly we trailed a walker log and kept spare spinners as these occasionally disappeared.

Sat nav: we bought one after five years and it certainly took the anxiety out of difficult, poor-visibility landfalls. It didn't change our navigating habits. David continued to take sunsights across the oceans.

Radio – VHF: used mainly as an anchorage 'phone', but useful in the U.S.A. for weather channels.

Short Wave: invaluable for B.B.C. world service, time

signals, W.W.V. ocean weather and listening to 'ham' radio networks. We eventually bought an old 'ham' radio transceiver to keep in touch with friends during ocean crossings.

DINGHY

This was our workhorse which had to be stable, rugged, capable of being loaded with jerricans etc., and at the same time, not too heavy for me to drag up the beach. The most satisfactory was one we bought in New Zealand – g.r.p., cathedral-hulled with aluminium runners on the keels.

It stowed on the the flat coachroof, upright and filled with warps, fenders, washtubs etc., but with a cover to protect it from sunlight and keep out the rain.

Outboard Engine: This was a six h.p., the maximum size we felt we could load and store. We used the dinghy much like a car, for pleasure trips to outer reefs and up rivers, and as shore-commuting and load-carrying transport. To us, having no outboard would seem like having a bicycle instead of a car, with similar pros and cons. Eventually we replaced the six h.p. with a two h.p. model which was much smaller and lighter and, surprisingly, drove us only a shade slower.

GALLEY ARRANGEMENTS

Cooker: the standard caravan model with two burners, oven and grill, proved very satisfactory. The cast iron burners eventually disintegrated but we were able to replace them in Fiji.

We carried propane in three 10 kg. bottles in the rear cockpit locker. The supply could be turned off at the bottle by a remote solenoid switch beside the cooker. Propane fuel was the most widely available but we carried various adaptors which allowed us to switch to butane or camping gas.

Fresh Food Storage: for the first four years we used our

cool box as a larder (with the lid slightly open for ventilation) On rare occasions when block ice was available we closed the lid and used it as designed. Not that there was much to put in it – dairy products, salad vegetables and meat were scarce in the Tropics.

However, in Australia David finally turned the cold box into a fridge/freezer, run off a compressor driven by the engine. We were surprised at how much this improved our quality of life. The bottom of the box was used as a deep freeze, mainly for the fish we caught, and the top layers for cheese, canned butter and water. We stored water in two sets of litre plastic bottles and each day swopped a set between the freezer and an insulated box under the companionway steps. This gave us a cool 'day fridge' where we considerably extended the life of fruit and small vegetables.

In the tropics we kept the freezer happy with two half-hour runs of the engine each day – a recipe, my Engineer stresses, for healthy batteries and a functioning engine.

WATER

We carried 270 litres in three stainless steel tanks, each capable of being filled and emptied independently. There were also two plastic jerricans, (three quarters full, to float in salt water) permanently stowed in the cockpit for a dire emergency, like abandoning ship.

In the initial months we conscientiously used our carbon filter purifier for drinking water, until we realised how quickly it used up filters. We found that the time-honoured method of adding chlorine (a teaspoon of domestic bleach to 50 litres water) kept our water bug-free. A slight taste of chlorine sometimes lingered, but only for a couple of days.

Most of our supply in the tropics was rainwater, run off the awning we rigged when at anchor. Two sections of the full-length awning were fitted at a couple of strategic points with drainholes from which plastic piping led into wash tubs and water carriers.

For showering we used a garden pump-up spray with a shower head attachment. We washed our selves and hair in salt water, and rinsed off with the fresh water shower. Shampoos and shower soaps lather perfectly well in salt water.

FISHING

We used 100 kilo-test nylon line with a large hook on a steel trace and spinner. The lure we made from spinnaker cloth, silver foil or anything colourful that might look, from a tuna's point of view, like a flying fish.

Landing a heavy, fighting tuna or dorado on board a rolling deck required practice for us novice fisherfolk. The line was wound on a large wooden drum mounted on the mast pulpit and run out from amidships. This meant we could bring the fish alongside and haul it in with a long-handled gaff. We quickly tied a rope round its tail and hung it from the ratlines with a bucket underneath. An incision behind its head killed it immediately and we were able to cut all the messy stuff, head etc, straight into the bucket. Before we perfected this technique, fishing was more of a gory battle.

Sometimes we caught something every few days, sometimes two weeks went by before a bite. Before we had refrigeration we could only keep enough of the fish for one meal. The rest, often ninety per cent of it, had to be thrown back, no doubt to appreciative mouths.

Only once, in the South Atlantic, did we ever find sufficient flying fish on deck sizeable enough to eat. They were full of fine bones but very tasty.

Every yacht is a collection of compromises. It will do some things well but at the expense of others. We viewed *Moongazer* as a good-looking, comfortable, self-contained home which was safe to sail in most seas. For this we sacrificed a degree of speed and performance which out in the ocean didn't seem to matter that much. We travelled hopefully and we arrived!